P9-CBZ-595

Frommer's®

P O R T A B L E

Washington, D.C.

2nd Edition

by Elise Hartman Ford

Macmillan • USA

ABOUT THE AUTHOR

Elise Hartman Ford has been a freelance writer in the Washington, D.C.,
area since 1985. She contributes regularly to such newspapers as the
Washington Post, and to *Washingtonian* and other magazines. In addition to
this guide, she is the author of two books about places to rent for special
events and meetings: *Unique Meeting, Wedding and Party Places in Greater
Washington*, now in its fourth edition, and *Unique Meeting Places* in Greater
Baltimore.

MACMILLAN TRAVEL

A Simon & Schuster Macmillan Company
1633 Broadway
New York, NY 10019

Find us online at **www.frommers.com**

ISBN 0-02-862959-0
ISSN 1092-3918

Editor: Vanessa Rosen
Production Editor: Mark Enochs
Design by Michele Laseau
Digital Cartography by Gail Accardi and Ortelius Design
Page Creation by John Bitter, Natalie Evans, and Angel Perez
Photo Editor: Richard Fox

SPECIAL SALES

Bulk purchases (10+ copies) of Frommer's and selected Macmillan travel
guides are available to corporations, organizations, mail-order catalogs,
institutions, and charities at special discounts, and can be customized to suit
individual needs. For more information, write to Special Sales, Macmillan
General Reference, 1633 Broadway, New York, NY 10019.

Manufactured in the United States of America

Contents

List of Maps

An Invitation to the Reader

In researching this book, we discovered many wonderful places—hotels, restaurants, shops, and more. We're sure you'll find others. Please tell us about them, so we can share the information with your fellow travelers in upcoming editions. If you were disappointed with a recommendation, we'd like to know that, too. Please write to:

Frommer's Portable Washington, D.C. '99
Macmillan Travel
1633 Broadway
New York, NY 10019

An Additional Note

Please be advised that travel information is subject to change at any time—and this is especially true of prices. We therefore suggest that you write or call ahead for confirmation when making your travel plans. The authors, editors, and publisher cannot be held responsible for the experiences of readers while traveling. Your safety is important to us, however, so we encourage you to stay alert and be aware of your surroundings. Keep a close eye on cameras, purses, and wallets, all favorite targets of thieves and pickpockets.

What the Symbols Mean
✪ Frommer's Favorites

Our favorite places and experiences—outstanding for quality, value, or both.

The following abbreviations are used for credit cards:

AE	American Express	JCB	Japan Credit Bank
CB	Carte Blanche	MC	MasterCard
DC	Diners Club	V	Visa
DISC	Discover		

Find Frommer's Online

Arthur Frommer's Outspoken Encyclopedia of Travel (www.frommers.com) offers more than 6,000 pages of up-to-the-minute travel information—including the latest bargains and candid, personal articles updated daily by Arthur Frommer himself. No other Web site offers such comprehensive and timely coverage of the world of travel.

Planning a Trip to Washington, D.C.

*T*he thing about Washington is there's never a bad time of year to visit. This fact alone allows for some flexibility as you plan your trip. But no matter when you go, you can help maximize the pleasure of your trip and minimize hassles by doing a certain amount of advance planning. A number of sightseeing attractions (see below) permit you to obtain tickets as far as 6 months in advance. If you have your heart set on seeing one of these well-liked sites, you can avoid the wait of a long line or the ultimate disappointment of missing a tour altogether by simply reserving advance tickets.

1 Visitor Information

Before you leave, contact the **Washington, D.C., Convention and Visitors Association,** 1212 New York Ave. NW, Washington, D.C. 20005 (☎ **202/789-7000**), www.washington.org, and ask them to send you a free copy of the *Washington, D.C., Visitors Guide,* which details hotels, restaurants, sights, shops, and more. They'll also be happy to answer specific questions. **The D.C. Committee to Promote Washington** (☎ **800/422-8644**) will send you free copies of brochures listing additional information about Washington.

MAKING ADVANCE RESERVATIONS FOR POPULAR ATTRACTIONS

Based on ticket availability, senators and/or representatives can provide their constituents with advance tickets for tours of the Capitol, the White House, the FBI, the Bureau of Engraving and Printing, the Supreme Court, and the Kennedy Center. This is no secret. Thousands of people know about it and do write, so make your request as far in advance as possible—even 6 months ahead is not too early—specifying the dates you plan to visit and the number of tickets you need. Their allotment of tickets for each site is limited, so there's no guarantee you'll secure them, but it's worth a try. (Advance tickets are not necessary to tour an attraction; but they can be helpful in avoiding long waits.)

What Things Cost in Washington, D.C.	U.S. $
Taxi from National Airport to downtown	$10–$11
Bus from National Airport to downtown	$8
Metro from National Airport to Farragut West (downtown) (non-rush hour)	$1.10
Local telephone call	.35¢
Double room at the Jefferson Hotel (very expensive)	$175–$310
Double room at the J.W. Marriott Hotel (expensive)	$139–$234
Double room at the Radisson Barceló Hotel (moderate)	$110–$199
Double room at the Embassy Inn (inexpensive)	$59–$110
Dinner for one, without wine, at the Willard Room (very expensive)	$45
Dinner for one, without wine, at Jaleo (moderate)	$25–$30
Dinner for one, without wine, at Il Radicchio (inexpensive)	$6–$15
Bottle of beer in a restaurant	$3.50–$4
Coca-Cola in a restaurant	$1.50
Cup of coffee in a restaurant	$1.25
Roll of ASA 100 film, 36 exposures	$6.50
Admission to all Smithsonian museums	Free
Theater ticket at the National	$25–$75

Address requests to representatives as follows: name of your congressperson, U.S. House of Representatives, Washington, D.C. 20515; or name of your senator, U.S. Senate, Washington, D.C. 20510. Don't forget to include the exact dates of your Washington trip. When you write, also request tourist information and literature.

Note: Before writing, you might try calling a senator or congressperson's local office; in some states you can obtain passes by phone.

THE CAPITOL   Congressional passes are required if you plan to sit and observe Congress in session. You also may be able to obtain VIP passes to tour the Capitol between 8 and 8:45am without waiting in line; see chapter 5 for details. (Regular guided tours, for which you need no ticket, take place Monday through Saturday, from 9am to 3:45pm, and last 45 minutes.) To see what's in session, call ☎ **202/225-3121** to check the House schedule and ☎ **202/224-3121** to check the Senate schedule.

THE WHITE HOUSE   Tuesday through Saturday between 8 and 8:45am, the doors of the White House are open for special VIP tours to those with tickets. Once again, write far, far in advance, because each senator and congressperson receives no more than 10 tickets a week to distribute. These early tours ensure your entrance during the busy tourist season when thousands line up during the 2 hours daily that the White House is open to the public. The VIP tours are also more extensive than those held later; U.S. Secret Service guides provide explanatory commentary as you proceed through the ground floor and state floor rooms. On the later tours, you see the same rooms but you don't get the commentary; however, attendants and Secret Service agents are on hand to answer questions.

THE FBI   The line for this very popular tour can be extremely long; March through September you can expect to wait for 1 or 2 hours. Guided congressional tours take place on the quarter hour, from 9:45 to 11:45am and from 1:45 to 2:45pm. Contact your senator or representative at least 3 months ahead to schedule an appointment for constituent groups of six or fewer.

BUREAU OF ENGRAVING & PRINTING   Guided VIP tours are offered weekdays at 8am, except on holidays, and last about 45 minutes. Write at least 3 months in advance for tickets.

THE KENNEDY CENTER   Congressional tours depart Monday through Saturday at 9:30am and 4:45pm year-round and at 9:45am April through September. These tours are free, but you must have a letter from your senator or congressperson. Call ☎ **202/416-8303** at the Kennedy Center for more information on these tours.

THE SUPREME COURT   Contact your senator or congressperson at least 2 months in advance to arrange for guided tours of the building led by a Supreme Court staff member. Self-guided and guided tours are allowed when the court is not in session. Call the Supreme Court information line to find out days and times that court arguments will take place.

2 When to Go

CLIMATE

If you have a choice of when you can visit, I'd recommend the fall. The weather is lovely, Washington's scenery is awash in fall foliage colors, and the tourists have thinned out.

If you hate crowds and want to get the most out of Washington sights, winter is your season: There are no long lines or early morning dashes to avoid them, and hotel prices tend to be lower.

Spring weather is delightful, and, of course, there are those cherry blossoms. Along with autumn, it's the nicest time to enjoy D.C.'s outdoor attractions, to get around to museums in comfort, and to laze away an afternoon or evening at the ubiquitous Washington street cafes. But the city is also crowded with visitors and school groups.

The throngs remain in summer, and anyone who's ever spent a summer in D.C. will tell you how hot and steamy it can be. The advantage: This is the season (especially June and July) to enjoy numerous outdoor events—free concerts, festivals, parades, and more.

WASHINGTON CALENDAR OF EVENTS

The district is the scene of numerous daily special events, fairs, and celebrations. Listed below are some major annual events. When in town, check the *Washington Post,* especially the Friday "Weekend" section. **The Smithsonian Information Center,** 1000 Jefferson Dr. SW (☎ **202/357-2700**), is another good source.

January

- **Martin Luther King, Jr.'s Birthday.** Events include speeches by prominent civil rights leaders and politicians; readings; dance, theater, and choral performances; prayer vigils; a wreath-laying ceremony at the Lincoln Memorial; and concerts. Many events take place at the Martin Luther King Memorial Library, 901 G St. NW (☎ **202/727-0321**). Call ☎ **202/789-7000** for further details. Third Monday in January.

February

- **Chinese New Year Celebration.** A friendship archway, topped by 300 painted dragons and lighted at night, marks Chinatown's entrance at 7th and H streets NW. The celebration begins the day of the Chinese New Year and continues for 10 or more days, with traditional firecrackers, dragon dancers, and colorful street parades. Some area restaurants offer special menus. For details, call ☎ **202/638-1041.** Mid-February.

- **Abraham Lincoln's Birthday, Lincoln Memorial.** Marked by the laying of a wreath and a reading of the Gettysburg Address at noon. Call ☎ **202/619-7222.** February 12.
- **George Washington's Birthday, Washington Monument.** Similar celebratory events. Call ☎ **202/619-7222** for details. Both presidents' birthdays also bring annual citywide sales. February 22. Mount Vernon also marks Washington's birthday with free admission and activities that include music and military performances on the bowling green. Call ☎ **703/780-2000.** President's Day, third Monday in February.

March

✪ **Cherry Blossom Events.** Washington's best-known annual event is the blossoming of the 3,700 famous Japanese cherry trees by the Tidal Basin in Potomac Park. Festivities include a major parade (marking the end of the festival) with princesses, floats, concerts, celebrity guests, and more. There are also special ranger-guided tours departing from the Jefferson Memorial. For parade information—or tickets for grandstand seating ($12 per person)—call the D.C. Downtown Jaycees (☎ **202/728-1137**). For other cherry-blossom events, check the *Washington Post* or call ☎ **202/789-7038** or 202/547-1500. Late March or early April (national news programs monitor the budding).

- **Smithsonian Kite Festival.** A delightful event if the weather cooperates—an occasion for a trip in itself. Throngs of kite enthusiasts fly their unique creations on the Washington Monument grounds and compete for ribbons and prizes. To compete, just show up with your kite and register between 10am and noon. Call ☎ **202/357-2700** or 202/357-3030 for details. Last weekend in March.

April

- **White House Easter Egg Roll.** The biggie for little kids. In past years, entertainment on the White House South Lawn and the Ellipse has included clog dancers, clowns, Ukrainian egg-decorating exhibitions, puppet and magic shows, military drill teams, an egg-rolling contest, and a hunt for 1,000 or so wooden eggs, many of them signed by celebrities, astronauts, or the president. *Note:* Attendance is limited to children ages 3 to 6, who must be accompanied by an adult. Hourly timed tickets are issued at the National Parks Service Ellipse Visitors Pavilion just behind the White House at 15th and E streets NW beginning at 7am. Call ☎ **202/456-2200** for details. Easter Monday between 10am and 2pm; enter at the southeast gate on East Executive Avenue, and arrive early.

- **White House Spring Garden Tours.** These beautifully landscaped creations are open to the public for free afternoon tours. Call ☎ **202/456-2200** for details. Two days only, in mid-April.

- **Filmfest D.C.** The 13th celebration of this annual international film festival takes place in 1999. The festival lasts about 2 weeks in mid- to late April and presents as many as 75 works produced by filmmakers from around the world. Screenings are staged throughout the festival at movie theaters, embassies, and other venues. Tickets are usually $7 per movie; some events are free. Call ☎ **202/628-FILM;** Web site www.capaccess.org/fillmfestdc.

- **Taste of the Nation.** An organization called Share Our Strength (SOS) sponsors this fund-raiser, which takes place in more than 100 cities throughout the nation every April. In Washington, anywhere from 70 to 90 major restaurants and many wineries set up tasting booths at Union Station and offer some of their finest fare. For the price of admission, you can do the circuit, sampling everything from barbecue to bouillabaisse; wine flows freely, and there are dozens of great desserts. The evening also includes a silent auction. Tickets are $65 if purchased in advance, $75 at the door, and 100% of the profits go to feed the hungry. To obtain tickets, call ☎ **800/955-8278.** Late April.

- ✪ **The Smithsonian Craft Show** features one-of-a-kind, limited-edition crafts by more than 100 noted artists (it's a juried show) from all over the country. It takes place at the National Building Museum, 401 F St. NW, during 4 days in late April. There's an entrance fee of about $10 per adult, $7 per child, each day. For details, call ☎ **202/357-2700** (TDD 202/357-1729) or 202/357-4000.

May

- **Georgetown Garden Tour.** View the remarkable private gardens of one of the city's loveliest neighborhoods. Admission (about $18) includes light refreshments. Some years there are related events such as a flower show at a historic home. Call ☎ **202/333-4953** for details. Early to mid-May.

- ✪ **Washington National Cathedral Annual Flower Mart,** on the cathedral grounds. Includes displays of flowering plants and herbs, decorating demonstrations, ethnic food booths, children's rides and activities (including an antique carousel), costumed characters, puppet shows, and other entertainment. Free. Call ☎ **202/537-6200** for details. First Friday and Saturday in May.

- **Memorial Day.** At 11am, a wreath-laying ceremony takes place at the Tomb of the Unknowns in Arlington National Cemetery, followed by military band music, a service, and an address by a high-ranking government official (sometimes the president); call ☎ **202/685-2851** for details. There's also a ceremony at 1pm at the Vietnam Veterans Memorial, including a wreath-laying, speakers, and the playing of taps (call ☎ **202/619-7222** for details), and there are activities at the U.S. Navy Memorial (call ☎ **202/737-2300**). On the Sunday before Memorial Day, the National Symphony Orchestra performs a free concert at 8pm on the West Lawn of the Capitol to officially welcome summer to Washington. Call ☎ **202/619-7222** for details.

June

- **Shakespeare Theatre Free for All.** This free theater festival presents a different Shakespeare play each year, for a 2-week run at the Carter Barron Amphitheatre in upper northwest Washington. Tickets are required and free. Evenings, mid-June. Call ☎ **202/ 547-3230.**

- **Smithsonian Festival of American Folklife.** A major event with traditional American music, crafts, foods, games, concerts, and exhibits. Past performances have ranged from Appalachian fiddling to Native American dancing, and demonstrations from quilting to coal mining. All events are free; most events take place outdoors on the Mall. Call ☎ **202/357-2700,** or check the listings in the *Washington Post* for details. For 5 to 10 days, always including July 4.

July

- **Independence Day.** There's no better place to be on the Fourth of July than in Washington, D.C. The festivities include a massive National Independence Day Parade down Constitution Avenue, complete with lavish floats, princesses, marching groups, and military bands. There are also celebrity entertainers and concerts. (Most events take place on the Washington Monument grounds.) A morning program in front of the National Archives includes military demonstrations, period music, and a reading of the Declaration of Independence. In the evening the National Symphony Orchestra plays on the west steps of the Capitol with guest artists (for example, Leontyne Price). Big-name entertainment also precedes the fabulous fireworks display behind the Washington Monument. *Note:* You can also attend an 11am free organ recital at Washington's National Cathedral. Consult the *Washington Post* or call ☎ **202/789-7000** for details. July 4, all day.

August/September

- **Labor Day Concert.** The National Symphony Orchestra closes its summer season with a free performance at 8pm on the West Lawn of the Capitol; call ☎ **202/619-7222** for details. Labor Day. (Rain date: same day and time at Constitution Hall.)

- **Washington National Cathedral's Open House.** Celebrates the anniversary of the laying of the foundation stone in 1907. Events include demonstrations of stone carving and other crafts utilized in building the cathedral; carillon and organ demonstrations; and performances by dancers, choirs, strolling musicians, jugglers, and puppeteers. This is the only time visitors are allowed to ascend to the top of the central tower to see the bells; it's a tremendous climb, but you'll be rewarded with a spectacular view. For details, call ☎ **202/537-6200.** A Saturday in late September or early October.

- **Black Family Reunion.** Performances, food, and fun are part of this celebration of the African-American family and culture on the National Mall. Free. Call ☎ **202/383-9104.** Mid-September.

- **Kennedy Center Open House Arts Festival.** A daylong festival of the performing arts in early to mid-September, featuring local and national artists on the front plaza and river terrace (which overlooks the Potomac) and throughout the stage halls of the Kennedy Center. Admission is free, but you may have to stand in a long line to gain admittance to the inside performances. Check the *Washington Post* or call ☎ **800/444-1324** or 202/467-4600 for details. A Sunday, in early to mid-September, noon to 6pm.

October

- **Taste of D.C. Festival,** Pennsylvania Avenue between 9th and 14th streets NW. Dozens of Washington's restaurants offer international food-tasting opportunities, along with live entertainment, dancing, storytelling, and games. Admission is free; purchase tickets for tastings. Call ☎ **202/724-5430** for details. Three days, including Columbus Day weekend.

- **White House Fall Garden Tours.** For 2 days, visitors have an opportunity to see the famed Rose Garden and South Lawn.

Admission is free. A military band provides music. For details, call
☎ **202/456-2200.** Mid-October.

- **Marine Corps Marathon.** More than 16,000 runners compete
  in this 26.2-mile race (the fourth-largest marathon in the United
  States). It begins at the Marine Corps Memorial (the Iwo Jima
  statue) and passes major monuments. Call ☎ **800/RUN-USMC**
  or 703/784-2225 for details. Anyone can enter; register up to a
  week ahead. Fourth Sunday in October.

November

- **Veterans Day.** The nation's war dead are honored with a wreath-
  laying ceremony at 11am at the Tomb of the Unknowns in
  Arlington National Cemetery, followed by a memorial service.
  The President of the United States or a very high-ranking government personage officiates. Music is provided by a military band.
  Call ☎ **202/685-2851** for information. At the Vietnam Veterans Memorial (☎ **202/619-7222**), observances include speakers,
  a wreath-laying, a color guard, and the playing of taps. November 11.

December

- ✪ **Christmas Pageant of Peace/National Tree Lighting,** at the
  northern end of the Ellipse. The president lights the national
  Christmas tree to the accompaniment of orchestral and choral
  music. The lighting inaugurates the 3-week Pageant of Peace, a
  tremendous holiday celebration with seasonal music, caroling, a
  Nativity scene, 50 state trees, and a burning Yule log. Call
  ☎ **202/619-7222** for details. A select Wednesday or Thursday
  in early December, at 5pm.

- **White House Candlelight Tours.** On 3 evenings after Christmas from 5 to 7pm, visitors can see the president's Christmas
  holiday decorations by candlelight. String music enhances the
  tours. Lines are long; arrive early. Call ☎ **202/456-2200** for
  dates and details.

3 Tips for Travelers with Special Needs

FOR TRAVELERS WITH DISABILITIES

Two helpful travel organizations, **Accessible Journeys** (☎ **800/
TINGLES** or 610/521-0339; Web site www.disabilitytravel.com)
and **Flying Wheels Travel** (☎ **800/535-6790** or 507/451-5005;
Web site www.flyingwheels.com), offer group tours, cruises, and
custom vacations worldwide for people with physical disabilities;
Accessible Journeys can also provide nurse-companions for travelers.

The Guided Tour Inc. (☎ 800/783-5841 or 215/782-1370; Web site www.guidedtour.com) offers tours for people with physical or mental disabilities.

Mobility International USA, P.O. Box 10767, Eugene, OR 97440 (☎ **541/343-1284,** TDD is the same number; Web site www.miusa.org), provides accessibility and resource information to its members. Individual membership costs $35 a year; the quarterly newsletter, "Over the Rainbow," is included in the membership.

The Society for the Advancement of Travel for the Handicapped (SATH), 347 Fifth Ave., Suite 610, New York, NY 10016 (☎ 212/447-7284; fax 212/725-8253; Web site www.sath.org/), offers travel information for people with disabilities and charges $5 for individual requests for information, $45 for adult memberships, and $30 for seniors and student memberships. SATH's quarterly magazine, *OPEN WORLD for Accessible and Mature Travel* is free to members and $13 annually to nonmembers.

Visually impaired travelers can obtain large-print and braille atlases of the Washington area (though they're slightly out of date) from Washington Ear, 35 University Blvd., E. Silver Spring, MD 20901 (☎ **301/681-6636**).

SIGHTSEEING ATTRACTIONS   Washington, D.C., is one of the most accessible cities in the world for travelers with disabilities. The Washington, D.C., Convention & Visitors Association publishes a fact sheet detailing general accessibility of Washington hotels, restaurants, shopping malls, and attractions. For a free copy, call ☎ **202/789-7064** or write to WCVA, 1212 New York Ave. NW, Suite 600, Washington, D.C. 20005.

Here is some accessibility information for specific attractions.

White House visitors in wheelchairs should come to the East Executive Avenue visitors' entrance; visitors arriving in wheelchairs do not need tickets. For details, call ☎ **202/456-2322.**

All Smithsonian museum buildings are accessible to visitors using wheelchairs. A comprehensive free publication called *Smithsonian Access* lists all services available to visitors with disabilities, including parking, building access, and more. To obtain a copy, contact the VIARC, SI Building, Smithsonian Institution, Washington, D.C. 20560 (☎ **202/357-2700** or TTY 202/357-1729). You can also use the TTY number to obtain information on all Smithsonian museums and events.

The Lincoln, Jefferson, and Vietnam Memorials and the Washington Monument are also equipped to accommodate visitors with disabilities and keep wheelchairs on the premises. There's limited parking for visitors with disabilities on the south side of the Lincoln Memorial.

Call your senator or representative to arrange wheelchair-accessible tours of the Capitol; or to arrange special tours there for visitors who are blind or deaf.

GETTING AROUND TOWN   Before you arrive in Washington, you may want to order Metro's free guide on bus and rail system accessibility for the elderly and physically disabled; call ☎ **202/ 635-6434.**

Each Metro station is equipped with an elevator (complete with braille number plates) to train platforms, and rail cars are fully accessible. By the end of 1999, Metro will have installed 24-inch sections of punctuated terra-cotta tiles leading up to the granite-lined platform edge to warn visually impaired Metro riders that they are nearing the tracks. Train operators make station and on-board announcements of train destinations and stops. Most of the district's Metrobuses have wheelchair lifts and kneel at the curb (this number will increase as time goes on). The TDD number for Metro information is ☎ **202/628-2033.** For other questions about Metro services for travelers with disabilities, call ☎ **202/ 962-1100.**

Regular Tourmobile trams are accessible to visitors with disabilities. The company also operates special vans for immobile travelers, complete with wheelchair lifts. Tourmobile recommends that you call a day ahead to ensure that the van is available for you when you arrive. For information, call ☎ **202/554-5100.**

FOR SENIORS

Bring some form of photo ID that includes your birth date, since many city attractions, theaters, transportation facilities, hotels, and restaurants grant special senior discounts.

Contact the D.C. Office on Aging, 441 4th St. NW (☎ **202/ 724-5626**) to request its free directory, *Golden Washingtonian Club Gold Mine.* It lists numerous establishments offering 10% to 15% discounts to seniors on goods and services.

Elderhostel, a national nonprofit organization that offers low-cost educational programs for people 55 or older and their adult companions, sponsors frequent weeklong residential programs in Washington. Some of these focus on government and American history, others on art, literature, and other subjects. Cost averages about $460 per person, including meals, room, and classes. For information, call ☎ **410/830-3437** or contact Elderhostel headquarters at

75 Federal St., Boston, MA 02110 (☎ **617/426-7788;** Web site www.elderhostel.org).

Saga International Holidays, 222 Berkeley St., Boston, MA 02116 (☎ **800/343-0273**), offers tours in the United States and abroad designed for travelers over 50. In Washington, D.C., their 5-night, 6-day Smithsonian Odyssey Tours program offers a behind-the-scenes look at several museums and other major D.C. institutions. For this specific program, call ☎ **800/258-5885.** Prices are moderate.

Amtrak (☎ **800/USA-RAIL**) offers a 15% discount off the full, one-way coach fare (with certain travel restrictions) to people 62 or older.

Greyhound also offers discounted fares for senior citizens. Call your local Greyhound office for details.

FOR GAYS & LESBIANS

The complete source for the gay and lesbian community is *The Washington Blade*, a comprehensive weekly newspaper distributed free at about 700 locations in the district. Every issue provides an extensive events calendar and a list of hundreds of resources, such as crisis centers, health facilities, switchboards, political groups, religious organizations, social clubs, and student activities; it puts readers in touch with everything from groups of lesbian bird-watchers to the Asian Gay Men's Network. Gay restaurants and clubs are, of course, also listed and advertised. You can subscribe to the *Blade* for $45 a year or pick up a free copy around town. One final source: Washington's gay bookstore, **Lambda Rising,** 1625 Connecticut Ave. NW (☎ **202/462-6969**), also informally serves as an information center for the gay community, which centers in the Dupont Circle neighborhood.

FOR FAMILIES

Perhaps more than any other city, Washington is crammed with historic buildings, arts and science museums, parks, and recreational outlets to interest young and old alike. Some of the museums, like the **National Museum of Natural History** and the **Daughters of the American Revolution (DAR) Museum**, have hands-on exhibits for children. Many more sponsor regular, usually free, family-oriented events, such as the **Corcoran Gallery of Art's** "Family Days" and the **Folger Shakespeare Library's** seasonal activities.

Washington, D.C., is easy to get around with children. The Metro covers the city, taking you nearly anywhere you'd want to go, and it's safe. Children under 4 ride free. Remember, however, that eating or drinking on the subway or in the station is prohibited.

Once you arrive, get your hands on a copy of the most recent *Washington Post* "Weekend" section, published each Friday. The section covers all possible happenings in the city, with a weekly feature, called "Saturday's Child," and a column, called "Carousel," devoted to children's activities.

4 Getting There

BY PLANE
D.C.'S AREA AIRPORTS

Ronald Reagan Washington National Airport (which everyone still calls National), lies across the Potomac River in Virginia, about 20 minutes from downtown in non-rush-hour traffic. **Washington Dulles International Airport** (Dulles), lies 26 miles outside the capital, in Chantilly, VA, a 35- to 45-minute ride to downtown in non-rush-hour traffic. **Baltimore-Washington International Airport (BWI),** is about 45 minutes from downtown, a few miles outside of Baltimore. Often overlooked by Washingtonians, BWI's bargain fares make it worth considering.

BEST-FOR-THE-BUDGET FARES   Think about flying into Baltimore-Washington International Airport (see above). The airport lies closer to Baltimore than Washington, but the inconvenience of adding about 20 more minutes to get into Washington may be well outweighed by the savings you receive in booking seats on the low-cost airlines that fly into BWI: **Southwest Airlines** (☎ **800/435-9792**) is the main one.

If you can do without frills, find out whether your city is served by any of the other low-cost airlines that serve Washington: **AirTran** (formerly ValuJet) (☎ **800/247-8726**); **Delta Express** (☎ **800/325-5205**); **Midway Airlines** (☎ **800/446-4392**); and **Western Pacific Airlines** (☎ **800/930-3030**). All but Midway use Washington Dulles International Airport; Midway uses National.

SHUTTLES TO & FROM NEW YORK   The **Delta Shuttle** (☎ **800/221-1212**), which runs between its own terminal at New York's LaGuardia Airport and Ronald Reagan Washington National Airport, departs New York every hour on the half hour weekdays 6:30am to 8:30pm, plus an extra 9pm flight; Saturday from 7:30am to 8:30pm; and Sunday from 8:30am to 8:30pm, plus an extra 9pm flight. On weekdays, the first flight leaves Washington at 6:45am, with flights every hour on the half hour after that until 9:30pm; on Saturday, hourly on the half hour from 7:30am to 8:30pm; and on Sunday, from 8:30am to 9:30pm. The **US Airways Shuttle** (☎ **800/428-4322**) flies from the US Airways terminal at LaGuardia Airport in New York to National Airport. Weekday and Saturday departures from LaGuardia Airport are hourly from 7am to 9pm and Sunday from 9am to 9pm. Washington to New York hourly departures weekdays and Saturday are 7am to 9pm and Sunday 9am to 9pm. Ask about student (12 to 24) and senior (62 and older) discounts.

GETTING DOWNTOWN FROM THE AIRPORT

The cheapest and probably the fastest way to get into town from National Airport is by using the **Metro:** $1.10 (non-rush-hour) or $1.40 (rush hour) and a 15- to 20-minute ride, and you're there.

SuperShuttle (☎ **800/258-3826**) operates seven-passenger blue vans that provide shared-ride, door-to-door service between all three airports and downtown and suburban locations in both Baltimore, Washington, and Virginia. Fares are based on ZIP code, so expect to pay anywhere from $6 to $13 to and from downtown, and about $25 for Maryland and Virginia suburbs.

The Washington Flyer (☎ **703/685-1400**) operates buses between the centrally located Airport Terminal Building at 1517 K St. NW and Dulles Airport, and provides transportation between Dulles and National airports. Fares to and from Dulles, to either downtown or National, are $16 one way; $26 round-trip. Children 6 and under ride free.

The Airport Connection II (☎ **800/284-6066** or 301/441-2345) runs a door-to-door van service between BWI and Washington, D.C.; Prince George's County, MD; and Montgomery County, MD. A minimum of 24 hours' notice is required. Fares run between $18 and $30 for one person; $26 and $37 for two people. Children 5 and younger ride free.

Amtrak (☎ **800/USA-RAIL**) offers daily train service ($13 per person, one-way), while **Maryland Rural Commuter System** (MARC) ($5 per person, one-way) (☎ **800/325-RAIL**) provides weekday service at the BWI Rail Station, 5 minutes from the airport. A courtesy shuttle runs between the airport and the train station.

Taxi fares are about $10 to $14 between National Airport and the White House, $42 to $45 between the White House and Dulles or BWI.

BY TRAIN

Amtrak offers daily service to Washington from New York, Boston, Chicago, and Los Angeles (you change trains in Chicago). Amtrak trains arrive at historic Union Station, 50 Massachusetts Ave. NE, a turn-of-the-century beaux arts masterpiece that was magnificently restored in the late 1980s at a cost of more than $180 million. Offering a three-level marketplace of shops and restaurants, this stunning depot is conveniently located and connects with Metro service. There are always taxis available there. For rail reservations, contact Amtrak (☎ **800/USA-RAIL;** Web site www.amtrak.com).

I suggest that you inquire about money-saving packages that include hotel accommodations, car rentals, tours, and so on with your train fare. Call ☎ **800/321-8684** for details about these "Amtrak Vacations" packages. For example, Amtrak's Air Rail program is a joint venture of Amtrak and United Airlines, allowing passengers to travel one way of a round-trip by train, the other by plane, with three stops permitted on the rail portion.

Metroliner service—which costs a little more but provides faster transit and roomier, more comfortable seating—is available between New York and Washington, D.C., and points in between.

BY BUS

Greyhound buses connect almost the entire United States with Washington, D.C. They arrive at a terminal at 1005 1st St. NE at L Street (☎ **800/231-2222;** Web site www.greyhound.com). The closest Metro stop is Union Station, 4 blocks away. The bus terminal area is not a showplace neighborhood, so if you arrive at night, take a taxi. If you're staying in the suburbs, you should know that Greyhound also has service to Silver Spring, MD, and Arlington and Springfield, VA.

The fare structure on buses is not necessarily based on distance traveled. The good news is that when you call Greyhound to make a reservation, the company will always offer you the lowest fare options. Call in advance and know your travel dates, since some discount fares require advance purchase.

BY CAR

Major highways approach Washington, D.C., from all parts of the country. Specifically, these are I-270, I-95, and I-295 from the north; I-95, Route 1, and Route 301 from the south; Route 50/301 and Route 450 from the east; and Route 7, Route 50, I-66, and

Route 29/211 from the west. No matter what road you take, you are going to have to navigate the Capital Beltway (I-495 and I-95) to gain entry to D.C. The Beltway girds the city, 66 miles around, with 56 interchanges or exits, and is nearly always congested, but especially weekdays, during the morning and evening rush hours, roughly 7 to 9am and 3 to 7pm.

If you're planning to drive to Washington, get yourself a good map before you do anything else. **The American Automobile Association** (AAA) (☎ **800/222-4357** or 703/222-6000) provides its members with maps and detailed Trip-Tiks that give travelers precise directions to a destination, including up-to-date information about areas of construction along the nation's highways and within city boundaries.

The district is 240 miles from New York City, 40 miles from Baltimore, 150 miles from Philadelphia, 700 miles from Chicago, nearly 500 miles from Boston, and about 630 miles from Atlanta.

2

Getting to Know Washington, D.C.

*U*nlike other big, scandalous cities, Washington, with its compact size, excellent subway system, trio of nearby airports, and bounty of free attractions, is a great city for visitors. Before you hit the streets, though, you'll need to know the basics about the city's layout, neighborhoods, transportation, and general ways and means.

1 Orientation

VISITOR INFORMATION

INFORMATION CENTERS If you haven't already called ahead for information from the **Washington, D.C., Convention & Visitors Association** (☎ 202/789-7038), stop in at their headquarters, 1212 New York Ave. NW, Suite 600, weekdays 9am to 5pm.

Another walk-in visitors center has opened at the accessible and convenient **Ronald Reagan Building and International Trade Center**, the very large and newly built structure at 1300 Pennsylvania Ave. NW, next door to the White House Visitor Center (see below). The center occupies space on the ground floor of the building, off the Wilson Plaza entrance, near the Federal Triangle Metro.

The **White House Visitors Center**, on the first floor of the Herbert Hoover Building, Department of Commerce, 1450 Pennsylvania Ave. NW (between 14th and 15th Streets) (☎ **202/208-1631** or 202/456-7041 for recorded information), is open daily 7:30am to 4pm.

The **Smithsonian Information Center**, in the "Castle," 1000 Jefferson Dr. SW (☎ **202/357-2700** or TTY 202/357-1729), is open every day but Christmas, 9am to 5:30pm. For a free copy of the Smithsonian's "Planning your Smithsonian Visit," which is full of valuable tips, write to Smithsonian Institution, VIARC, SI Building, Room 153, MRC 010, Washington, D.C. 20560, or stop at the Castle for a copy.

The **American Automobile Association (AAA)** has a large central office near the White House, at 701 15th St. NW, Washington,

Washington, D.C. at a Glance

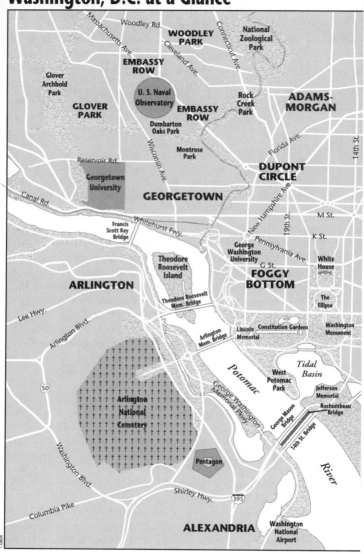

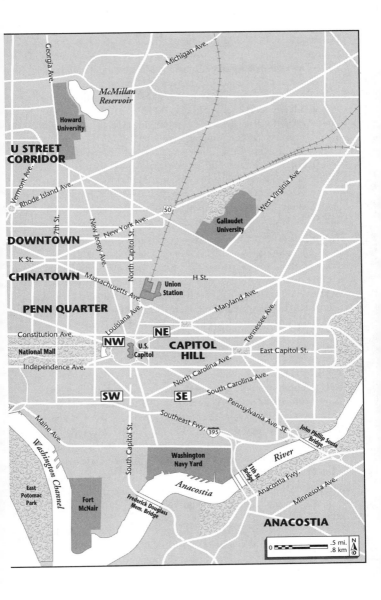

Georgia Ave.

Michigan Ave.

McMillan Reservoir

Howard University

U STREET CORRIDOR

Vermont Ave.

Rhode Island Ave.

West Virginia Ave.

50

Gallaudet University

7th St.

New Jersey Ave.

New York Ave.

North Capitol St.

DOWNTOWN

K St.

CHINATOWN Massachusetts Ave.

H St.

PENN QUARTER

Louisiana Ave.

Union Station

Maryland Ave.

Constitution Ave.

NW **NE**

National Mall

U.S. Capitol

CAPITOL HILL

East Capitol St.

Tennessee Ave.

Independence Ave.

SW **SE**

North Carolina Ave.

South Carolina Ave.

Pennsylvania Ave. SE

Maine Ave.

Southeast Fwy. 395

John Phillip Sousa Bridge

Washington Channel

South Capitol St.

Washington Navy Yard

River

11th St. Bridge

Anacostia Fwy.

Minnesota Ave.

East Potomac Park

Fort McNair

Anacostia

Frederick Douglass Mem. Bridge

ANACOSTIA

0 .5 mi.
.8 km

N

D.C. 20005-2111 (☎ **202/331-3000**). Hours are weekdays 9am to 6pm.

The **Travelers Aid Society** is a nationwide network of volunteer, nonprofit, social-service agencies providing help to travelers in difficulty. In Washington, Travelers Aid has a central office in the Capitol Hill area at 512 C St. NE (☎ **202/546-3120**), where professional social workers are available to provide assistance. It's open only on weekdays 9am to 5pm; please call first.

There are also Travelers Aid desks at Ronald Reagan National Airport (open weekdays 9am to 9pm, weekends 9am to 6pm, ☎ **703/417-3972**); at Dulles International Airport (open weekdays 10am to 9pm, weekends 10am to 6pm, ☎ **703/572-8296**); and at Union Station (open Monday through Saturday 9:30am to 5:30pm, Sunday 12:30 to 5:30pm; ☎ **202/371-1937**).

NEWSPAPERS   Washington has two daily newspapers: the *Washington Post* and the *Washington Times*. The Friday "Weekend" section of the *Post* is essential for finding out what's going on, recreation-wise. *City Paper*, published every Thursday and available free at downtown shops and restaurants, covers some of the same material but is a better guide to the club and art-gallery scene. If you're staying in the suburbs, the *Friday Journal Papers* (one for each area county) provide comprehensive coverage of activities beyond the downtown.

CITY LAYOUT

The U.S. Capitol marks the center of the city, which is divided into quadrants: **northwest (NW), northeast (NE), southwest (SW), and southeast (SE).** If you look at your map, you'll see that some addresses—for instance, the corner of G and 7th Streets—appear in four different places. There's one in each quadrant. Hence you must observe the quadrant designation (NW, NE, SW, or SE) when looking for an address.

FINDING AN ADDRESS   Once you understand the city's layout, it's easy to find your way around. As you read this, have a map handy.

Each of the four corners of the District of Columbia is exactly the same distance from the Capitol dome. The White House and most government buildings and important monuments are west of the Capitol (in the northwest and southwest quadrants), as are important hotels and tourist facilities.

Numbered streets run north-south, beginning on either side of the Capitol with First Street, northeast (NE) and southeast (SE). Lettered streets run east-west and are named alphabetically, beginning with A Street. (Don't look for a B, a J, an X, Y, or Z Street, however.) After W Street, one-syllable, two-syllable, and three-syllable street names come into play; the more syllables in a name, the farther the street will lie from the Capitol.

Avenues, named for U.S. states, run at angles across the grid pattern and often intersect at traffic circles. For example, New Hampshire, Connecticut, and Massachusetts Avenues intersect at Dupont Circle.

With this in mind, you can easily find an address. On lettered streets, the address tells you exactly where to go. For instance, 1776 K Street NW is between 17th and 18th Streets (the first two digits of 1776 tell you that) in the northwest quadrant (NW). Note: I Street is often written Eye Street to prevent confusion with 1st Street.

To find an address on numbered streets, you'll probably have to use your fingers. For instance, 623 8th Street SE is between F and G Streets (the sixth and seventh letters of the alphabet; the first digit of 623 tells you that) in the southeast quadrant (SE). One thing to remember: You count B as the second letter of the alphabet even though no B Street exists today (Constitution and Independence Avenues were each at one time the original B Streets), but since there's no J Street, K becomes the 10th letter, L the 11th, and so on.

NEIGHBORHOODS IN BRIEF

Adams-Morgan   This increasingly trendy, multiethnic neighborhood is about a minute long, centered around 18th Street and Columbia Road NW. Parking during the day is OK, but forget it at night. You can easily walk (and be alert; the neighborhood is edgy) or take a taxi here for a taste of Malaysian, Ethiopian, Spanish, or some other international cuisine. On Friday and Saturday nights, it's a hot nightlife district, rivaling Georgetown and Dupont Circle.

Capital Hill   Everyone's heard of "the Hill," the area crowned by the Capitol. When people speak of Capitol Hill, they refer to a large section of town, extending from the western side of the Capitol to the D.C. Armory going east, bounded by H Street NE and the

Southwest Freeway north and south. It contains not only the chief symbol of the nation's capital, but the Supreme Court building, the Library of Congress, the Folger Shakespeare Library, Union Station, and the U.S. Botanic Garden. Much of it is a quiet residential neighborhood of tree-lined streets and Victorian homes.

Downtown   The area roughly between 7th and 22nd Streets NW going east to west, and P Street and Pennsylvania Avenue going north to south, is a mix of the Federal Triangle's government office buildings, K Street ("Lawyer's Row"), Connecticut Avenue restaurants and shopping, historic hotels, the city's poshest small hotels, and the White House. Also here is a quadrant known as the Historic Penn Quarter, a part of downtown that is taking on new life with the opening of the MCI Center, trendy new restaurants, and art galleries. The total downtown area takes in so many blocks and attractions that I've divided discussions of accommodations (chapter 3) and dining (chapter 4) into two sections: "Downtown, 16th Street NW and West," and "Downtown, east of 16th Street NW"; 16th Street and the White House form a natural point of separation.

Dupont Circle   My favorite part of town, the Dupont Circle area is a fun place to be any time of day or night. It takes its name from the traffic circle minipark, where Massachusetts, New Hampshire, and Connecticut Avenues collide. The streets extending out from the circle are lively with all-night bookstores, really good restaurants, wonderful art galleries and art museums, nightspots, movie theaters, and Washingtonians at their loosest. It is also the hub of D.C.'s gay community.

Foggy Bottom   The area west of the White House to the edge of Georgetown, Foggy Bottom was Washington's early industrial center. Its name comes from the foul fumes emitted in those days by a coal depot and gasworks, but its original name, Funkstown (for owner Jacob Funk), is perhaps even worse. There's nothing foul about the area today. The Kennedy Center and George Washington University are located here. Constitution and Pennsylvania Avenues are Foggy Bottom's southern and northern boundaries, respectively.

Georgetown   This historic community dates from colonial times. It was a thriving tobacco port long before the District of Columbia was formed, and one of its attractions, the Old Stone House, dates from pre-Revolutionary days. Georgetown action centers on M Street and Wisconsin Avenue NW, where you'll find numerous boutiques, chic restaurants, and popular pubs (lots of nightlife here). But get off the main drags and see the quiet tree-lined streets of restored colonial row houses, stroll through the beautiful gardens of Dumbarton Oaks, and check out the C&O Canal. One of the reasons so much activity flourishes in Georgetown is because of Georgetown University and its students.

Glover Park   Mostly a residential neighborhood, this section of town, just above Georgetown and just south of the Washington National Cathedral, is worth mentioning because of the increasing number of good restaurants opening along its main stretch, Wisconsin Avenue NW. Glover Park sits between the campuses of Georgetown and American Universities, so there's a large student presence here.

The Mall   This lovely tree-lined stretch of open space between Constitution and Independence Avenues, extending for 2$^{1}/_{2}$ miles from the Capitol to the Lincoln Memorial, is the hub of tourist attractions. It includes most of the Smithsonian Institution museums and many other nearby visitor attractions. The 300-foot-wide Mall is used by natives as well as tourists—joggers, food vendors, kite-flyers, and picnickers among them.

U Street Corridor   D.C.'s newest nightlife neighborhood between 12th and 15th Streets NW is rising from the ashes of nightclubs and theaters frequented decades ago by African Americans. At the renovated Lincoln Theater, where legends like Duke Ellington, Louis Armstrong, and Cab Calloway once performed, patrons today can enjoy performances by popular though less famous black artists. The corridor offers at least six alternative rock and contemporary music nightclubs and several restaurants (see chapter 7 for details).

Woodley Park   Home to Washington's largest hotel (the Washington Marriott Wardman Park—formerly known as the Sheraton Washington) and another really big one (the Omni Shoreham), Woodley Park also is the site of the National Zoo, many good restaurants, and some antique stores. Washingtonians are used to seeing conventioneers, still wearing their name tags, wandering the neighborhood's pretty residential area.

2   Getting Around

Washington is one of the easiest U.S. cities in which to get around. Only New York rivals its comprehensive transportation system, but Washington's clean, efficient subways put the Big Apple's underground nightmare to shame. A complex bus system covers all major D.C. arteries, as well, and it's easy to hail a taxi anywhere at any time. But because Washington is of manageable size and marvelous beauty, you may find yourself shunning transportation and getting around on foot.

BY METRO

Metrorail stations are immaculate, cool, and attractive. Cars are air-conditioned and fitted with upholstered seats; tracks are rubber-cushioned so the ride is quiet; service is frequent enough so you usually get a seat, at least during off-peak hours (basically weekdays 10am to 3pm and weeknights after 8pm); and the system is so simply designed that a 10-year-old can understand it. Eating, drinking, and smoking are strictly prohibited on the Metro and in stations.

There are five lines in operation—red, blue, orange, yellow, and green—with extensions planned for the future. The lines connect at several points, making transfers easy. All but yellow- and green-line trains stop at Metro Center; all except red-line trains stop at L'Enfant Plaza; all but blue- and orange-line trains stop at Gallery Place/Chinatown.

Metro stations are indicated by discreet brown columns bearing the station's name and topped by the letter M. Below the M is a colored stripe or stripes indicating the line or lines that stop there. When entering a Metro station for the first time, go to the kiosk and ask the station manager for a free "Metro System Pocket Guide" (available in six languages: English, German, Spanish, Korean, Japanese, and French). It contains a map of the system, explains how it works, and lists the closest Metro stops to points of interest. The station manager can also answer questions about routing or purchase of fare cards. Some Metro riders will soon be able to turn to Metro station computers for help.

To enter or exit a Metro station, you need a computerized fare card, available at vending machines near the entrance. Don't throw away your fare card after you enter, you'll need it to get out of the station. The minimum fare to enter the system is $1.10, which pays for rides to and from any point within 7 miles of boarding during off-peak hours; during peak hours (weekdays 5:30 to 9:30am and 3 to 8pm), $1.10 takes you for only 3 miles. The machines take nickels, dimes, quarters, and bills from $1 to $20; they can return up to $4.95 in change (coins only). If you plan to take several Metrorail trips during your stay, put more value on the fare card to avoid having to purchase a new card each time you ride. There's a 10% bonus on all fare cards of $20 or more. Up to two children under 5 can ride free with a paying passenger. Senior citizens (65 and older) and people with disabilities (with valid proof) ride Metrorail and Metrobus for a reduced fare.

Discount passes, called "**One-Day Rail passes**," cost $5 per person and allow you unlimited passage for the day, after 9:30am weekdays, and all day on weekends and holidays. You can buy them at most stations; at Washington Metropolitan Transit Authority, 600 5th St. NW (☎ **202/637-7000**); at Metro Center, 12th and G sts. NW; or at a Giant or Safeway grocery store.

When you insert your card in the entrance gate, the time and location are recorded on its magnetic tape, and your card is returned. Don't forget to snatch it up and keep it handy; you have to reinsert it in the exit gate at your destination, where the fare will automatically be deducted. The card will be returned if there's any value left on it. If you arrive at a destination and your fare card doesn't have enough value, add what's necessary at the Exitfare machines near the exit gate.

Metrorail operates weekdays 5:30am to midnight, weekends and holidays 8am to midnight. Call ☎ **202/637-7000** for information on Metro routes. *Warning:* The line is often busy, so just keep trying.

BY BUS

While a 10-year-old can understand the Metrorail system, the Metrobus system is considerably more complex. The 15,800 stops on the 1,489-square-mile route (it operates on all major D.C. arteries as well as in the Virginia and Maryland suburbs) are indicated by red, white, and blue signs. However, the signs tell you only what buses pull into a given stop, not where they go. For routing information, call ☎ **202/637-7000.** Calls are taken weekdays 6am to 10:30pm, weekends and holidays 8am to 10:30pm. This is the same number you call to request a free map and time schedule, information about parking in Metrobus fringe lots, and for locations and hours of those places where you can purchase bus tokens.

Base fare in the district is $1.10; bus transfers cost 10¢. There are additional charges for travel into the Maryland and Virginia suburbs. Bus drivers are not equipped to make change, so be sure to carry exact change or tokens. If you'll be in Washington for a while and plan to use the buses a lot, consider buying a $20 2-week pass, also available at the Metro Center station and other outlets.

Metro Stops in Georgetown & Downtown

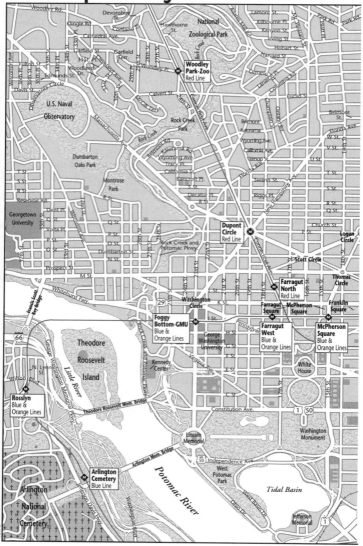

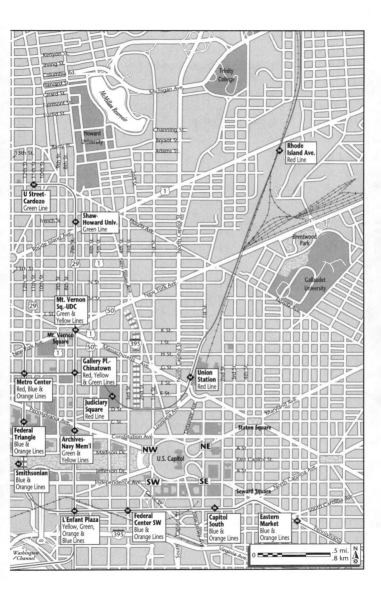

Rhode Island Ave.
Red Line

Trinity College

McMillan Reservoir

Howard University

Brentwood Park

Gallaudet University

U Street-Cardozo
Green Line

Shaw-Howard Univ.
Green Line

Mt. Vernon Sq.-UDC
Green & Yellow Lines

Mt. Vernon Square

Gallery Pl.-Chinatown
Red, Yellow & Green Lines

Metro Center
Red, Blue & Orange Lines

Judiciary Square
Red Line

Union Station
Red Line

Staton Square

Federal Triangle
Blue & Orange Lines

Archives-Navy Mem'l
Green & Yellow Lines

NW

NE

U.S. Capitol

Smithsonian
Blue & Orange Lines

Seward Square

SW

SE

L'Enfant Plaza
Yellow, Green, Orange & Blue Lines

Federal Center SW
Blue & Orange Lines

Capitol South
Blue & Orange Lines

Eastern Market
Blue & Orange Lines

Washington Channel

0 .5 mi.
.8 km

N

27

Most buses operate daily almost around the clock. Service is quite frequent on weekdays, especially during peak hours. You may not be as lucky late at night or on the weekends.

Up to two children under 5 ride free with a paying passenger on Metrobus, and there are reduced fares for senior citizens (☎ **202/ 962-7000**) and people with disabilities (☎ **202/962-1245** or 202/ 962-1100). If you should leave something on a bus, train, or in a station, call Lost and Found at ☎ **202/962-1195.**

BY CAR

More than half of all visitors to the district arrive by car. If you're one of them, you should know that traffic is always thick during the week, parking spaces are often hard to find, and parking lots are ruinously expensive.

Even if you don't drive in D.C., you will want a car to get to most attractions in Virginia and Maryland. All major car-rental companies are represented here. Here are the phone numbers for those rental companies with locations at all three airports: **Alamo** (☎ **800/327-9633**); **Avis** (☎ **800/331-1212**); **Budget** (☎ **800/ 527-0700**); **Hertz** (☎ **800/654-3131**); and **Thrifty** (☎ **800/ 367-2277**). **Kemwel Holiday Auto** (☎ **800/678-0678**) offers discounted rates for major car-rental companies.

BY TAXI

District cabs operate on a zone system instead of meters. By law, basic rates are posted in each cab. If you take a trip from one point to another within the same zone, you pay just $4, regardless of the distance traveled. So it will cost you $4 to travel a few blocks from the U.S. Capitol to the National Museum of American History, but the same $4 could take you from the Capitol all the way to Dupont Circle. They're both in Zone 1. Also in Zone 1 are most other tourist attractions: the White House, most of the Smithsonian, the Washington Monument, the FBI, the National Archives, the Supreme Court, the Library of Congress, the Bureau of Engraving and Printing, the Old Post Office, and Ford's Theatre. If your trip takes you into a second zone, the price is $5.50, $6.90 for a third zone, $8.25 for a fourth, and so on.

The fares seem modest, but they can add up. There's a $1.50 charge for each additional passenger after the first, so a $4 Zone 1 fare can become $8.50 for a family of four (although one child under 5 rides free). There's also a rush-hour surcharge of $1 per trip weekdays between 7 and 9:30am and 4 and 6:30pm. Surcharges are also added for large pieces of luggage and for arranging a pickup by telephone ($1.50).

The zone system is not used when your destination is an out-of-district address (such as an airport); in that case, the fare is based on mileage covered—$2 for the first half mile or part thereof and 70¢ for each additional half mile or part. You can call ☎ **202/331-1671** to find out the rate between any point in D.C. and an address in Virginia or Maryland. Call ☎ **202/645-6018** to inquire about fares within the district.

It's generally easy to hail a taxi, although the *Washington Post* has reported that taxi cabs, even those driven by black cabbies, often ignore African Americans to pick up white passengers; African-American friends corroborate that this is true. Unique to the city is the practice of allowing drivers to pick up as many passengers as they can comfortably fit, so expect to share (unrelated parties pay the same as they would if they were not sharing). You can also call a taxi, though there's that $1.50 charge. Try **Capitol Cab** (☎ **202/546-2400**), **Diamond Cab Company** (☎ **202/387-6200**), or **Yellow Cab** (☎ **202/544-1212**).

BY TOURMOBILE

The best way to get acquainted with any city, I'm convinced, is by hopping on a tour bus that circles the major parts of town while a guide narrates. A good one to try is **Tourmobile** (☎ **202/554-5100** or 888/868-7707; Web site www.tourmobile.com), whose comfortable red, white, and blue sightseeing trams travel to as many as 25 sites, as far out as Arlington National Cemetery and even (with coach service) Mount Vernon. (Tourmobile is the only narrated sightseeing shuttle tour authorized by the National Park Service.) You can take the **Washington/Arlington Cemetery** tour or tour only **Arlington Cemetery.** The former stops at 21 different sites on or near the Mall and four sights at Arlington Cemetery: the Kennedy grave sites, the Tomb of the Unknowns, Arlington House, and the Women in Military Service Memorial.

Here's how the system works: You pay the driver when you first board the bus (you can also purchase a ticket inside the Arlington National Cemetery Visitor Center or, for a small surcharge, order your ticket in advance from Ticketmaster, ☎ **800/551-SEAT**). Along the route, you may get off at any stop to visit monuments or buildings. When you finish exploring each area, step aboard the next Tourmobile that comes along without extra charge (as long as you can show your ticket). The buses travel in a loop, serving each stop about every 15 to 30 minutes. One fare allows you to use the buses for a full day. The charge for the Washington/Arlington Cemetery tour is $14 for anyone 12 and older, $7 for children 3 to 11. For Arlington Cemetery only, those 12 and older pay $4.75, children $2.25. Children under 3 ride free. Buses follow figure-eight circuits from the Capitol to Arlington Cemetery and back. You can also buy an advance ticket after 3pm June 15–Labor Day or after 1pm the rest of the year, that is valid for the rest of the afternoon plus the following day; these tickets cost $16 per adult, $8 for children 3 to 11. Well-trained narrators give commentaries about sights along the route and answer questions.

Tourmobiles operate daily year-round, except Christmas. From June 15 to Labor Day, they ply the Mall between 9am and 6:30pm. After Labor Day, the hours are 9:30am to 4:30pm. In Arlington Cemetery, between November and March, they start at 8:30am and end at 4:30pm; from April through October, the hours are 8:30am to 6:30pm.

From April through October, Tourmobiles also run round-trip to **Mount Vernon.** Coaches depart from the Arlington National Cemetery Visitor Center at 10am, noon, and 2pm, with a pickup at the Washington Monument shortly thereafter. The price is $22 for those 12 and older, $11 for children ages 3 to 11, including admission to Mount Vernon. A combination tour of Washington, Arlington Cemetery, and Mount Vernon (good for 2 days) is $37 for anyone 12 and older, $18.50 for children ages 3 to 11. Another offering (June 15 to Labor Day) is the **Frederick Douglass National Historic Site Tour,** which includes a guided tour of Douglass's home, Cedar Hill, in southeast Washington. Departures are from Arlington National Cemetery at noon, with a pickup at the Washington Monument shortly thereafter. Those 12 and older pay $7, and children ages 3 to 11 pay $3.50. A 2-day Combination Frederick Douglass Tour and Washington/Arlington National Cemetery Tour is also available for $28 for those 12 and older, $14 for children ages 3 to 11. For both the Mount Vernon and Frederick Douglass tours, you must reserve in person at either Arlington Cemetery or the Washington Monument at least an hour in advance.

Tourmobile's newest offering is a **Twilight Tour** that departs each evening at 6:30pm March through December from Union Station, stopping at the Jefferson, FDR, and Lincoln Memorials, the White House, and the Capitol, before returning to Union Station. The tour lasts nearly 4 hours, includes narrated touring on the bus and at each site, and costs $14 per adult, $7 per child ages 3 to 11.

BY OLD TOWN TROLLEY   Another standard is **Old Town Trolley Tours** (☎ **202/832-9800**), which offers 2¹/₂-hour narrated tours aboard green-and-orange trolleys that stop at more than 19 sites. Both the Tourmobiles and the trolleys are open-air in summer—meaning not air-conditioned. For a fixed price, you can get on and off these green-and-orange vehicles as often as you like for an entire loop around the city. Following a loop, the trolleys stop at 19 locations in the district, including Georgetown; they also go out to Arlington National Cemetery. They operate Memorial Day to Labor Day daily from 9am to 5pm; the rest of the year 9am to 4pm. The cost is $20 for adults, $11 for children 4 to 12, free for children under 4. You can board without a ticket and purchase it en route.

Old Town Trolley also offers a 2¹/₂-hour "Washington After Hours" tour of illuminated federal buildings and memorials from mid-March to the end of December. Call above for details.

FAST FACTS: Washington, D.C.

Airports   See "Getting Around," above.

American Express   There's an American Express Travel Service office at 1150 Connecticut Ave. NW (☎ **202/457-1300**), another at Metro Center, 1001 G St. NW (☎ **202/393-2368**), and a third in upper northwest Washington at 5300 Wisconsin Ave. NW, in the Mazza Gallerie (☎ **202/362-4000**). Each office functions as a full travel agency and currency exchange; of course, you can also buy traveler's checks here.

Area Code   Within the District of Columbia, it's 202. In suburban Virginia, it's 703. In suburban Maryland, it's 301.

Baby-sitters   Most hotels can arrange for sitters. If your hotel does not offer a baby-sitting service, you can contact **White House Nannies** (☎ **301/652-8088**).

Congresspersons   To locate a senator or congressional representative, call the Capitol switchboard (☎ **202/224-3121**).

Convention Center   The Washington, D.C., Convention Center, 900 9th St. NW, between H St. and New York Ave. (☎ **202/789-1600**), is a vast multipurpose facility with 381,000 square feet of exhibition space and 40 meeting rooms.

Crime See "Safety," below.

Doctors/Dentists **Prologue** (☎ 800/DOCTORS) can refer you to any type of doctor or dentist you need. Its roster includes just about every specialty. Hours are weekdays 8:30am to 8pm, Saturday 9:30am to 4pm. **The Washington Hospital Center** (☎ 202/877-DOCS) referral service operates weekdays 8am to 4pm and will point you to a doctor located as close as possible to where you are staying.

Drugstores **CVS,** Washington's major drugstore chain (with more than 40 stores), has two convenient 24-hour locations: 14th St. and Thomas Circle NW, at Vermont Ave. (☎ 202/628-0720), and at Dupont Circle (☎ 202/785-1466), both with round-the-clock pharmacies. These drugstores also carry miscellaneous goods ranging from frozen food and basic groceries to small appliances. Check your phone book for other convenient locations.

Emergencies/Hotlines Dial ☎ 911 to contact the police or fire department or to call an ambulance. See also "Hospitals," below. To reach a 24-hour **poison control hotline,** call ☎ 202/ 625-3333; to reach a **24-hour crisis line,** call ☎ 202/561-7000; and to reach the **drug and alcohol abuse hotline,** which operates daily 10am to 2am, call ☎ 1-888/294-3572.

Hospitals **George Washington University Hospital,** 901 23rd St. NW (entrance on Washington Circle; ☎ 202/994-3211 for emergency room or 202/994-1000 for general information); **Georgetown University Hospital,** 3800 Reservoir Rd. NW (☎ 202/784-2119 for emergency room or 202/687-2000 for general information).

Laundry/Dry Cleaning Most hotels provide laundry and dry-cleaning services and/or have coin-operated facilities. Otherwise, try **Washtub Laundromat,** 1511 17th St. NW (☎ 202/ 332-9455), for self-service coin-operated laundering. For complete laundry and dry-cleaning services with free pickup and delivery, contact **Bergmann's** (☎ 703/247-7600). For same-day dry-cleaning service, try **MacDee Quality Cleaners,** at 1639 L St. NW (☎ 202/296-6100), open Monday through Saturday.

Liquor Laws The minimum drinking age is 21. Liquor stores are closed on Sunday.

Police In an emergency, dial ☎ 911. For a nonemergency, call ☎ 202/727-1010.

Post Office   Post offices are located throughout the city, including the one in the National Postal Museum building, opposite Union Station at 2 Massachusetts Ave. NE, at G and North Capitol streets. (☎ **202/523-2628**). It's open weekdays 7am to midnight, and weekends until 8pm.

Safety   In Washington, you're quite safe throughout the day in all the major tourist areas described in this book, and you can also safely visit the Lincoln Memorial after dark. At nighttime, be alert anywhere you go in Washington. Riding the Metro is quite safe.

Taxes   Sales tax on merchandise is 5.75% in the district, 5% in Maryland, and 4.5% in Virginia. The tax on restaurant meals is 10% in the district, 5% in Maryland, and 4.5% in Virginia.

In the district, in addition to your hotel rate, you pay 13% sales tax and $1.50 per night occupancy tax. The state sales tax on a hotel room is 9.75% in suburban Virginia and 10% in Maryland (where you can expect an additional 5% to 7% in city or local taxes).

Taxis   See "Getting Around," earlier in this chapter.

Tickets   A service called **TICKETplace** (☎ **202/TICKETS**) sells half-price tickets, on the day of performance only, to most major Washington-area theaters and concert halls. It also functions as a Ticketmaster outlet. A same-day half-price ticket booth operates at the Old Post Office Pavilion. For advance sale tickets, call Ticketmaster (☎ **202/432-SEAT**) or Protix (☎ **703/218-6500**).

Transit Information   See "Getting Around," earlier in this chapter.

Weather   Call ☎ 202/936-1212.

3

Where to Stay in Washington, D.C.

*N*ot so long ago, up until 1997, in fact, Washington's peak seasons coincided generally with two activities: the sessions of Congress and springtime, starting with the appearance of the cherry blossoms along the Potomac. Specifically, when Congress was "in," from about the second week in September until Thanksgiving and again from about mid-January through June, hotels were reasonably full with guests whose business took them to Capitol Hill or to conferences scheduled here. The period April through June traditionally has been the peak-peak season, when families and school groups descend upon the city to see the cherry blossoms and enjoy Washington's sensational spring. Weekdays, too, have always been considered prime time, with hotels emptying out on weekends.

A NOTE ABOUT PRICE CATEGORIES　The hotels listed in this chapter are grouped first by location, then alphabetically by price. I've used the following guide for per-night prices: **Very Expensive,** more than $215; **Expensive,** $150 to $215; **Moderate,** $100 to $149; and **Inexpensive,** less than $100.

HOW TO GET THE BEST RATE

As you peruse this chapter, you should keep certain things in mind. First, consider all the hotels, no matter the rate category. The accepted wisdom is that no one pays the advertised "rack" rate. Even the best and most expensive hotels may be ready to negotiate and often offer bargain rates at certain times or to guests who are members of certain groups, and you may be eligible. If you can be flexible about the time you are traveling, all the better. Second, as a rule, when you call a hotel, you should ask whether there are special promotions or discounts available.

It pays to know what you want and to do some research. For example, by calling hotels and simply asking if there were special weekend rates, I was quoted the following low prices: about $155 at the posh Watergate Hotel; $125 (as much as $34 off the regular rate) for a "Weekend Superbe" package available through the Hotel Sofitel, entitling couples to a one-night stay with a continental breakfast of croissants and pastries served in the room; and $99, including continental breakfast served in the restaurant, at the Morrison-Clark Inn.

RESERVATION SERVICES   If you don't have the time or energy to find yourself the right accommodation, these Washington reservations services will do it for you, for free. Because each of these businesses is Washington-based, you can specify your needs and ask for details about neighborhoods that only local people would know.

Capitol Reservations, 1730 Rhode Island Ave. NW, Suite 1114, Washington, D.C. 20036 (☎ **800/VISIT-DC** or 202/452-1270; fax 202/452-0537; www.hotelsdc.com), will find you a hotel that meets your specific requirements and is within your price range, and they'll do the bargaining for you. **Washington D.C. Accommodations,** 2201 Wisconsin Ave. NW, Suite C110, Washington, D.C. 20007 (☎ **800/554-2220** or 202/289-2220; fax 202/338-4517; www.dcaccommodations.com), has been in business for 14 years and provides the same service.

GROUPS   If you're planning a meeting, convention, or other group function requiring 10 rooms or more, contact **U.S.A. Groups** (☎ **800/872-4777** or 202/861-1900; fax 703/440-9705). This free service represents hotel rooms at almost every hostelry in the Washington, D.C., and suburban Virginia–Maryland region in all price categories..

A similar service, **Bed & Breakfast Accommodations Ltd.,** P.O. Box 12011, Washington, D.C. 20005 (☎ **202/328-3510;** fax 202/332-3885; www.bnbaccom.com), has more than 80 homes, inns, guest houses, and unhosted furnished apartments in its files. Most are in historic districts.

1   Best Bets

- **Best Historic Hotel:** The grande dame of Washington hotels is the magnificent **Renaissance Mayflower,** 1127 Connecticut Ave. NW (☎ **800/HOTELS-1** or 202/347-3000), which, when it was built in 1925, was considered not only the last word in luxury and beauty, but also "the second-best address" in town. Harry S Truman preferred it over the White House.
- **Best Location:** The **Willard Inter-Continental,** 1401 Pennsylvania Ave. NW (☎ **800/327-0200** or 202/628-9100), is within walking distance of the White House; museums; theaters;

downtown offices; good restaurants; and the Metro. It's also a
quick taxi ride to Capitol Hill.

- **Best Place for a Romantic Getaway:** The posh **Jefferson,** 16th
  and M Sts. NW (☎ **800/368-5966** or 202/347-2200), is just
  enough off the beaten track, but still conveniently downtown, to
  feel like you've really escaped. Because the service, bar, and restaurant (see chapter 4 for a review of The Restaurant at the
  Jefferson) are outstanding, you have no need to leave the premises. The restaurant itself has one of the most romantic nooks
  in the city.

- **Best Moderately Priced Hotel:** The newly renovated **Hotel
  Lombardy,** 2019 Pennsylvania Ave. NW (☎ **800/424-5486** or
  202/828-2600), is now slightly more than moderately priced
  but still conveniently located, with spacious and charmingly decorated accommodations, and concierge-like service from the front
  desk.

- **Best Inexpensive Hotel: The Days Inn Premier,** 1201 K St.
  NW (☎ **800/562-3350** or 202/842-1020), near the Convention
  Center and the MCI Center, even has a small rooftop pool. If you
  reserve far in advance, you may be able to get the special $59 per
  night "Super Saver" rate.

- **Best Inn:** The stunning **Morrison-Clark Inn,** Massachusetts
  Avenue and 11th Street NW (☎ **800/332-7898** or 202/898-
  1200), housed in two beautifully restored Victorian town houses,
  has exquisite rooms and an acclaimed restaurant.

- **Best B&B: Swann House,** 1808 New Hampshire Ave. NW
  (☎ **202/265-7677**) is remarkably pretty and comfortable, in a
  great neighborhood (Dupont Circle), and not outrageously
  priced.

- **Best Service:** The staff at **The Four Seasons,** 2800 Pennsylvania
  Ave. NW (☎ **800/332-3442** or 202/342-0444), pampers you
  relentlessly and greets you by name. The hotels also offers an "I
  Need It Now" program that delivers any of 100 or more left-at-
  home essentials (tweezers; batteries; cufflinks; electric hair curlers;
  and so on) to you in 3 minutes, at no cost.

- **Best for Business Travelers: The Grand Hyatt** Washington,
  1000 H St. NW (☎ **800/233-1234** or 202/582-1234), wins for
  its convenient central location (in the business district between
  the White House and the Capitol, directly across from the Convention Center, and 3 blocks from the MCI Center, with direct
  underground access to the subway) and for its ample on-site
  meeting facilities. The hotel also offers a inviting, $15-extra

"Business Plan," which accommodates travelers in 8th- and 9th-floor rooms equipped with a large desk, fax machine, and computer hookup, with access to printers and other office supplies. Continental breakfast is included in the plan.

- **Best Health Club:** The **West End Fitness Center,** at the ANA Hotel, 2401 M St. NW (☎ **800/ANA-HOTELS** or 202/429-2400), is the model against which all other hotels measure their own. The 17,500-square-foot center offers classes in yoga and aerobics; seminars in stress management and weight loss; and equipment that includes virtual-reality bike machines, stair climbers with telephones and TV/VCR units, NordicTraks, rowing machines, exercise bikes with telephones, and assorted other torturous machines. The health club also has squash and racquetball courts; a swimming pool; a steam room; a whirlpool; saunas; and a minispa. Personal trainers, fitness evaluation, and workout clothes are available.
- **Best Views: The Hay-Adams,** 16th and H sts. NW (☎ **800/424-5054** or 202/638-6600), has such a great, unobstructed view of the White House that the Secret Service comes over regularly to do security sweeps of the place.

2 Capitol Hill/The Mall

EXPENSIVE

Capitol Hill Suites. 200 C St. SE, Washington, D.C. 20003. ☎ **800/424-9165** or 202/543-6000. Fax 202/547-2608. 152 units. A/C TV TEL. Weekdays and weekends $89–$199 double. Extra person $20. Rates include continental breakfast. Children under 18 stay free. AE, CB, DC, DISC, MC, V. Valet parking $15. Metro: Capitol South.

This well-run all-suite property (on the House of Representatives side of the Capitol) comprises two contiguous converted apartment houses on a residential street near the Library of Congress, the Capitol, and Mall attractions—hence its popularity with numerous congresspeople, whose photographs are displayed in the pleasant lobby. Spacious accommodations, ideal for families, offer full kitchens or kitchenettes and dining areas, and you'll find complete living and dining rooms in the one-bedroom units. Decor is residential, with 18th-century mahogany reproduction furnishings and museum art prints adorning the walls. The hotel provides a helpful guide to local shops and services. A food market and about 20 nearby restaurants (many of which deliver to the hotel) compensate for the lack of on-premises dining facilities. Guests enjoy free use of extensive facilities at the nearby Washington Sports Club.

Georgetown & Downtown Accommodations

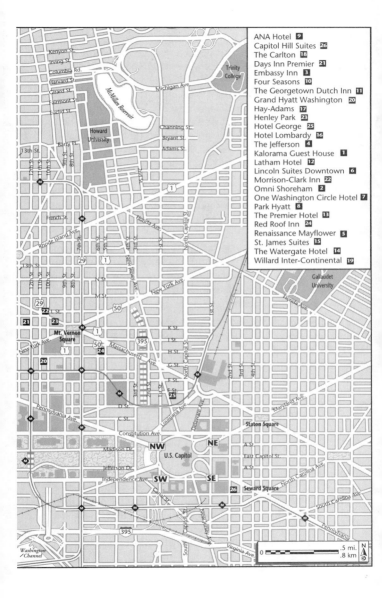

ANA Hotel **9**
Capitol Hill Suites **26**
The Carlton **18**
Days Inn Premier **21**
Embassy Inn **3**
Four Seasons **10**
The Georgetown Dutch Inn **11**
Grand Hyatt Washington **20**
Hay-Adams **17**
Henley Park **23**
Hotel George **25**
Hotel Lombardy **16**
The Jefferson **4**
Kalorama Guest House **1**
Latham Hotel **12**
Lincoln Suites Downtown **6**
Morrison-Clark Inn **22**
Omni Shoreham **2**
One Washington Circle Hotel **7**
Park Hyatt **8**
The Premier Hotel **13**
Red Roof Inn **24**
Renaissance Mayflower **5**
St. James Suites **15**
The Watergate Hotel **14**
Willard Inter-Continental **19**

✪ **The Hotel George.** 15 E St. NW, Washington, D.C. 20001. ☎ **800/ 576-8331** or 202/347-4200. Fax 202/347-4213. www.hotelgeorge.com. 147 units. A/C MINIBAR TV TEL. Weekdays $185–$220, weekends $129, suites $375–$500. Ask about seasonal rates. Extra person $20. Children under 14 stay free. AE, CB, DC, DISC, MC, V. Parking $18. Metro: Union Station.

Out with the old, in with the funk. Posters throughout this new hotel, housed in a 1928 building, depict a modern-day interpretation of George Washington, sans wig—and that's the theme of this hotel. Rather than stick to old-style traditions, this place with a hip attitude brings you Washington à la 2000. The lobby isn't fancy, but it's comfortable, and the decor is "cool retro." The large rooms offer modern amenities.

Dining/Diversions: The hotel's restaurant, bis, opened in May 1998 and serves French bistro food, the creation of chef Jeff Buben, who co-owns bis and the acclaimed Vidalia (see chapter 4) with his wife, Sallie.

Amenities: 24-hour concierge; overnight shoe shine; weekday delivery of *Washington Post;* laundry and valet; nightly turndown; room service during restaurant hours; express checkout; VCR and CD player rentals; cigar-friendly billiard room; business/secretarial services; 1,600 square feet of meeting/banquet space; fitness center.

3 Downtown, East of 16th Street NW

VERY EXPENSIVE

Grand Hyatt Washington. 1000 H St. NW, Washington, D.C. 20001. ☎ **800/233-1234** or 202/582-1234. Fax 202/637-4781. 900 units. A/C MINIBAR TV TEL. Weekdays $290 double, weekends $119–$139 double. Extra person $25. Children under 18 stay free. AE, CB, DC, DISC, MC, V. Parking $12. Metro: Metro Center.

There's always something going on in the vast lobby—whose atrium is 12 stories high and enclosed by a glass, mansard-style roof. By contrast to its public areas, guest rooms seem rather tame. Each room has a 25-inch cable TV with free HBO service, hair dryers, irons, and ironing boards. One of the best things about the Grand Hyatt is the potpourri of special plans and packages the hotel offers, especially for business travelers. For example, an extra $15 qualifies you for the business plan, which includes an 8th- or 9th-floor room equipped with a large desk, fax machine, computer hookup, and coffeemaker; access to printers and other office supplies on the floor; and complimentary continental breakfast. Tourists should ask about seasonal deals, like the annual winter holiday package.

♨ Family-Friendly Hotels

The Premier Hotel (see p. 64)   Near the Kennedy Center, this property has a rooftop pool and Ping-Pong area, coin-operated washers and dryers, and a family-friendly diner. Rooms have small refrigerators and TVs equipped with Nintendo games.

Omni Shoreham (see p. 65)   Adjacent to Rock Creek Park, the Omni is also within walking distance of the zoo and is equipped with a large outdoor pool and kiddie pool.

One Washington Circle Hotel (see p. 63)   A great location in a safe neighborhood; bright and airy suites with full kitchens and sofa beds; an outdoor pool; a coin-operated washer and dryer; a good restaurant on the premises; and a great price that includes continental breakfast—and a hospital across the street for emergencies—all for a great price, which, if more than $135, includes continental breakfast.

Dining/Diversions: The Hyatt offers three restaurants: The Zephyr Deli, the informal Grand Cafe, and the smaller Via Pacifica, which features American, Italian, and Asian cuisine; and three bars, the lobby Via's Bar, the large Grand Slam sports bar, and Butler's—The Cigar Bar.

Amenities: Concierge; room service (Mon–Thurs 6am–1am, Fri–Sat 6am–2am); dry cleaning and laundry service; twice daily maid service; express checkout; courtesy car available on a first come, first served basis that takes guests within a 2-mile or 10-minute radius of the hotel; two-story health club with Jacuzzi, lap pool, exercise room, steam and sauna room, and aerobics program; business services that include two large ballrooms, a 102-seat theater, and 40,000 square feet of meeting space; an American Express Travel Center for traveler's checks and ticketing; and direct underground access to the Metro.

✪ **Willard Inter-Continental.** 1401 Pennsylvania Ave. NW, Washington, D.C. 20004. ☎ **800/327-0200** or 202/628-9100. Fax 202/637-7326. 341 units. A/C MINIBAR TV TEL. Weekdays $410–$440 double, weekends $199 double. Extra person $30. Children under 18 stay free. AE, DC, DISC, JCB, MC, V. Parking $20. Metro: Metro Center.

Billed as the "crown jewel of Pennsylvania Avenue," the Willard is the crown jewel of all Washington hotels. Its designation as a

National Historic Landmark in 1974 and magnificent restoration in the 1980s helped revitalize Pennsylvania Avenue and this part of town.

Rooms are sumptuous, spacious, and furnished in Edwardian and Federal-period reproductions. Because of the large number of foreign visitors, many of whom still smoke, six of the Willard's 12 floors are no-smoking, and, because of the many heads of state (more than 100 in the last decade) who bunk here, the hotel offers the 6th floor as "Secret Service–cleared. Eight rooms are outfitted to accommodate guests with disabilities. The "02" suites on each floor allow a partial look at the White House, but perhaps the best rooms are the ones perched in the curve of the 12th floor's southeast corner—the ones with the round "bull's eye" windows that capture glimpses of the Capitol. Phones have dual lines with voice mail, and cable TVs (with pay-movie channels and video message, data-port plugs, retrieval/checkout) are concealed in armoires. Each room has an in-room safe, an iron, and an ironing board. In the marble bathrooms are a hair dryer, scale, phone, and TV speaker.

Dining/Diversions: The Willard Room (the term power lunch originated here) is simply stunning (see p. 44 for a review). The circular Round Robin Bar is where Henry Clay mixed the first mint julep in Washington (see box, this chapter, for more about the Round Robin and bartender Jim Hewes). The Café Espresso offers croissant sandwiches, pastas, pastries, and vintage wines by the glass. The Nest Lounge offers live jazz on weekends.

Amenities: Twice-daily maid service; 24-hour room service; concierge; currency exchange; airline/train ticketing; express checkout; choice of newspaper delivery; fax and cellular phone rental; full business center; complete fitness center; VCRs in suites; upscale boutiques.

EXPENSIVE

Henley Park. 926 Massachusetts Ave. NW (at 10th St.), Washington, D.C. 20001. ☎ **800/222-8474** or 202/638-5200. Fax 202/638-6740. 95 units. A/C MINIBAR TV TEL. Weekdays $145–$225 double. Summer and weekends $98 double (including parking and continental breakfast). Junior suite $315, one-bedroom suite $395–$475, Ambassador Suite $725 weekdays and weekends. Senior discounts. Extra person $20. Children under 14 stay free. AE, CB, DC, DISC, MC, V. Parking $16. Metro: Metro Center, Gallery Place, or Mt. Vernon Square.

The Henley Park caters to a high-end corporate clientele who are not put off by its location: It's off by itself in an iffy part of town, although within walking distance of the Convention

Center, restaurants, and nightlife. This is an intimate, English-style hotel housed in a converted 1918 Tudor-style apartment house with 119 gargoyles on its facade. The lobby, with its exquisite Tudor ceiling, archways, and leaded windows, is particularly evocative of the period. Luxurious rooms make this a good choice for upscale romantic weekends. They are decorated in the English country house mode, with Hepplewhite-, Chippendale-, and Queen Anne–style furnishings, including lovely period beds. Bathrooms offer phones, cosmetic mirrors, and luxury toiletries, and in-room amenities include terry-cloth robes, cable TVs with pay-movie options, and, in some rooms, fax machines.

Dining/Diversions: The hotel's posh restaurant, Coeur de Lion, serves classic continental cuisine; the menu highlights seafood; and the wine list is excellent. Adjoining the Coeur de Lion, Marley's, a delightful cocktail lounge, is the setting for piano bar entertainment (and complimentary hors d'oeuvres) weeknights, live jazz nightly, and dancing Friday and Saturday. Afternoon tea is served daily in the octagonal Wilkes Room, a charming parlor with a working fireplace.

Amenities: 24-hour concierge and room service; *Washington Post* delivery each weekday morning; complimentary shoe shine; nightly bed turndown with gourmet chocolate; complimentary weekday 7:30–9:30am limo service to downtown and Capitol Hill locations; access to a fitness room in the Morrison-Clark Inn (see listing below) across the street.

MODERATE

✪ **Morrison-Clark Historic Inn and Restaurant.** 1015 L St. NW, at 11th St. and Massachusetts Ave. NW, Washington, D.C. 20001. ☎ **800/332-7898** or 202/898-1200. Fax 202/289-8576. 66 units. A/C MINIBAR TV TEL. Weekdays $155–$185 double; weekends $99–$129 double; suites $175–$205 weekdays and weekends. Rates include continental breakfast. Extra person $20. Children under 16 stay free. AE, CB, DC, DISC, MC, V. Parking $15. Metro: Metro Center or Mt. Vernon Square.

This magnificent inn, occupying twin 1865 Victorian brick town houses—with a newer wing in converted stables across an interior courtyard—is listed in the National Register of Historic Places. Guests enter via a turn-of-the-century parlor, with velvet- and lace-upholstered Victorian furnishings and lace-curtained bay windows. A delicious continental breakfast is served in the adjoining Club, which is furnished with an original white marble fireplace and 13-foot windows flanking gilded mirrors. In warm weather, you can

Behind Hotel Bars: The Willard's Round
Robin Bartender Tells All

On one hand, a good hotel bar is a haven. Whether you are a woman alone, a couple in love, old friends catching up with each other, colleagues talking business, or a journalist interviewing a subject, a hotel bar can offer a comfortable, relaxing place for quiet conversation and a well-mixed drink or glass of wine. And at the best hotel bars, you will find yourself agreeably looked after but unbothered. In Washington, exceptional bars include those at the **Jefferson, Westin-Fairfax, Hay-Adams, Mayflower,** and the **Canterbury.**

In a class of its own, largely because of bartender Jim Hewes, is the **Willard Hotel's Round Robin Bar.** Hewes, who, with colleagues Carol Randall and Shawn Carey, has bartended at the Round Robin since the renovated Willard reopened in 1986, is steeped in nearly 2 centuries' worth of knowledge of presidential drink preferences and Washington political and social life. A cast of characters from Hewes's stories are depicted in the black-and-white portraits that line the green felt–lined walls of the bar: Charles Dickens, Samuel Clemens, Warren Harding, and Abraham Lincoln are just some of the many famous people who have stopped in or stayed at the Willard. If you care for an easy, amiably given history lesson along with that classically mixed gin and tonic, grab a stool at the round mahogany bar here and listen as the ponytailed Hewes fills you in.

"In the old days, everything took place within 10 blocks of the White House. The center of activity was supposed to be the Capitol, but it was really around here, and the Willard, starting in the 1840s and 1850s, gained a reputation as a meeting place. Presidents Zachary Taylor, Millard Fillmore, James Buchanan, Calvin Coolidge, Warren Harding, and Abraham Lincoln each lived or stayed for a time at the Willard. Washington Irving brought Charles Dickens (a port, brandy, and

breakfast in the lovely, two-level, brick-paved courtyard, enclosed by the inn and neighboring buildings.

High-ceilinged guest rooms are individually decorated with original artworks, sumptuous fabrics, and antique or reproduction 19th-century furnishings. Most popular—and the grandest—are the wine drinker) here for a drink. Samuel Clemens (better known as Mark Twain) palled around with Senator Stewart from Nevada, imbibing bourbon at the bar. Walt Whitman wrote a poem about the Willard bar. Nathaniel Hawthorne, in the capital to cover the Civil War for *The Atlantic* magazine, wrote 'You adopt the universal habit of the place, and call for a mint-julep, a whiskey-skin, a gin cocktail, a brandy smash, or a glass of pure old Rye, for the conviviality of Washington sets in at an early hour and, so far as I have had the opportunity to observe, never terminates at any hour.'

"Throughout the 19th century, and up until World War I, people drank constantly throughout the day," says Hewes. "Popular in the 1840s was the Mamie Taylor, a potent mix of Scotch whiskey, lime juice, and ginger soda that was invented in Washington to honor Old Rough and Ready's sweetie, a hard-drinking, corn-cob-smoking first lady," notes Hewes. The mint julep, introduced at the Round Robin by statesman Henry Clay in 1850, quickly caught on and has been associated with the Round Robin ever since. (For the past few Kentucky Derby Days, Hewes has discussed the history of the mint julep for National Public Radio's *All Things Considered*.) Ulysses S. Grant was among the presidents to enjoy the julep.

"President Clinton is a Tanqueray and tonic man, and he likes his beer, though usually he'll have what the others in his party are having. Bush liked martinis. Reagan, and Nixon, too, introduced the city to California wines and Schramsburg sparkling wine," says Hewes.

And Hewes's favorite drink? "A good Irish whiskey, or a beer," he says. If you're intent on hitting the Round Robin when Hewes is tending bar, better call ahead (☎ 202/637-7348) since he's not there everyday.

Victorian-style rooms, which have acquired new chandeliers and bedspreads in the past year. Four Victorian rooms have private porches; many other rooms have plant-filled balconies. All have cable TVs, two phones (bed and bathroom) equipped with computer jacks, and hair dryers.

Room service is available from the inn's highly acclaimed restaurant (see chapter 4 for a review). Other amenities include twice-daily maid service with Belgian chocolates at bed turndown, complimentary *Washington Post*, business services, and fresh flowers in every room. A fitness center is on the premises. Look for ads in the *New York Times* to obtain the best rate of $79.

INEXPENSIVE

Days Inn Premier. 1201 K St. NW, Washington, D.C. 20005. ☎ **800/ 562-3350,** 800/325-2525, or 202/842-1020. Fax 202/289-0336. 219 units. A/C TV TEL. Weekdays $99–$125 double; weekends $69–$99 double. Extra person $15. Children under 18 stay free. AE, CB, DC, DISC, MC, V. Parking $14. Metro: McPherson Square, Metro Center.

Proximity to the Convention Center makes this eight-floor Days Inn a perfect choice for visitors attending events there. A small rooftop pool will appeal to families with young children. Newly renovated rooms are cheerfully decorated and equipped with remote-control satellite TVs (with free and pay-movie channels) in armoires, hair dryers, and coffeemakers. On the top two "executive floors," guests get king-size beds; minirefrigerators; microwaves; views of the Capitol (corner room 919 is probably best); and access to the Executive Club, with its computer, TV, continental breakfast, and kitchen. Rooms are split between smoking and no-smoking. Four rooms are equipped for wheelchair accessibility.

The lobby is always crowded with conventioneers checking in, along with families during the summer. The facility has 12,000 square feet of meeting space, a full-service restaurant, and adjoining lounge. Inquire about special packages when you reserve. Lower "Super Saver" rates (about $59) are sometimes available if you reserve in advance (the earlier the better) via the central toll-free number, ☎ **800/325-2525**—it's worth a try (you may find better rates by calling this number instead of the one listed above).

Red Roof Inn. 500 H St. NW, Washington, D.C. 20001. ☎ **800/THE-ROOF** or 202/289-5959. Fax 202/682-9152. 197 units. A/C TV TEL. Weekdays $97.99– $102 double; weekends $70–$102 double. Children under 18 stay free AE, CB, DC, DISC, MC, V. Parking $8.50. Metro: Gallery Place.

Reserve early. This popular hotel, with endearingly considerate staff, sits in the heart of Chinatown, within walking distance of many attractions, including two (off the Mall) Smithsonian museums; it's also just 1 block from the MCI Center and 3 blocks from the Convention Center. Red Roof Inns purchased the 10-story property (which used to be a Comfort Inn) in 1996 and renovated the rooms, which are attractively decorated and equipped with cable TVs offering free Showtime and pay-movie options plus Nintendo. There's a reasonably priced cafe open 6:30am–2pm and 5:30–10pm. On-premises facilities include coin-operated washers and dryers and a sunny 10th-floor exercise room with sauna. *USA Today* newspapers are free at the front desk.

4   Downtown, 16th Street NW & West

VERY EXPENSIVE

✪ **The Carlton.** 923 16th St. NW, Washington, D.C. 20006. ☎ **800/ 562-5661** or 202/638-2626. Fax 202/638-4231. 192 units. A/C MINIBAR TV TEL. Weekdays $285–$325 double; $450–$2,500 suite; weekends $265–$285 double. Extra person $15. Children under 10 stay free. AE, CB, DC, DISC, JCB, MC, V. Parking $22. Metro: Farragut West or McPherson Square.

Ah, luxury! Palladian windows dressed in rich damask draperies, elaborately gilded ceilings, Louis XVI chandeliers, plush green over-sized sofas, and cozy arrangements of comfortable chairs: This is the lobby of the Carlton, designed to resemble a Milan palazzo. Guest rooms are quietly opulent and decorated in tastefully coordinated colors (for instance, grays and royal blues), with desks set in alcoves, a mirror-covered armoire, and creamy silk moiré wall coverings. Guests have included everyone from Queen Elizabeth to the Rolling Stones.

Dining/Diversions: The Carlton's Lespinasse is quite the elegant restaurant (see chapter 4 for a review). The Library Lounge, which might be the best hotel bar in Washington, has a working fireplace and paneled walls lined with bookcases. High tea is offered daily in the posh lobby.

Amenities: Dual telephone lines; voice mail and modem capabilities; personal safes; terry robes; and hair dryers; 24-hour concierge and room service; pressing service; complimentary coffee or tea with wake-up call; complimentary newspaper and shoe shine; complimentary bottled water with turndown service; no charge for credit-card calls and local faxes; state-of-the-art fitness room and access to a complete health club (at the University Club); 10,000 square feet of meeting space; ballroom.

Hay-Adams. 16th and H sts. NW, Washington, D.C. 20006. ☎ **800/ 424-5054** or 202/638-6600. Fax 202/638-3803. 136 units. A/C MINIBAR TV TEL. Weekdays $265–$485 double, weekends $199–$329. Extra person $30. Children under 12 stay free. AE, CB, DC, JCB, MC, V. Parking (valet only) $22. Metro: Farragut West or McPherson Square.

Reserve a room on the 5th through 8th floor, H Street side of the hotel, pull back the curtains from the windows, and enjoy a full frontal view of the White House—with the Washington Monument behind it. One block from the president's abode, the Hay-Adams offers the best vantage point in town. Between the hotel and the White House is Lafayette Square, another landmark.

Rooms are individually furnished with antiques and superior appointments. A typical accommodation might include 18th-century–style furnishings; silk-covered walls hung with botanical prints and fine art; a gorgeous molded plaster ceiling; and French silk floral-print bedspreads, upholstery, and curtains. Many rooms have ornamental fireplaces.

Dining/Diversions: The sunny Lafayette Restaurant (overlooking the White House) is an exquisite dining room that serves contemporary American/continental fare at all meals, plus afternoon tea. The adjoining lounge features nightly piano-bar entertainment. Off the Record is the hotel's newly opened wine and champagne bar.

Amenities: Hair dryers, cosmetic mirrors, and phones in the bathrooms; terry-cloth robes; and cable TVs equipped with HBO; 24-hour room and concierge service; nightly bed turndown; complimentary shoe shine; guest access to a local health club; secretarial and business services; in-room fax on request; meeting rooms.

✪ **The Jefferson.** 1200 16th St. NW (at M St.), Washington, D.C. 20036. ☎ **800/368-5966** or 202/347-2200. Fax 202/223-9039. 100 units. A/C MINIBAR TV TEL. Weekdays $300–$310 double, $350–$1,200 suite; weekends $175 double, $350 and up for suite. Extra person $25. Children under 12 stay free. AE, CB, DC, JCB, MC, V. Parking $20. Metro: Farragut North.

Opened in 1923 just 4 blocks from the White House, the Jefferson is one of the city's three most exclusive venues (along with the Hay-Adams and the Carlton), proffering discreet hospitality to political personages, royalty, literati, and other notables. With a very high staff-to-guest ratio, the Jefferson puts utmost emphasis on service.

Each antique-filled guest room evokes a European feel. Yours might have a four-poster bed with plump eyelet-trimmed comforter and pillow shams (many are topped with canopies), or a cherry-wood bookstand from the Napoleonic period filled with rare books. In-room amenities include two-line speaker phones with hold buttons; fax machines (you get your own fax number when you check in); cable TVs with VCRs; CD players; and, in the bathrooms, terry robes, hair dryers, and phones.

Dining/Diversions: Off the lobby is The Restaurant at the Jefferson, one of the city's premier dining rooms (see chapter 4 for a review) and a cozy bar/lounge. In the paneled lounge, whose walls are hung with framed letters and documents written by Thomas Jefferson, you can sink into a red leather chair and enjoy a marvelous high tea daily from 3 to 5pm, or cocktails anytime—the bar stocks a robust selection of single-malt scotches and a fine choice of Davidoff cigars.

Amenities: 24-hour butler service; overnight shoe shine; nightly bed turndown with Godiva chocolate; morning delivery of *Washington Post* or any other major newspaper; 24-hour room and multilingual concierge service; video and CD rentals; express checkout; business/secretarial services and meeting rooms; for a fee of $20, guests have access to full health club facilities (including Olympic-size pool) at the University Club across the street.

Renaissance Mayflower. 1127 Connecticut Ave. NW (between L and M sts.), Washington, D.C. 20036. ☎ **800/228-7697** or 202/347-3000. Fax 202/466-9082. 738 units. A/C MINIBAR TV TEL. Weekdays $275–$335 double; weekends $139–$199 double. Extra person $25. Children under 18 stay free. AE, CB, DC, DISC, JCB, MC, V. Parking $12. Metro: Farragut North.

This hotel is quite historic. Among other things, the Mayflower was the site of Calvin Coolidge's inaugural ball in 1925, the year it opened. (Coolidge didn't attend—he was mourning the death of his son from blood poisoning.) President-elect FDR and family lived in rooms 776 and 781 while waiting to move into the White House, and this is where FDR penned the words, "The only thing we have to fear is fear itself."

Graciously appointed guest rooms have high ceilings, cream moiré wall coverings, and mahogany reproduction furnishings (Queen Anne, Sheraton, Chippendale, Hepplewhite). Handsome armoires hold 25-inch remote-control TVs. Amenities include ironing board and iron; three phones; a terry robe; hair dryer; and a small color TV in the bathroom. Inquire about "summer value rates."

Dining/Diversions: Washington lawyers and lobbyists gather for power breakfasts in the Café Promenade. Under a beautiful domed skylight, the restaurant is adorned with Edward Laning's murals, crystal chandeliers, marble columns, and lovely flower arrangements. A full English tea is served here afternoons Mon–Sat. The clubby, mahogany-paneled Town and Country is the setting for light buffet lunches and complimentary hors d'oeuvres during cocktail hour.

Bartender Sambonn Lek has quite a following and is famous for his magic tricks and personality. The Lobby Court, a Starbucks espresso bar just opposite the front desk, serves coffee and fresh-baked pastries each morning, and becomes a piano bar serving cocktails later in the day.

Amenites: Coffee, tea, or hot chocolate and *USA Today* with wake-up call; 24-hour room service; twice-daily maid service; complimentary overnight shoe shine; concierge; courtesy car takes you within 3-mile radius; express checkout; valet parking; business center; full on-premises fitness center; florist; gift shop.

MODERATE

Lincoln Suites Downtown. 1823 L St. NW, Washington, D.C. 20036. ☎ **800/424-2970** or 202/223-4320. Fax 202/223-8546. 99 suites. A/C TV TEL. Weekdays $129–$159, weekends $99–$129. Children under 16 stay free. AE, CB, DC, DISC, MC, V. Parking $9 (in adjoining garage). Metro: Farragut North or Farragut West.

Lots of long-term guests stay at this all-suite, 10-story hotel in the heart of downtown, just 5 blocks from the White House. A multi-million dollar renovation was completed in May 1997, refurbishing the large, comfortable suites and sprucing up hallways. About 36 suites offer full kitchens; others have refrigerators, wet bars, coffeemakers, and microwaves. Rooms are fairly spacious, well-kept, attractive, and equipped with cable TVs with free HBO, shower massagers, hair dryers, and irons and ironing boards. The property also has a coin-operated washer and dryer and a small meeting room.

Samantha's, next door (and leased from the hotel), offers reasonably priced American fare. The hotel's own Beatrice is a grotto-like Italian restaurant open for all meals and providing room service Mon through Sat 7am to 2pm and 5 to 10pm, Sun 7 to 11am for breakfast only. In the lobby are complimentary copies of the *Washington Post* Monday through Saturday (and for sale on Sunday), complimentary milk and homemade cookies each evening, and complimentary continental breakfast weekend mornings; guests enjoy free use of the well-equipped Bally's Holiday Spa nearby.

INEXPENSIVE

Embassy Inn. 1627 16th St. NW (between Q and R sts.), Washington, D.C. 20009. ☎ **800/423-9111** or 202/234-7800. Fax 202/234-3309. 38 units (all with bathroom). A/C TV TEL. Weekdays $79–$110 double, weekends $59 double based on availability. Rates include continental breakfast, evening sherry, and snacks. Smoking rooms on lower level. Extra person $10. Children under 14 stay free. AE, CB, DC, MC, V. Metro: Dupont Circle.

This four-story 1910 brick building, a former inn, was rescued from demolition some years back, spruced up, and restored to become a quaint, homey, small hotel. Its Federal-style architecture harmonizes with other turn-of-the-century town houses along this block, falling within a district designated "historic" in 1964. Accommodations are comfortable, clean, and a little quirky in design: the sink is in the bedroom, not the bathroom; bathrooms have only shower stalls, no tubs; and middle rooms have no windows. Cable TV with free HBO and hair dryers, are unexpected perks. The recently redone lobby doubles as a parlor where breakfast (including fresh-baked muffins and croissants) is served daily and fresh coffee brews all day; tea, cocoa, and evening sherry are also complimentary. You can pick up maps and brochures, read a complimentary *Washington Post*, or request sundries you may have forgotten (toothbrush, razor, and the like). *Note:* There is no elevator, and there's street parking only.

5 Georgetown

VERY EXPENSIVE

✪ **The Four Seasons.** 2800 Pennsylvania Ave. NW, Washington, D.C. 20007. ☎ **800/332-3442** or 202/342-0444. Fax 202/944-2076. 260 units. A/C MINIBAR TV TEL. Weekdays $370–$465 double; $775–$3,500 suite; weekends $275 double, starting at $550 for suites. Extra person $40. Children under 16 stay free. AE, DC, JCB, MC, V. Parking $22. Metro: Foggy Bottom.

Since it opened in 1979, this most glamorous of Washington's haute hotels has hosted everyone from Tom Hanks to Aretha Franklin, Puff Daddy to King Hussein. Open the front door and you enter a plush setting where thousands of plants and palm trees grow and large floral arrangements enhance the garden-like ambience.

Service is what sets this hotel apart. Staff are trained to know the names, preferences, even allergies of guests, and repeat clientele rely on this attention. Accommodations, many of them overlooking Rock Creek Park or the C&O Canal, have walls hung with gilt-framed antique prints, beds outfitted with down-filled bedding, dust ruffles, and scalloped spreads, and large desks and plump cushioned armchairs with hassocks to drive home the residential atmosphere. In-room amenities include cable TVs with free HBO and Spectravision movie options; VCRs (movies and video games are available); CD players (the concierge stocks CDs); bathrobes; and, in the bathrooms, hair dryers, lighted cosmetic mirrors, and upscale toiletries. Under construction now, in an adjoining building, are 40 luxury suites for clients who want state-of-the-art business amenities (each suite will be soundproofed and have an office equipped with fax machine, at least 3 telephones with 2-line speakers, portable telephones, and headsets for private TV listening).

Dining/Diversions: The elegant and highly acclaimed Seasons is reviewed in chapter 4. The delightful Garden Terrace is bordered by tropical plants, ficus trees, and flower beds and has a wall of windows overlooking the canal. It's open for lunch, a lavish Sunday jazz brunch, and classic English-style afternoon teas.

Amenities: Twice-daily maid service; 24-hour room service and concierge; complimentary sedan service weekdays within the district; gratis newspaper of your choice; car windows washed when you park overnight; complimentary shoe shine; beauty salon; gift shop; jogging trail; business facilities; children's programs; extensive state-of-the-art fitness club that includes personal trainers; and a spa that offers a Vichy shower, hydrotherapy, and synchronized massage (two people work on you at the same time).

EXPENSIVE

The Latham. 3000 M St. NW, Washington, D.C. 20007. ☎ **800/528-4261** or 202/726-5000. Fax 202/337-4250. 143 units. A/C TV TEL. Weekdays $160–$180 double; weekends $119–$139; suites $175–$290. Extra person $20. Children under 18 stay free. AE, DC, DISC, MC, V. Valet parking $14.

The Latham is at the hub of Georgetown's trendy nightlife/restaurant/shopping scene, but since its accommodations are set back from the street, none of the noise of nighttime revelers will reach your room. It's also the only Georgetown hotel with a swimming pool. Charming earth-tone rooms are decorated in French-country motif, with pine furnishings and multipaned windows; cable TVs (offering cable and pay-per-view movie selections) are housed in forest-green armoires. All rooms are equipped with large desks; hair dryers; terry robes; irons; and ironing boards. Tenth-floor rooms offer gorgeous river views; third-floor accommodations, all two-room suites, have windows facing a hallway designed to replicate a quaint Georgetown street. Most luxurious are two-story carriage suites with cathedral ceilings, full living rooms, and stocked minibars. Fax printers are in all suites and in one-third of the guest rooms; CD players with headphones are in third-floor and carriage suites.

Dining/Diversions: The highly acclaimed Citronelle, one of D.C.'s hottest restaurants, is on the premises (see chapter 4 for a review). And fronting the hotel is the country-French La Madeleine.

Amenities: Room service during restaurant hours; concierge; valet parking; nightly turndown; free delivery of morning newspaper; business services; express checkout; small outdoor pool and bilevel sundeck May–Sept; fitness room; jogging and bike path along the C&O Canal, next to hotel; meeting rooms and audiovisual services.

MODERATE

The Georgetown Dutch Inn. 1075 Thomas Jefferson St. NW (just below M St.), Washington, D.C. 20007. ☎ **800/388-2410** or 202/337-0900. Fax 202/333-6526. 47 units. A/C TV TEL. Weekdays $125–$195 one-bedroom suite for 2; $250–$320 two-bedroom duplex penthouse (sleeps 6); weekends $105–$115 one-bedroom suite for 2; $195–$250 penthouse suite. Rates include continental breakfast. Extra person $20. Children under 14 stay free. AE, CB, DC, DISC, MC, V. Limited free parking for small to midsize cars. Metro: Foggy Bottom, with a 10-minute walk. Bus: Bus no. 32, 34, and 36 go to all major Washington tourist attractions.

Many European and South American guests, usually embassy folks, stay at this inn. It's also a favorite for families here to celebrate weddings or graduations; they book several suites, or maybe a whole floor. Personalized service is a hallmark of the hotel, whose staff greet you by name and protect your privacy, should you be a celebrity of some sort—which many guests are.

Accommodations are spacious one- and two-bedroom, apartment-like suites, nine of them duplex penthouses with $1^{1}/_{2}$ bathrooms; all have full kitchens but no microwaves. Amenities include cable TVs with HBO; irons and ironing boards; coffeemakers with free coffee; and three phones (bedside, living room, and bathroom). You'll also find a cosmetic mirror in the bathroom; a hair dryer is provided on request.

6 Adams-Morgan/North Dupont Circle

EXPENSIVE

✪ **Hotel Sofitel.** 1914 Connecticut Ave. NW, Washington, D.C. 20009. ☎ **800/424-2464** or 202/797-2000. Fax 202/462-0944. 144 units. A/C MINIBAR TV TEL. Weekdays from $199–$259; weekends $139–$159 for double or suite. Extra person $20. Children under 12 stay free. AE, CB, DC, MC, V. Valet parking $15. Metro: Dupont Circle.

Housed in a building dating back to 1906, which is a registered historic property on a hill, the hotel is a short walk from lively Dupont Circle; its elevated position allows for great city views from rooms on the upper level, Connecticut Avenue–side of this eight-floor hotel. You're also a short walk away from trendy Adams-Morgan:

cross Connecticut and walk up Columbia Road. Rooms are spacious, each with a breakfast/study alcove and many with sitting areas, and are decorated in muted shades of champagnes and peach. A multilingual staff sees to the needs of an international clientele of diplomats, foreign delegations, and corporate travelers.

Dining/Diversions: The Trocadero is open for breakfast, lunch, and dinner; the adjoining Pullman Lounge features a pianist weeknights starting at 5:30pm.

Amenities: Full-service concierge; room service (5:30am–11pm); dry cleaning and laundry; secretarial services including faxing and copying; express checkout; courtesy limo available weekdays 7–9am and 5–7pm for city jaunts, but not to the airport; fitness center with Nautilus and other equipment; newly renovated conference rooms.

MODERATE

✪ **Normandy Inn.** 2118 Wyoming Ave. NW (at Connecticut Ave.), Washington, D.C. 20008. ☎ **800/424-3729** or 202/483-1350. Fax 202/387-8241. 75 units. A/C TV TEL. Weekdays and weekends $79–$155 double. Extra person $10. Children under 18 stay free. AE, DC, DISC, MC, V. Parking $10 plus tax. Metro: Dupont Circle.

This gracious small hotel is a gem. It has pretty twin and queen guest rooms, all remodeled in 1998, with tapestry-upholstered mahogany and cherry-wood furnishings in 18th-century styles, pretty floral-print bedspreads, and gilt-framed botanical prints gracing the walls. Amenities include minirefrigerators; coffeemakers; remote-control cable TVs; access to the neighboring Washington Courtyard Hotel's pool and exercise room; and complimentary *Washington Post* (in lobby). The Normandy is an easy walk from both Adams-Morgan and Dupont Circle.

7 Dupont Circle

VERY EXPENSIVE

Westin-Fairfax. 2100 Massachusetts Ave. NW, Washington, D.C. 20008. ☎ **800/325-3589** or 202/293-2100. Fax 202/293-0641. 206 units. A/C MINIBAR TV TEL. Weekdays $215–$235 double, suites $350–$2,100 for Presidential Suite; weekends $195 double, including breakfast. Children under 18 stay free. AE, CB, DC, MC, V. Valet parking $23. Metro: Dupont Circle.

A 1994 renovation gussied up the hotel's top-drawer appearance, from canopied entrance angled on Embassy Row, to the rich, walnut-paneled lobby, to pristine Oriental-carpeted hallways and lovely rooms. The latter are handsomely appointed with traditional dark-wood pieces; rich, brocade draperies; and French architectural

Adams-Morgan & Dupont Circle Accommodations

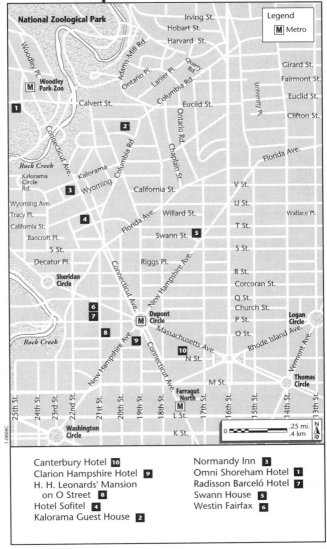

Canterbury Hotel **10**
Clarion Hampshire Hotel **9**
H. H. Leonards' Mansion
  on O Street **8**
Hotel Sofitel **4**
Kalorama Guest House **2**

Normandy Inn **3**
Omni Shoreham Hotel **1**
Radisson Barceló Hotel **7**
Swann House **5**
Westin Fairfax **6**

watercolor renderings. Front-of-the-house rooms overlook Embassy Row. Some 6th- to 8th-floor rooms at the back of the house give you a glimpse of the Washington Monument and Georgetown. In-room amenities include cable TVs (with HBO) concealed in armoires; safes; three phones; and terry robes. Gorgeous marble bathrooms are equipped with hair dryers and upscale toiletries (some also have small black-and-white TVs). The seventh floor of the eight-story hotel is the Club level, with its own lounge, and is where a concierge attends you.

Dining/Diversions: The Jockey Club is one of Washington's most prominent restaurants. The elegant Fairfax Club, with a working fireplace, is an intimate setting for cocktails, light fare, and piano music. The back room of the bar is an exclusive club and disco for certain wealthy Washingtonians. The Terrace Court Salon is the setting for daily continental breakfast and afternoon tea ($16 for traditional, $23 with champagne).

Amenities: Complimentary morning newspaper delivery and shoe shine; nightly turndown with imported chocolates; 24-hour concierge and room service; in-room massage; twice daily maid service; express checkout; dry cleaning and laundry service; fitness room with Stairmasters, Life-cycles,treadmills, sauna, massage, and separate locker areas; meeting rooms and services.

EXPENSIVE

Canterbury Hotel. 1733 N St. NW, Washington, D.C. 20036. ☎ **800/ 424-2950** or 202/393-3000. Fax 202/785-9581. 99 units. A/C MINIBAR TV TEL. Weekdays $160–$400 suite for 2 (most are under $200); weekends and off-season weekdays $119–$140. Rates include continental breakfast served in restaurant. Extra person $35. Children under 12 stay free. AE, CB, DC, DISC, MC, V. Parking $15. Metro: Dupont Circle.

Located on a lovely residential street, this small, European-style hostelry is close to many tourist attractions. Enter the hotel via a graciously appointed lobby hung with British prints that conjure up shades of Jane Austen. Classical music is played in public areas.

Each room is actually a junior suite and differently appointed, although all have a sofa/sitting area, dressing room, and kitchenette or full kitchen. Attractively decorated, these spacious accommodations sport 18th-century mahogany English-reproduction furnishings (a few have four-poster beds). Among the amenities: cable TVs with CNN and pay-movie stations; iron and ironing board; coffeemakers; electronic locks; and multifeature phones with voice mail. Bathrooms are supplied with cosmetic mirrors; hair dryers; phones; and baskets of fine toiletries.

Dining/Diversions: The hotel's wonderful new restaurant, Brighton (see chapter 4 for details), serves American-regional fare at all meals; and the Tudor-beamed Union Jack Pub, complete with dartboard and a menu featuring fish-and-chips, is the perfect place to relax after a busy day on the town. English beers on tap are served in pint mugs.

Amenities: Nightly turndown with fine chocolate; room service during restaurant hours; morning delivery of the *Washington Post;* complimentary *Wall Street Journal* available in lobby and restaurant; express checkout; secretarial services; meeting space for up to 75 people. Guests enjoy free use of the nearby YMCA/National Capital Health Center's extensive workout facilities, including an indoor lap pool.

Radisson Barceló Hotel. 2121 P St. NW, Washington, D.C. 20037. ☎ **800/ 333-3333** or 202/293-3100. Fax 202/857-0134. 301 units. A/C TV TEL. Weekdays $155–$180 double; weekends $99–$139 double; suites $250–$500 weekdays in season, $150–300 weekends and off-season. Extra person $20. Children under 18 stay free. AE, CB, DC, DISC, MC, V. Parking $14. Metro: Dupont Circle.

The first American venture for a Mallorca-based firm, the 10-story Barceló offers friendly European-style service, an unbeatable location midway between Dupont Circle and Georgetown, and a superb restaurant. The Barceló's art deco–style, marble-floored lobby is inviting, and its accommodations (formerly apartments) are enormous (the hotel claims these are the largest sleeping rooms in Washington). All offer workspaces with desks and living room areas containing sofas and armchairs. In-room amenities include cable TVs with HBO and more than 200 pay-movie options; three phones with voice-mail and modem jacks; marble bathrooms with hair dryers and shaving mirrors; irons and ironing boards; coffee and coffeemakers. *Note:* Weekend "bed-and-breakfast" packages on Friday and Saturday nights in summer can go as low as $89 for a double.

Dining/Diversions: Gabriel features first-rate Latin American/ Mediterranean cuisine (see chapter 4 for a review); its simpatico bar/ lounge (featuring tapas and sherry) is popular with sophisticated Washingtonians.

Amenities: Concierge; room service (6:30am–11pm); complimentary *Washington Post* in the morning at the front desk; nightly turndown; faxing and other secretarial services; express checkout; rooftop sundeck; swimming pool in the courtyard; sauna; small fitness room; bike rentals; gift shop.

MODERATE

Clarion Hampshire Hotel. 1310 New Hampshire Ave. NW (at N St.), Washington, D.C. 20036. ☎ **800/368-5691** or 202/296-7600. Fax 202/293-2476. 82 units. A/C MINIBAR TV TEL. Weekdays $109–$159 suite for 2; weekends and off-season weekdays $79–$109 per suite. Extra person $20. Children under 12 stay free. AE, CB, DC, DISC, JCB, MC, V. Parking $12. Metro: Dupont Circle.

The Hampshire is within easy walking distance of Georgetown and 2 blocks from Dupont Circle, convenient to numerous restaurants, nightspots, and offices. The hotel serves mostly an association, corporate, and government clientele, so you should inquire about low summer rates.

Spacious, junior-suite accommodations are furnished with 18th-century reproductions and offer lots of closet space; big dressing rooms; couches; coffee tables; and desks. Fifty of the 82 rooms have kitchenettes, which come with microwaves and coffeemakers; some have cooking ranges. Balconies at the front of the hotel offer city views. Amenities include a hair dryer; chocolates on arrival; multifeature, data port–equipped phones; cable TVs; and morning delivery of the *Washington Post*. Guests also receive free passes to a large health club with indoor pool, 10 minutes away.

The hotel's Peacock Bistro, with an outdoor cafe, a fresh juice bar, and a coffee bar, serves fresh salads, pastas, grilled meats, and sandwiches. Room service is available during restaurant hours.

✪ **H. H. Leonards' Mansion on O Street.** 2020 O St. NW, Washington, D.C. 20036. ☎ **202/496-2000.** Fax 202/659-0547. E-mail mansion@ erols.com. 6 suites and a 5-bedroom guest house. A/C TV TEL. $150–$1,000. Government and nonprofit rates available. Except for the guest house, rates include breakfast, whatever you want. MC, V. Parking $15 and $6 (for garage a block away). Metro: Dupont Circle.

A legend in her own time, H. H. Leonards operates this Victorian property, made up of three five-story town houses, as an event space, an art gallery, an antiques emporium, and—oh, yeah—a B&B. If you stay here, you may find yourself buying a sweater, a painting, or (who knows?) an antique bed. Everything's for sale. Guest rooms are so creative they'll blow you away; most breathtaking is a log cabin loft suite, with a bed whose headboard encases an aquarium. The art deco–style penthouse takes up an entire floor and has its own elevator, 10 phones, and seven televisions. The International Room has a nonworking fireplace and three TVs (one in the bathroom). All rooms have king-size beds, computer-activated telephones that can hook you up to the Internet, at least one television, and out-of-this-world decor; most have a whirlpool, and some have kitchens.

Elsewhere on the property are an outdoor pool; eight office/conference spaces; 21 far-out bathrooms; art and antiques everywhere; an exercise room; and thousands and thousands of books. Full business services are available, including multiline phones; fax machines; IBM and Mac computers; and satellite feeds. The Light House (guest house) has a separate entrance and five bedrooms, all white walls with light streaming in from windows and skylights; rates include maid service.

✪ **Swann House.** 1808 New Hampshire Ave. NW, Washington, D.C. 20009. ☎ **202/265-7677.** Fax 202/265-6755. E-mail SwannHousse@aol.com. 11 units. A/C TV TEL. $110–$235 depending on rm and season. Extended stay and government rates available. Extra person $20. Rates include expanded continental breakfast. Limited off-street parking. No pets. MC, V. Metro: Dupont Circle.

This stunning 1883 mansion angled prominently on a corner 4 blocks north of Dupont Circle has nine exquisite guest rooms, two with private entrances. The coolest is the Blue Sky Suite, which has the original rose-tiled (working) fireplace, a queen-size bed and sofa bed, a gabled ceiling, and its own roof deck. The most romantic room is probably the Il Duomo, with Gothic windows; cathedral ceiling; working fireplace; and a turreted bathroom with angel murals. The Jennifer Green Room has a queen-size bed; another working fireplace; an oversized marble steam shower; and a private deck overlooking the pool area and garden. The Regent Room has a king-size bed in front of a carved working fireplace; a whirlpool; double shower; outdoor hot tub; TV; VCR; and stereo. The beautiful window treatments and bed coverings are the handiwork of innkeeper Mary Ross. You'll want to spend some time on the main floor of the mansion, which has 12-foot ceilings; fluted woodwork; inlaid wood floors; a turreted living room; columned sitting room; and a sunroom (where breakfast is served) leading through three sets of French doors to the garden and pool. Laundry facilities, meeting space, and business services are available.

8   Foggy Bottom/West End

VERY EXPENSIVE

ANA Hotel. 2401 M St. NW, Washington, D.C. 20037. ☎ **800/ANA-HOTELS** or 202/429-2400. Fax 202/457-5010. 415 units. A/C MINIBAR TV TEL. Weekdays $280 double; weekends $139 double, suite $700–$1,700. Extra person $30. Children under 18 stay free. AE, CB, DC, DISC, JCB, MC, V. Valet parking $19. Metro: Foggy Bottom.

The ANA is famous for its newly remodeled 17,500-square-foot West End Executive Fitness Center, which includes a pool and spa facilities, squash and racquetball courts, and every kind of exercise equipment. When in town, this is where Arnold Schwarzenegger stays, and where other visiting celebrities come to work out, even if they don't stay here. Guests pay $10 a day to use exercise equipment or to take aerobics classes but may use the pool, sauna, steam room, and whirlpool for free.

The ANA's lobby and public areas are especially pretty, thanks to the central interior garden courtyard. The 146 guest rooms that overlook this courtyard are probably the best. An $8 million renovation in late 1998 spruced up all the guest rooms and the lobby. Amenities in guest rooms include large writing desks; terry robes; iron and ironing board; three phones (one in the bathroom) with voice mail; safes; remote-controlled TVs; and Caswell Massey toiletries. The ninth floor is a secured executive club level, popular with many of the business travelers who stay here.

Dining/Diversions: *Washingtonian* magazine's readers' poll named ANA's Sunday brunch the best in Washington; it's served in the lovely Colonnade, which is also a popular site for wedding receptions. The Bistro serves American cuisine with a Mediterranean flair; for Japanese guests (the Japanese-owned hotel is named for its owners, All Nippon Airways, and draws a fair number of travelers from Japan), the Bistro offers an authentic Japanese breakfast daily. Cocktails, coffee, and pastries are available in the Lobby Lounge.

Amenities: 24-hour room service; concierge (7am–11pm); dry cleaning and laundry service; nightly turndown; twice daily maid service; express checkout; valet parking; complimentary shoe shine; fitness center; business center; 5,500-square-foot ballroom; 186 fixed-seat auditorium; more than 29,000 square feet of meeting space.

✪ **Park Hyatt.** 1201 24th St. NW, Washington, D.C. 20037. ☎ **800/ 922-PARK** or 202/789-1234. Fax 202/457-8823. 223 units. A/C MINIBAR TV TEL. Weekdays $255–$320 double, $295–$360 suite; weekends $179–$199 double, $202–$224 suite. Extra person $25. Children under 17 free. Family plan offered, based on availability: 2nd rm for children under 17 is half price. AE, CB, DC, DISC, JCB, MC, V. Valet parking $20 weekdays, $8 weekends. Metro: Foggy Bottom or Dupont Circle.

At this luxury hotel, museum-quality modern art hangs on the walls of the handsome public areas (including a David Hockney lithograph) and the framed reproductions in guest rooms are of works hanging in the National Gallery and other museums in town. Each room has an iron and ironing board, and each bathroom has a TV and radio, telephone, hair dryer, and makeup mirror. You won't see maid carts in the hallways because housekeeping staff use handheld baskets. The 11-year-old, 10-story hotel prides itself on going the extra mile to please a customer, even if it means taking out a wall to enlarge a suite, as the Park Hyatt did for Lily Tomlin, right after the hotel opened. Guests include big names, royal families (who use the Presidential Suite, with its fireplace and grand piano), lobbyists, and tour bus travelers. Executive suites have separate living and dining areas, fax machines, and a second TV. Rooms are handsome and service is superb.

Dining/Diversions: Melrose's bright and lovely dining room offers four-star cuisine with an emphasis on seafood (see chapter 4 for a review); look for the amiable chef, Brian McBride, who's been known to pop into the dining room from time to time to make sure all is well. From Thursday through Sunday in the lounge, afternoon tea is served (traditional $15.95, with champagne cocktail $19), including finger sandwiches, scones, Devon cream, and pastries, plus the services of a palmist ($10 extra). Adjoining Melrose is a bar; outdoors is a smashingly beautiful cafe.

Amenities: 24-hour concierge; room service; business center; valet/laundry service; foreign currency exchange; shoe shine; twice-daily maid service; delivery of *Washington Post* weekdays; nightly turndown; express checkout; gift shop; hair and skin salon; health club, including indoor pool, heated whirlpool, sauna and steam rooms, and extensive exercise room.

✪ **The Watergate Hotel.** 2650 Virginia Ave. NW, Washington, D.C. 20037. ☎ **800/424-2736** or 202/965-2300. Fax 202/337-7915. 231 units. A/C MINIBAR TV TEL. Weekdays $230–$320 double; weekends $155 double; suites from $420 double, with greatly reduced weekend rates. Extra person $25. Children under 17 stay free. AE, CB, DC, DISC, JCB, MC, V. Parking $20 (valet only). Metro: Foggy Bottom.

Year-round, the Watergate's clientele includes high-level diplomats, business travelers, and Kennedy Center performers (the Kennedy Center is adjacent). Its spa facilities, indoor lap pool and sundeck, state-of-the-art health club, entertainment options, and dozens of adjacent shops are popular with sophisticated travelers, including couples in search of a romantic weekend.

Rooms and suites are spacious—suites are said to be the largest in the city. River-facing rooms give splendid views of the Potomac, and of these, all but the 8th- and 14th-floor rooms have balconies. All rooms have writing desks and fax machines, and most have wet bars; most executive suites have kitchenettes. TVs offer Showtime movies and more than 50 cable stations. In your bathroom you'll find Gilchrist & Soames toiletries; a cosmetic mirror; hair dryer; phone; and terry robes.

Dining/Diversions: Chef Robert Wiedemaier (who ran the Four Seasons's premier restaurant for 7 years) presides over Aquarelle, winning accolades for his Euro-American cuisine. The elegant Potomac Lounge serves British-style afternoon teas Tues–Sun and features special early evening events, such as caviar tastings, sushi/Japanese beer nights, and salmon nights, while a pianist plays on.

Amenities: 24-hour room service and concierge; full business services; nightly turndown; complimentary shoe shine; daily newspaper of your choice; complimentary weekday morning limo to downtown; complimentary coffee in Potomac Lounge; Jacuzzi; steam, sauna, massage and spa treatments; barber/beauty salon (Zahira's, the stylist to three presidents); 10 meeting rooms; gift shop; ballroom overlooking the Potomac; and, in the adjacent complex, dozens of shops including jewelers, designer boutiques, a supermarket, drugstore, and post office.

EXPENSIVE

St. James Suites. 950 24th St. NW (off of Washington Circle), Washington, D.C. 20037. ☎ **800/852-8512** or 202/457-0500. Fax 202/466-6484. 195 units. A/C MINIBAR TV TEL. Weekdays $165–$185, weekends $89–$129. Rates include breakfast. Extra person $20. Children under 17 stay free. AE, DC, DISC, MC, V. Parking $17. Metro: Foggy Bottom.

The St. James is a home away from home for many of its guests, about one-third of whom book these luxury suites for more than 30 days at a time. The suites are all one-bedrooms, with separate living and sleeping areas, marble bathrooms, two-line telephones with modem capability, and kitchens equipped with everything from china and flatware to cooking utensils. Each living room includes a queen-size pullout sofa. Unlike other hotels in this residential neighborhood of old town houses, the St. James is fairly new (only 11 years old), which means accessibility was a factor in its design: A ramp in the lobby leads to the reception area, and 10 suites are available for travelers with disabilities. The St. James is near Georgetown, George Washington University, and the Kennedy Center. Corporate club members receive extra perks, such as evening cocktails and hors d'oeuvres served in the club's pleasant second-floor quarters.

Amenities: Room service (11am–11pm); dry cleaning; laundry service; *Washington Post, New York Times, Wall Street Journal, USA Today* available in breakfast room or delivered to room on request; nightly turndown on request; baby-sitting; business services including faxing and courier service; daily shoe shine; full kitchens;

outdoor pool; 24-hour, state-of-the-art fitness center; nearby tennis courts and jogging/biking paths; conference rooms.

MODERATE

✪ Hotel Lombardy. 2019 Pennsylvania Ave. NW, Washington, D.C. 20006. ☎ **800/424-5486** or 202/828-2600. Fax 202/872-0503. 125 units. A/C MINIBAR TV TEL. Weekdays $140–$180 double, $160–$180 suite for 2; weekends (and sometimes off-season weekdays) $69–$99 double, $119–$140 suite for 2. Extra person $20. Children under 16 stay free in parents' room. AE, CB, DC, DISC, MC, V. Self-parking $17. Metro: Farragut West or Foggy Bottom.

From its handsome walnut-paneled lobby with carved Tudor-style ceilings to its old-fashioned nonautomatic elevator (the hotel is not well suited for travelers with disabilities), the 11-story Lombardy offers a lot of character and comfort for the price and the location (about 5 blocks west of the White House). George Washington University's campus is just across Pennsylvania Avenue, which means this part of town remains vibrant at night, when other downtown neighborhoods have shut down. Peace Corps, World Bank, and corporate guests make up a large part of the clientele, but other visitors will also appreciate the Lombardy's warmly welcoming ambience and the attentive service of the multilingual staff.

Spacious rooms, entered via pedimented louver doors, have undergone a recent redecoration , and each one is slightly different, although all share a 1930s northern Italian motif. Large desks, precious dressing rooms, and roomy walk-in closets are other assets.

Moderately priced and open for all meals, the Café Lombardy, a sunny, glass-enclosed restaurant, serves authentic northern Italian fare. You can also dine in the newly opened Venetian Room, an exquisitely decorated haven with velvet upholstery, antique lanterns, mother-of-pearl-inlaid Moorish cocktail tables, and a custom-made cherry-wood bar. The Venetian Room shares a menu with the cafe, or you may choose from a special menu of appetizers. Amenities include a free overnight shoe shine; fully equipped kitchens and dining nooks in all but 20 rooms; Spectravision pay-per-view movie channel; access to health club 1 block away ($5 per visit); and two small meeting rooms.

One Washington Circle Hotel. 1 Washington Circle NW, Washington, D.C. 20037. ☎ **800/424-9671** or 202/872-1680. Fax 202/887-4989. 151 suites. A/C TV TEL. Weekdays $135–$165 for smallest suite, $170–$285 for largest suite; weekends $59–$99 for smallest suite, $109–$149 for largest. Extra person $15. Guests paying rates of $135 or higher receive free continental breakfast weekdays and cocktails/hors d'oeuvres Mon–Thurs. Children under 18 stay free. AE, CB, DC, MC, V. Underground valet parking $8–$15. Metro: Foggy Bottom.

Built in 1960, this building was converted into a hotel in 1976, making it the city's first all-suite hotel property. Five types of suites are available, ranging in size from 390 to 710 square feet. Every suite has a comfortable decor that includes a sofa bed and dining area, kitchens, and walk-out balconies, some overlooking the circle with George Washington's statue, but keep in mind that across the circle is George Washington University Hospital's emergency room entrance, which is busy with ambulance traffic; although the hotel is well insulated, you may want to ask for a suite on the L Street side. President Nixon liked to stay here on his visits to Washington after Watergate; he preferred Suite 615. Clientele is mostly corporate, but families like the outdoor pool; in-house restaurant; prime location near Georgetown and the Metro; free shuttle to the Kennedy center; and the kitchens. Ask about bargain room rates available to groups, AAA members, and senior citizens, or through a special value ad for the hotel in the *New York Times*. The well-reviewed West End Cafe serves contemporary American cuisine in a garden room/greenhouse setting. Locals frequently dine here, but guests sometimes benefit from special rates. A pianist plays jazz Tuesday through Saturday nights.

INEXPENSIVE

The Premier Hotel. 2601 Virginia Ave. NW (at New Hampshire Ave.), Washington, D.C. 20037. ☎ **800/965-6869** or 202/965-2700. Fax 202/337-5417. www.premierdc.com. E-mail dcpremier@aol.com. 192 units. A/C TV TEL. Weekdays and weekends $89–$139 double, concierge floor $30 additional. Extra person $10. Children under 18 stay free. AE, DC, DISC, JCB, MC, V. Parking $9 (maximum height 6'2"). Metro: Foggy Bottom.

A short walk from the Kennedy Center, with an entrance through a nicely landscaped porte cochere, this former Howard Johnson's property has an upscale look following a $3.5 million renovation. It now offers many assets unusual in its price range, including a concierge and a business center. Pluses include a large L-shaped rooftop pool with a sundeck and adjoining Ping-Pong area; a 24-hour workout room; secured underground parking; coin-operated washers and dryers; sightseeing bus tours; and a gift shop. Rooms, attractively decorated in rich earth tones (half with balconies overlooking the Potomac), offer refrigerators, coffeemakers, safes, and cable TVs with HBO, pay-movie options, and Nintendo. Rooms on the executive floor (the seventh) are larger and have either a sofa bed or chair with ottoman. Room 723 on this floor is dubbed the "Watergate Room," commemorating its use by a lookout for the Watergate burglars, who on June 17, 1972, were across the street breaking in to the

Democratic National Committee Headquarters, in the Watergate Hotel. You may stay in this room ($250 per night), which is decorated with memorabilia from the Watergate time.

Local calls are free. America's Best, a contemporary diner with an exhibition kitchen, serves all meals and provides room service during breakfast hours only, 6 to 9:30am.

9 Woodley Park

EXPENSIVE

Omni Shoreham. 2500 Calvert St. NW (at Connecticut Ave.), Washington, D.C. 20008. ☎ **800/843-6664** or 202/234-0700. Fax 202/265-7972. 860 units. A/C TV TEL. Weekdays and weekends $109–$299 double, depending on availability. Extra person $22. Children under 18 stay free. AE, CB, DC, DISC, JCB, MC, V. Parking $14. Metro: Woodley Park–Zoo.

A massive, $74-million renovation of all guest rooms and the lobby is underway at the Omni and is scheduled for completion by May 1999. The spacious guest rooms will remain twice the size of normal hotel rooms, but their new decor will restore a traditional, elegant look through the use of chintz fabrics, mahogany furnishings, and porcelain fixtures. A new air-conditioning system is being installed throughout the hotel, the pools are being torn out and restructured, and the already excellent health club is being refitted to include extras like a steam room and whirlpool.

Business travelers will appreciate the new two-line telephones with voice mail and the ability to program one's own wake-up-call. Leisure travelers should consider the Shoreham for its recreational facilities, such as the large swimming pool with children's pool, and its proximity to the National Zoo and excellent restaurants. Its 11-acre location on Rock Creek Park is a special asset, because of the spectacular views it affords and its immediate access to bike and jogging paths. Built in 1930, the Shoreham has been the scene of inaugural balls for every president since FDR. Do you believe in ghosts? Ask about Room 800G, the haunted suite (available for $2,500 a night).

Dining/Diversions: The elegant Monique Café et Brasserie, reminiscent of the famed La Coupole in Paris, specializes in continental/American fare with an emphasis on steak and seafood. Rock Creek Park provides a fitting backdrop for the lushly planted cocktail lounge, which is housed under a 35-foot vaulted ceiling.

Amenities: Room service (6am–2am); concierge; dry cleaning and laundry service; express checkout; shops; travel/sightseeing desk; business center and conference rooms; 10 miles of jogging, hiking, and bicycle trails; health and fitness center; $1^1/_2$-mile Perrier parcourse with 18 exercise stations.

INEXPENSIVE

Kalorama Guest House. 2700 Cathedral Ave. NW (entrance on 27th St.), Washington, D.C. 20008. ☎ **202/667-6369.** Fax 202/319-1262. 19 units, 12 with bathrooms. A/C. $45–$75 double with shared bathroom, $65–$105 double with private bathroom. Rates include continental breakfast. AE, CB, DC, DISC, MC, V. Limited parking $7. Metro: Woodley Park–Zoo.

This is the Woodley Park location of the bed-and-breakfast based in Adams-Morgan.

4

Where to Dine in Washington, D.C.

*T*o say that the Washington dining scene is diverse is to state the obvious. Take a look at the list of restaurants by cuisine in the second section of this chapter and you'll see what I mean: from first entry "America" to last entry "Miss Saigon," the capital's restaurants represent a world of tastes. Not quite so obvious, perhaps, is the degree of sophistication you'll find here. For example, not only does Washington have many wonderful Italian restaurants, but the city is also home to many that specialize in the cuisine of a particular region or city, like **Galileo** (Piedmontese), **Villa Franco** (the Amalfi Coast), or **I Ricchi** (Tuscan). Washington has not only superb French restaurants, but also superb inexpensive (**La Fourchette**) and expensive (**Lespinasse**); bistro (**Bistrot Lepic**) and haute cuisine (**Citronelle**); and Provençal (**Provence**) restaurants. Both red meat and fresh fish emporiums proliferate.

1 Best Bets

- **Best Spot for a Romantic Dinner:** Just ask for the "snug" (tables 39 and 40) at The Restaurant at the **Jefferson,** 1200 16th St. NW, at M St. (☎ **202/347-2200**). Two cozy seating areas in alcoves are secluded from the main dining room, complete with banquettes for cuddling. Follow your sumptuous dinner with drinks in front of the fireplace in the adjoining lounge.
- **Best Spot for a Business Lunch:** The upstairs dining room of the **Occidental Grill,** 1475 Pennsylvania Ave. NW (☎ **202/783-1475**), is quiet, with nice-sized booths that guarantee privacy in a restaurant that's centrally located near Capitol Hill and downtown offices. (The food's great, too.)
- **Best Spot for a Celebration: Goldoni,** 1113 23rd St. NW (☎ **202/293-1511**), has a festive air, thanks to the bits of opera bursting through the bubble of conversation in the skylit room. A fun place, and the food is excellent.

- **Best Decor: The Willard Room** (☎ 202/637-7440), in the Willard Hotel, is simply grand, decorated with paneling, velvet, and silk. (Consider this another contender for most romantic.)
- **Best Wine List:** At **Seasons,** in the Four Seasons Hotel, 2800 Pennsylvania Ave. NW (☎ **202/944-2000**). For the 11th consecutive year, its wine cellar has been chosen as one of the 100 best worldwide by *Wine Spectator* magazine.
- **Best for Kids:** The **Austin Grill,** 2404 Wisconsin Ave. NW (☎ **202/337-8080**), is a friendly, chattering place with a children's menu, spill-proof cups, and an atmosphere to please everyone. Go before 9pm.
- **Best American Cuisine: Kinkead's,** 2000 Pennsylvania Ave. NW (☎ **202/296-7700**), concentrates on seafood, but also offers a meat and poultry item on each menu; at any rate, you could eat here every day and not go wrong.
- **Best Chinese Cuisine: Full Kee,** 509 H St. NW (☎ **202/ 371-2233**), in the heart of Chinatown, is consistently good and a great value.
- **Best French Cuisine:** For fancy French food, **Lespinasse,** in the Carlton Hotel, 923 16th St. NW (**202/879-6900**), is the place to go. The luxuriously decorated dining room is a fitting backdrop for the divinely prepared (and enormously expensive) creations of chef Troy Dupuy. For French staples served with great enthusiasm and charm in a more relaxed setting, head for **Bistrot Lepic,** at 1736 Wisconsin Ave. NW (☎ **202/333-0111**).
- **Best Italian Cuisine:** Roberto Donna's **Galileo,** 1110 21st St. NW (☎ **202/293-7191**), serves the best fine Italian cuisine, preparing exquisite pastas, fish, and meat dishes with savory ingredients like truffles and porcini mushrooms. For more traditional (and affordable) classic Italian fare, Donna's **Il Radicchio,** 1211 Wisconsin Ave. NW (☎ **202/337-2627**) and 1509 17th St. NW ☎ **202/986-2627**), does the trick.
- **Best Seafood: Pesce,** 2016 P St. NW (☎ **202/466-3474**) offers reasonably priced, perfectly grilled or sautéed seafood in a convivial atmosphere.
- **Best Pizza:** At **Pizzeria Paradiso's,** 2029 P St. NW (☎ **202/ 223-1245**), peerless chewy-crusted pies are baked in an oak-burning oven and crowned with delicious toppings. You'll find great salads and sandwiches on fresh-baked focaccia here, too.
- **Best Desserts:** No frou-frou desserts served at **Café Berlin,** 322 Massachusetts Ave. NE (☎ **202/543-7656**). These cakes, tortes, pies, and strudels are the real thing.

- **Best Late-Night Dining:** To satisfy a yen for Chinese food, go to **Full Kee,** 509 H St. NW in Chinatown (☎ 202/371-2233), open until 3am on weekends; for more comfortable surroundings and good old American cuisine, try the **Old Ebbitt Grill,** 675 15th St. NW (☎ 202/347-4801), whose kitchen stays open until 1am on weekends.
- **Best Outdoor Dining:** **Les Halles,** 1201 Pennsylvania Ave. NW (☎ 202/347-6848), so much fun inside, carries the party outside in warm weather to its partly covered sidewalk cafe, excellently located on the avenue for people-watching and sightseeing (the Capitol lies down the street; the Old Post Office Pavilion is directly across the avenue).
- **Best Spot for a Night on the Town:** For an exuberant evening, you can dine to the rhythm of a Brazilian beat at **Coco Loco,** 810 7th St. NW (☎ 202/289-2626), and stay on to dance the night away.

2 Restaurants by Cuisine

AMERICAN

America (Capitol Hill, *M*)

Aquarelle (Foggy Bottom, *VE*)

Brighton (Dupont Circle, *E*)

Cashion's Eat Place (Adams-Morgan, *M*)

Martin's Tavern (Georgetown, *M*)

Melrose (Foggy Bottom, *E*)

Mrs. Simpson's (Woodley Park, *E*)

Morrison-Clark Inn (Downtown East, *E*)

Occidental Grill (Downtown East, *VE*)

Old Ebbitt Grill (Downtown East, *M*)

The Restaurant at the Jefferson (Downtown West, *VE*)

Ruppents (Downtown East, *VE*)

Seasons (Georgetown, *VE*)

The Willard Room (Downtown East, *VE*)

BARBECUE

Old Glory Barbecue (Georgetown, *I*)

CHINESE

City Lights of China (Dupont Circle, *I*)

Full Kee (Downtown East, *I*)

ETHIOPIAN

Meskerem (Adams-Morgan, *I*)

FRENCH

Bistrot Lepic (Georgetown, *M*)

Key to Abbreviations: *VE*=Very Expensive; *E*=Expensive; *M*=Moderate; *I*=Inexpensive

Citronelle (Georgetown, *VE*)
La Colline (Capitol Hill, *E*)
La Fourchette (Adams-Morgan, *M–E*)
Lespinasse (Downtown West, *VE*)
Provence (Foggy Bottom, *E*)

GERMAN

Café Berlin (Capitol Hill, *M*)

INDIAN

Bombay Club (Downtown West, *E*)

INTERNATIONAL

Cities (Adams-Morgan, *E*)
New Heights (Woodley Park, *E*)

ITALIAN

Barolo (Capitol Hill, *E–VE*)
Galileo (Downtown West, *VE*)
Goldoni (Foggy Bottom, *E*)
I Ricchi (Downtown West, *VE*)
Il Radicchio (Dupont Circle, *I*)
Obelisk (Dupont Circle, *E*)
Pizzeria Paradiso (Dupont Circle, *I*)
Sostanza (Dupont Circle, *E*)
Villa Franco (Downtown East, *VE*)

JAPANESE

Sushi-Ko (Glover Park, *M*)

LATIN

Café Atlantico (Downtown East, *M*)
Gabriel (Dupont Circle, *E*)

MEXICAN

Coco Loco (Downtown East, *M*)
Mixtec (Adams-Morgan, *I*)

SEAFOOD

Georgetown Seafood Grill on 19th Street (Downtown West, *E*)
Kinkead's (Foggy Bottom, *E*)
Pesce (Dupont Circle, *M*)

SOUTHERN/SOUTHWESTERN/AMERICAN

Austin Grill (Glover Park, Bethesda, *I*)
B. Smith's (Capitol Hill, *E*)
Music City Roadhouse (Georgetown, *I*)
Vidalia (Downtown West, *E*)

SPANISH

El Catalan (Downtown East, *VE*)
Taberna del Alabardero (Downtown West, *VE*)

STEAKHOUSES

Les Halles (Downtown East, *E*)
The Palm (Downtown West, *E*)

VIETNAMESE

Miss Saigon (Georgetown, *M*)

3 Capitol Hill

For information on eating at the Capitol and other government buildings, see "Dining at Sightseeing Attractions," later in this chapter.

EXPENSIVE

B. Smith's. Union Station, 50 Massachusetts Ave. NE. ☎ **202/289-6188.** Reservations recommended. Lunch and brunch $8.95–$18.95, $10.95–$21.95. AE, CB, DC, DISC, MC, V. Mon–Thurs 11:30am–4pm and 5–11pm, Fri–Sat 11:30am–4pm and 5pm–midnight, Sun 11:30am–8:30pm. Free validated parking for 2 hours. Metro: Union Station. TRADITIONAL SOUTHERN.

Union Station's most upscale restaurant, the creation of former model Barbara Smith, occupies the room where presidents once greeted visiting monarchs and dignitaries. The dining room has 29-foot ceilings, imposing mahogany doors, white marble floors, gold-leafed moldings, and towering Ionic columns. Background music is mellow (Nat King Cole, Ray Charles, Sarah Vaughan). The restaurant has live jazz on Friday and Saturday evenings and at Sunday brunch. Chef James Oakley's menu offers appetizers such as jambalaya or red beans and rice studded with andouille sausage and tasso (spicy smoked pork). Among the main dishes are sautéed Virginia trout piled high with crabmeat/vegetable "stuffing" and served atop mesclun with rice and a medley of roasted vegetables. A basket of minibiscuits, corn and citrus-poppyseed muffins, and sourdough rolls accompanies all dishes. Desserts include pecan sweet potato pie. An almost all-American wine list features many by-the-glass selections.

Barolo. 223 Pennsylvania Ave. NW. ☎ **202/547-5011.** Reservations recommended. Lunch $11–$14.50, dinner $13.95–$24. AE, DC, MC, V. Mon–Thurs 11:30am–2:30pm and 5:30–10pm, Fri 11:30am–2:30pm and 5:30–10:30pm, Sat 5:30–10:30pm. Free valet parking at dinner. Metro: Capitol South. ITALIAN.

Much needed on Capitol Hill is this excellent upscale Italian restaurant, another pearl in Roberto Donna's string of fine eateries in the area. Situated above another Donna creation, the inexpensive Il Radicchio (see write-up for Dupont Circle location), Barolo has three dining rooms, including a back room for private parties. The intimate main room is paneled and has wooden floors, a working fireplace, and tables placed discreetly apart; encircling the upper reaches of the room is a charming, narrow balcony set with tables for two. Although the menu changes daily, you can expect Piedmontese-style cuisine, such as white asparagus salad with fresh fava beans and slices of Parma prosciutto; saffron pappardelle pasta with fresh sautéed lobster, asparagus, roasted garlic, and fresh basil; or roasted filet of red snapper over sweet potato, rosemary, black olives, and fresh basil. You can also expect to see Washington notables dining here; among recent guests were Mary Bono and Jerry Lewis, both representatives of California, and the owner himself,

Georgetown & Downtown Dining

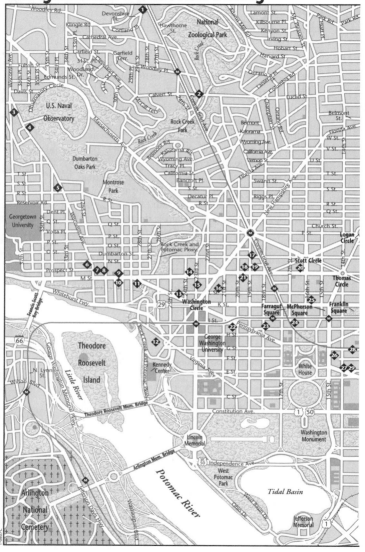

America 🛈
Aquarelle 🛈
Austin Grill 🛈
B. Smith's 🛈
Barolo 🛈
Bistrot Lepic 🛈
Bombay Club 🛈
Café Atlantico 🛈
Café Berlin 🛈
Citronelle 🛈
Coco Loco 🛈
El Catalan 🛈
Full Kee 🛈
Galileo 🛈
Georgetown Seafood
  Grill on 19th St. 🛈
Goldoni 🛈
I Ricchi 🛈
Kinkead's 🛈
La Colline 🛈
Les Halles 🛈
Lespinasse 🛈
Martin's Tavern 🛈

Melrose 🛈
Miss Saigon 🛈
Morrison-Clark Inn 🛈
Mrs. Simpson's 🛈
Music City
  Roadhouse 🛈
New Heights 🛈
Occidental Grill 🛈
Old Ebbitt Grill 🛈
Old Glory Barbecue 🛈
The Palm 🛈
Provence 🛈
Restaurant at
  the Jefferson 🛈
Rupperts 🛈
Seasons 🛈
Sushi-Ko 🛈
Taberna del
  Alabardero 🛈
Vidalia 🛈
Villa Franco 🛈
The Willard Room 🛈

73

Roberto Donna. The wine list is entirely Italian and focuses on wines of the Piedmont, with emphasis on those produced from the Barolo grape.

✪ **La Colline.** 400 N. Capitol St. NW. ☎ **202/737-0400.** Reservations recommended. Breakfast $5–$8.75, lunch $8.75–$16.25, dinner $18.75–$21. AE, CB, DC, MC, V. Mon–Fri 7–10am, 11:30am–3pm, and 6–10pm; Sat 6–10pm. Free garage parking after 5pm. Metro: Union Station. FRENCH.

Mornings are great here if you want to see breakfast fund-raisers in progress. Hill people like La Colline for its convenience to the Senate side of the Capitol; the great bar; the 4 private rooms; the high-backed leather booths that allow for discrete conversations; and, last but not least, the food. You'll always get a good meal here. The regular menu offers an extensive list of French standards, like the salad niçoise, the terrine of foie gras (a deal for under $9), and the fish—poached, grilled, or sautéed. Almost as long is the list of daily specials, which are worth considering—the soft-shell crab is superb here in season. The wine list concentrates on French and California wines; wine-by-the-glass choices change with the season to complement the menu. Don't let the dessert cart roll past you; the apple pie is a winner.

MODERATE

America. Union Station, 50 Massachusetts Ave. NE. ☎ **202/682-9555.** Reservations recommended. Main courses $6.95–$17.95; sandwiches, burgers, and salads $3.50–$13.95; brunch $7.25–$13.50. AE, DC, DISC, MC, V. Sun–Thurs 11:30am–midnight, Fri–Sat 11:30am–1am. Free validated parking for 2 hours. Metro: Union Station. AMERICAN REGIONAL.

Our helpful waiter gave us the lowdown: Candice Bergen, Justice Clarence Thomas, Newt Gingrich, and Alec Baldwin are among those who have eaten here at one time or another. People-watching is one reason to come to this vast, four-level restaurant, but sightseeing is another. Ask for a seat in the uppermost Capital Wine Room, where if you look out the window, you see the Capitol dome; look the other direction (between the Roman legionnaire statues), and you've got a grand view of Union Station. (This area seats parties of up to four, not large groups.) Walls are decorated with WPA-style murals, a large painting of the American West, and a whimsical frieze depicting surfers, athletes, astronauts, and superheroes in outer space.

A vast American-classic menu comprises about 150 items, each with the name of the city, state, or region in which the dish supposedly originated: spaghetti and meatballs (Cleveland?), chili dogs

(Fort Lee, NJ?). The BLT (Newport) is a safe bet, the nachos (Eagle Pass, TX) are too greasy, and you'll definitely find better crab cakes (Ocean City, MD) elsewhere in the city.

Café Berlin. 322 Massachusetts Ave. NE. ☎ **202/543-7656.** Reservations recommended. Main courses $11.95–$16.95 at lunch and dinner; soups, sandwiches, and salads $4.75–$6.95 at lunch. AE, DC, MC, V. Mon–Thurs 11am–10pm, Fri–Sat 11am–11pm, Sun 4–10pm. Metro: Union Station. GERMAN.

You have to walk past the dessert display on your way to your table at Café Berlin, so forget your diet. These delicious, homemade confections are the best reason to come here. The vast spread might include a dense pear cheesecake, raspberry Linzer torte, sour-cherry crumb cake, or vanilla custard cake. Entrees feature things like the Rahm Schnitzel, which is a center cut of veal topped with a light cream and mushroom sauce, or a wurstplatte of mixed sausages. Seasonal items highlight asparagus in spring, game in the fall, and so on. Lunch is a great deal: a simple chicken salad sandwich (laced with tasty bits of mandarin orange), the soup of the day, and German potato salad, all for $5.75. The owners and chef are German; co-owner Peggy Reed emphasizes that their dishes are "on the light side—except for the beer and desserts." The 12-year-old restaurant occupies two prettily decorated dining rooms on the bottom level of a Capitol Hill town house, whose front terrace serves as an outdoor cafe in warm weather.

4 Downtown, East of 16th Street NW

VERY EXPENSIVE

El Catalan. 1319 F St. NW. ☎ **202/628-2299.** Reservations recommended. Lunch $12.50–$21, dinner $13.50–$28. AE, DC, MC, V. Mon–Thurs 11:45am–2:30pm and 5:30–10:15pm, Fri 11:45am–2:30pm and 5:30–11:15pm, Sat 5:30–11:15pm. Metro: Metro Center. SPANISH.

This restaurant would be top-notch if it weren't for the service, which is so slow, it's agonizing. And throughout my meal, the waiter kept addressing me as "lady," not as in "Lady," but as in "hey lady." Restaurant reviews have pointed out the poor service ever since El Catalan opened in 1997, but management apparently doesn't care. The front dining area is the more casual room, the rear dining area elegantly beautiful with, somehow, a Casablanca feel about it. Emerging from the open kitchen are excellent tapas, such as octopus stew with potatoes or the squid sautéed with chorizo; and even more excellent entrees, the best of which is probably the beef rib stew with an orange-and-olive-flavored sauce. The desserts are heavenly; try the Catalan cream or the pear gratin.

✪ **Rupperts.** 1017 7th St. NW. ☎ **202/783-0699.** Reservations required. Main courses $25 at lunch and dinner. AE, DC, MC, V. Tues–Wed 6–10pm, Thurs 11:30am–2:30pm and 6–10pm, Fri–Sat 6–11pm. Metro: Mount Vernon Square–UDC, Gallery Place–Chinatown. AMERICAN.

Within spitting distance of the D.C. Convention Center, this one-room, understated restaurant with a casual atmosphere is in a marginal neighborhood; thankfully, a boom in downtown development is rapidly bringing other restaurants and nightlife a little closer.

The restaurant's success is a tribute to the chef's simple but excellent ways with seasonal produce. The chef changes the menu daily, sometimes three times a day, to work with the freshest ingredients. You may see a foie gras and figs dish on the menu in late fall or soft-shell crabs and grilled rhubarb in spring. The food is not heavy, nor laden with sauces. Three different freshly baked breads come with dinner. The wine list is eclectic, everything from a $210 bottle of Borgogno Riserva Barolo to a $15 Domaine Manoir Beaujolais Noveau. Desserts, however, are too hip; black rice with persimmon left me unimpressed. Most people are in business dress at lunch, less formal attire in the evening.

The Willard Room. In the Willard Inter-Continental Hotel, 1401 Pennsylvania Ave. NW. ☎ **202/637-7440.** Reservations recommended. Lunch $8–$22, dinner $10–$32. AE, DC, DISC, JCB, MC, V. Mon–Fri 7:30–10am and 11:30am–2pm; Mon–Sat 6–10pm. Metro: Metro Center. AMERICAN REGIONAL/CLASSIC EUROPEAN.

Like the rest of the hotel (see chapter 3), the Willard dining room has been restored to its original turn-of-the-century splendor, with gorgeous carved oak paneling, towering scagliola columns, brass and bronze torchères and chandeliers, and a faux-bois beamed ceiling. Scattered among the statesmen and diplomats dining here are local couples who have come for romance; the Willard has been the setting for more than one betrothal.

Chef de cuisine Gerard Madani, who changes the lunch menu daily and the dinner menu every 2 or 3 weeks, emphasizes lightness in cooking. Some examples: steamed Dover sole with a sorrel-flavored vermouth cream sauce; veal kidney with celery root mustard-seed sauce; beef tenderloin with bordelaise sauce; and grilled whole Maine lobster. Two of the most popular desserts are the double-vanilla crème brûlée and the chocolate tears, which combines dark chocolate and white chocolate in a tear-shaped, mousse-like confection. The wine list offers more than 250 fine selections.

EXPENSIVE

✪ **Les Halles.** 1201 Pennsylvania Ave. NW. ☎ **202/347-6848.** Reservations recommended. Lunch $11.75–$20, dinner $13.25–$22.50. AE, CB, DC, DISC, MC, V. Daily 11:30am–midnight. Metro: Metro Center, Federal Triangle. FRENCH/STEAKHOUSE.

Anyone who believes that red meat is passé should stop reading here. At lunch and dinner, people are eating the *onglet* (a boneless, French-cut steak hard to find outside France); steak au poivre; steak tartare; New York sirloin; and other cuts of cow—always accompanied by *frites,* of course. The menu isn't all beef, but it is classic French: cassoulet; confit de canard; escargots; onion soup; and such. I can never resist the *frisee aux lardons,* a savory salad of chicory studded with hunks of bacon and toast smeared thickly with Roquefort.

Les Halles is big and charmingly French, with French-speaking staff providing breezy, flirtatious service. The banquettes; pressed tin ceiling; mirrors; wooden floor; and the side bar capture the feel of a brasserie. A vast window overlooks Pennsylvania Avenue and the awning-covered sidewalk cafe, which is a superb spot to dine in warm weather. Les Halles is a favorite hangout for cigar smokers, but the smoking area is well ventilated.

Morrison-Clark Inn and Restaurant. Massachusetts Ave. NW (at 11th St.). ☎ **202/898-1200.** Reservations recommended. Lunch $12.50–$14.50, dinner $17.50–$23, 3-course Sun brunch (including unlimited champagne) $25. AE, CB, DC, DISC, MC, V. Mon–Fri 11:30am–2:30pm and 5:30–9:30pm, Sat 5:30–9:30pm, Sun 11:30am–2:30pm and 5:30–9pm. Metro: Metro Center. AMERICAN REGIONAL.

The *Washington Post* and *Gourmet* magazine often cite the Morrison-Clark restaurant as one of the best in the city. The dining room is a Victorian drawing room with ornately carved white-marble fireplaces. At night, soft lighting emanates from Victorian brass candelabras, crystal chandeliers, and candles. During the day, sunlight streams through floor-to-ceiling, mahogany- and gilt-trimmed windows, and, weather permitting, you can dine outdoors at courtyard umbrella tables.

Chef Susan McCreight Lindeborg's seasonally changing menus are elegant and inspired. An early spring menu may feature potato and leek soup with country ham toasts as a first course and sautéed salmon with risotto cakes and crimini mushroom butter sauce as a main course. The inn is known for its desserts, like the chocolate caramel tart topped with praline-studded whipped cream. Similar fare is available at lunch and brunch. A reasonably priced wine list offers a variety of premium wines by the glass, plus a nice choice of champagnes, dessert wines, and ports.

Villa Franco. 601 Pennsylvania Ave. NW. ☎ **202/638-2423.** Reservations recommended. Lunch $12–$16, dinner $13–$28. AE, MC, V. Mon–Thurs 11:30am–3pm and 5:30–11pm, Fri 11:30am–3pm and 5:30–11:30pm, Sat 5:30–11:30pm. Metro: Archives-Navy Memorial. ITALIAN.

Although it has a Pennsylvania Avenue address, Villa Franco's entrance is on Indiana Avenue, just a block up from Pennsylvania. The decor is colorful, with faux stucco wall treatments in bright pastels, trompe l'oeil statuary and fountains, and vividly decorated rotundas in the tiled bar and back dining room. The food represents cuisine from the Amalfi Coast of Italy, near Naples, Palermo, and Capri—think fresh mozzarella; tomatoes; basil; eggplant; and olives. Standouts include a fresh tuna tartare with a sun-dried tomato and black olive purée, a baby spinach salad with frisée and shavings of ricotta cheese, and pan-roasted yellow snapper in a tangy caponata sauce.

MODERATE

Café Atlantico. 405 8th St. NW. ☎ **202/393-0812.** Reservations required. Lunch $9.50–$14.50, dinner $13.95–$16.50, light fare $4.50–$7.50. AE, DC, MC, V. Mon–Tues 11:30am–2:30pm and 5:30–10pm, Wed–Sat 11:30am–2:30pm and 5:30–11pm (Fri 2:30–5:30pm for light fare), Sun 5:30–10pm. The bar stays open until 1am on weekends. Metro: Archives–Navy Memorial. LATIN AMERICAN/CARIBBEAN.

This place, a favorite hot spot in Washington's burgeoning downtown, rocks on weekend nights. The colorful, three-tier restaurant throbs with Latin, calypso, and reggae music, and everyone is having a good time—including, it seems, the staff. If the place is packed, see if you can snag a seat at the second-level bar, where you can watch the genial bartender mix the potent drinks for which Café Atlantico is famous: the caipirinha, made of limes, sugar, and *cachacha* (sugarcane liqueur); or the mojito, a rum and crushed mint cocktail.

After you are seated at the bar or table, your waiter makes fresh guacamole right in front of you. As for the main dishes, you can't get a more elaborate meal for the price. The ceviche, Ecuadorean seared scallops, and Argentine rib eye are standouts, and tropical side dishes and pungent sauces produce a burst of color on the plate. Since the menu changes every week, these items may not be available; ask your waiter for guidance.

✪ Coco Loco. 810 7th St. NW (between H and I sts.). ☎ **202/289-2626.** Reservations recommended. Tapas mostly $4.95–$12; *churrascaria* with antipasti bar $30 (dinner only); antipasti bar $14 (dinner only). AE, MC, V. Mon–Thurs 11:30am–2:30pm and 5:30–10pm, Fri 11:30am–2:30pm and 5:30–11pm, Sat 5:30–11pm. Metro: Gallery Place. BRAZILIAN/MEXICAN.

At 8pm on a Wednesday night, the dance floor is filled with young, well-dressed couples dancing to salsa. Weekends, you can't even get in the joint. Besides the music and dancing, much of the action emanates from the open kitchen and the U-shaped bar. If you want a quieter setting, head for the window-walled front room or the garden patio. The exuberantly tropical interior space centers on a daily changing buffet table. Cheeses; fresh fruits; salads (ranging from roasted tomatoes with mozzarella to garbanzos with figs); cold cuts; and other antipasti are temptingly arrayed on palm fronds and banana leaves.

An extensive selection of Mexican tapas includes interesting quesadillas and pan-roasted shrimp on chewy black (squid-infused) Chinese jasmine rice. Coco Loco's most popular dish is churrascaria, the Brazilian mixed grill. Waiters serve you chunks of the sausage; chicken; beef; and pork from skewers. It comes with salsa, fried potatoes, and coconut-flavored rice and includes antipasti bar offerings. All this and Mexican chocolate rice pudding for dessert, too. The wine list is small but well chosen. French chef Yannick Cam, also of Provence, is one of Coco Loco's owners.

Old Ebbitt Grill. 675 15th St. NW (between F and G sts.). ☎ **202/347-4801.** Reservations recommended. Breakfast $4.50–$6.95; brunch $5.95–$12.95; lunch $7.95–$12.95; dinner $9.95–$15.95; burgers and sandwiches $6.25–$10.95; raw bar $8.95–$18.50. AE, DC, DISC, MC, V. Mon–Fri 7:30am–1am, Sat 8am–1am, Sun 9:30am–1am. Bar Sun–Thurs to 2am, Fri–Sat to 3am. Raw bar open daily to midnight. Metro: McPherson Square or Metro Center. Complimentary valet parking from 6pm Mon–Sat, from noon Sun. AMERICAN.

Located 2 blocks from the White House, this is the city's oldest saloon, founded in 1856. Among its artifacts are animal trophies bagged by Teddy Roosevelt and Alexander Hamilton's wooden bears—one with a secret compartment in which it's said he hid whiskey bottles from his wife. The Old Ebbitt is an attractive place, with Persian rugs strewn on beautiful oak and marble floors; beveled mirrors; flickering gas lights; etched-glass panels; and paintings of Washington scenes. The long, dark mahogany Old Bar area gives it the feeling of a men's saloon.

You may see preferential treatment given to movers and shakers, and you'll always have a wait for a table if you don't reserve ahead.

The staff is friendly and professional in a programmed sort of way; service could be faster. Menus change daily but always include certain favorites: burgers; trout Parmesan (Virginia trout dipped in egg batter and Parmesan cheese, deep-fried); crab cakes; and oysters (there's an oyster bar). The tastiest dishes are usually the seasonal ones, whose fresh ingredients make the difference.

INEXPENSIVE

Full Kee. 509 H St. NW. ☎ **202/371-2233.** Reservations accepted. Lunch $4.25–$9, dinner $6.95–$14.95. No credit cards. Sun–Thurs 11am–1am, Fri 11am–3am, Sat 11am–3am. Metro: Gallery Place/Chinatown. CHINESE.

This is probably Chinatown's best restaurant, in terms of the actual food. Forget decor: Full Kee's two rooms are brightly lighted and crammed with Chinese-speaking customers sitting upon metal-legged chairs at plain rectangular tables. The restaurant does not have a no-smoking section. A cook works at the small open kitchen at the front of the room, hanging roasted pig parts on hooks and wrapping dumplings.

Chefs from some of Washington's best restaurants often congregate here after hours, and here's their advice: Order from the typed back page of the menu. Two selections are especially noteworthy: the jumbo breaded oyster casserole with ginger and scallions (I can second that) and the whole steamed fish. Check out the laminated tent card on the table and find the soups; if you love dumplings, order the Hong Kong—style shrimp dumpling broth (you get eight shrimp dumplings if you order the broth without noodles, only four if you order the broth with noodles). Bring your own wine or beer (and your own glasses in which to pour it) if you'd like to have a drink, since Full Kee does not serve any alcohol and accepts no responsibility for helping you imbibe.

5 Downtown, 16th Street NW & West

VERY EXPENSIVE

✪ **Galileo.** 1110 21st St. NW. ☎ **202/293-7191,** www.robertodonna.com. Reservations recommended. Breakfast $2.95–$9.95, lunch $11–$19, dinner $17–$30 at dinner. AE, CB, DC, DISC, MC, V. Mon–Fri 7:30–9:30am, 11:30am–2pm and 5:30–10pm, Sat 5:30–10:30pm, Sun 5–10pm. Complimentary valet parking in evening. Metro: Foggy Bottom. ITALIAN.

Food critics mention Galileo as one of the best Italian restaurants in the country and Roberto Donna as one of our best chefs. The likable Donna opened the white-walled, grotto-like Galileo in 1984; since then, he has opened several other restaurants in the area, including Il Radicchio and Pesce (see Dupont Circle listings), has written a cookbook, and has established himself as an integral part of Washington culture.

Galileo features the cuisine of Donna's native Piedmont region, an area in northern Italy influenced by neighboring France and Switzerland—think truffles, hazelnuts, porcini mushrooms, and veal. A SWAT team of male waiters attend.

I Ricchi. 1220 19th St. NW. ☎ **202/835-0459.** Reservations recommended. Lunch $10–$28, dinner $11.95–$32. AE, DC, MC, V. Mon–Fri 11:30am–1:30pm and 5:30–9:45pm, Sat 5:30–10pm. Free valet parking at dinner. Metro: Dupont Circle. ITALIAN.

This restaurant celebrates its 10th year in 1999, and it remains a popular and convivial place to enjoy Italian food à la Tuscany. An open kitchen with a blazing wood-burning grill creates a warming bustle in the large room. What's good here? If you're into fish, check out the daily specials; the minestrone; and the pastas, particularly the one stuffed with spinach and ground veal, the fat noodles wrapped in rabbit sauce, or the spaghettini covered with a thick tomato sauce, with mushrooms and crisp shrimp.

Lespinasse. 923 16th St. NW (in the Carlton Hotel). ☎ **202/879-6900.** Reservations recommended. Jacket required for men. Breakfast $8–$19; lunch prix fixe $36, à la carte $24–$27; tea $19; dinner prix fixe $75, à la carte $28–$39. AE, CB, DC, DISC, MC, V. Mon–Fri 7–10:30am noon–2pm and 6pm–10pm, Sat 7–11am and 6pm–10pm, Sun 7–11am; daily tea (in lobby) 3–5:30pm. Complimentary valet parking for lunch and dinner. Metro: Farragut North. FRENCH.

A $6-million renovation of Lespinasse's opulent dining room endowed it with a castlelike stenciled ceiling with wooden beams; creamy gold-hued walls; royal blue stamped banquettes and floral carpeting; and comfortable yellow leather chairs. The china is Limoges, the crystal Riedel. You pay for the embellishments: This Washington branch of New York's Lespinasse is now the most expensive restaurant in town. St. Regis chef Gray Kunz sent his sous-chef, Troy Dupuy, to command this kitchen. Sommelier Vincent Feraud is the best, having presided at Jean-Louis (now closed). One unexpected thing about the wine list is that it offers a nice selection of reasonably priced good wines by the glass.

The Restaurant at the Jefferson. 1200 16th St. NW (at M St.). ☎ **202/833-6206.** Reservations recommended. Lunch $13–$22, dinner $22–$28, Sun brunch $19.50–$28. AE, CB, DC, JCB, MC, V. Daily 6:30–10:30am, 11am–3pm, and 6–10:30pm. Free valet parking. Metro: Farragut North. NATURAL AMERICAN.

Cozy, rather than intimidatingly plush, the Jefferson Hotel's restaurant is very romantic (ask to be seated in "the snug," tables 39 or 40). The emphasis on privacy and the solicitous, but not imposing service also make it a good place to do business.

Chef James Hudock changes his menus seasonally. Appetizers we enjoyed from a late winter menu included a baby spinach salad sprinkled with goat cheese and dressed with tangerine-ginger dressing, and a warm artichoke heart salad with designer lettuce and scallops, resting upon a thin potato galette. Among the entrees were a caramelized black grouper with Kalamata olives, roasted peppers, English peas, and roasted potatoes, and perfectly done lamb chops. Our meal ended with a divine coffee crème brûlée. An extensive wine list includes many by-the-glass selections.

✪ **Taberna del Alabardero.** 1776 I St. NW (entrance on 18th St. NW). ☎ **202/429-2200.** Reservations recommended. Jacket and tie required for men. Lunch $10–$18, dinner $18–$28, pretheater $30. AE, DC, DISC, MC, V. Mon–Thurs 11:30am–2:30pm and 6–10pm, Fri 11:30am–2:30pm and 6–11pm, Sat 6–11pm. Metro: Farragut West. SPANISH.

Dress up to visit this elegant restaurant, where you receive royal treatment from the Spanish staff who are quite used to attending to the real thing: Spain's King Juan Carlos and Queen Sofia and their children regularly dine here when in Washington.

The dining room is old-world ornate, with lace antimacassars placed upon velvety banquettes and heavy brocade-like drapes framing the large front windows. Order a plate of tapas to start: lightly fried calamari; shrimp in garlic and olive oil; thin smoked ham; and marinated mushrooms. Although the à la carte menu changes with the seasons, the four paellas (each requires a minimum of two people to order) are always available.

EXPENSIVE

Bombay Club. 815 Connecticut Ave. NW. ☎ **202/659-3727.** Reservations recommended. Lunch and dinner $7.50–$18.50, Sun brunch $16.50, pretheater $24. AE, CB, DC, MC, V. Mon–Thurs 11:30am–2:30pm and 6–10:30pm, Fri 11:30am–2:30pm and 6–11pm, Sat 6–11pm, Sun 11:30am–2:30pm and 5:30–9pm. Free valet parking after 6pm. Metro: Farragut West. INDIAN.

The Clintons have eaten here many times, and diners know it; when the Secret Service swept the restaurant recently at lunch, the place was abuzz with anticipation, only to see Prince Bandar bin Sultan, the Saudi ambassador, enter the room.

The Indian menu here ranges from fiery green chili chicken (not for the fainthearted, the menu warns) to the delicately prepared lobster malabar, a personal favorite. Tandoori dishes, like the chicken marinated in a yogurt, ginger, and garlic dressing, are specialties, as is the vegetarian fare—try the black lentils cooked overnight on a slow fire. The staff seems straight out of *Jewel in the Crown,* attending to your every whim. This is one place where you can linger over a meal as long as you like. Slow-moving ceiling fans and wicker furniture accentuate the colonial British ambience.

✪ **Georgetown Seafood Grill on 19th Street.** 1200 19th St. NW. ☎ **202/530-4430.** Reservations recommended. Lunch $9.95–$17.95, dinner $10.95–$21.95, salads and sandwiches $8.95–$12.95. AE, DC, DISC, MC, V. Mon–Thurs 11:30am–10pm, Fri 11:30am–11pm, Sat 5:30–11pm, Sun 5:30–10pm. Metro: Dupont Circle. SEAFOOD.

In the heart of downtown is this hint of the seashore. Two big tanks of lobsters greet you as you enter, and the decor throughout follows a nautical theme: aquariums set in walls, canoes fastened to the ceiling, models of tall ships placed here and there. Meanwhile, music from another era is heard—"Young at Heart," and the like. It's enough to make you forget what city you're in.

A bar and sets of tables sit at the front of the restaurant, an open kitchen is in the middle, and tall wooden booths on platforms lie at the rear. The lobster thermidor special is a mix of Pernod, scallions, mushrooms, and cream mixed with bits of lobster, but if you want really healthier chunks of lobster, order the lobster club, served on brioche with apple-wood bacon and mayonnaise, or better yet, the fresh lobster delivered daily from Maine. As is the rule in many seafood restaurants, your best bets are the most simply prepared: Besides the lobster, you can choose from a list of at least eight "simply grilled" fish entrees. Raw-bar selections list oysters from Canada, Virginia, and Oregon, and these may be the freshest in town. Service is excellent.

✪ **The Palm.** 1225 19th St. NW. ☎ **202/293-9091.** Reservations recommended. Lunch $8.50–$17, dinner $15–$58. AE, DC, MC, V. Mon–Fri 11:45am–10:30pm, Sat 6–10:30pm, Sun 5:30–9:30pm. Complimentary valet parking at dinner. Metro: Dupont Circle. STEAKHOUSE.

The Palm is one in a chain that started 76 years ago in New York—but here in D.C., it feels like an original. The Washington Palm is 27 years old; its walls, like all Palms, are covered with the caricatures of regulars, famous and not-so. (Look for my friend, Bob Harris.) You can't go wrong with steak, whether it's offered as a 36-ounce, dry-aged New York strip, or sliced in a steak salad. Oversize lobsters are a specialty, and certain side dishes are a must: creamed spinach; onion rings; Palm fries (something akin to deep-fried potato chips);

and hash browns. Several of the longtime waiters like to joke around; service is always fast.

✪ **Vidalia.** 1990 M St. NW. ☎ **202/659-1990.** Reservations recommended. Lunch $13–$16.75, dinner $17–$27. AE, DC, DISC, MC, V. Mon–Thurs 11:30am–2:30pm and 5:30–10pm, Fri 11:30am–2:30pm and 5:30–10:30pm, Sat 5:30–10:30pm, Sun 5–9:30pm (closed Sun July 4–Labor Day). Complimentary valet parking at dinner. Metro: Dupont Circle. PROVINCIAL AMERICAN.

Down a flight of steps from the street, the charming Vidalia is a tiered dining room, with cream stucco walls hung with gorgeous dried-flower wreaths and works by local artists.

Chef Jeff Buben's "provincial American" menu (focusing on southern-accented regional specialties) changes frequently, but recommended constants include crisp East Coast lump crab cakes, a fried grits cake with portobello mushrooms, and something that fans refer to simply as "the onion": a roasted whole Vidalia onion that's cut and opened, like the leaves of a flower. Venture from the regular items, and you may delight in a timbale of roasted onion and foie gras.

A signature entree is the scrumptious sautéed shrimp on a mound of creamed grits and caramelized onions in a thyme and shrimp-cream sauce. Try to make room for side dishes like garlic mashed potatoes and the onion casserole. Corn bread and biscuits with apple butter are served at every meal. Vidalia is known for its lemon chess pie, which tastes like pure sugar; I prefer the pecan pie. A carefully chosen wine list highlights American vintages. *Note:* In early summer 1998, the Bubens opened bis, a French restaurant, in the Hotel George on Capitol Hill.

6 Georgetown

VERY EXPENSIVE

✪ **Citronelle.** In the Latham Hotel, 3000 M St. NW. ☎ **202/625-2150.** Reservations recommended. Breakfast $7–12. Lunch $16–$25, dinner $22–$32. AE, DC, MC, V. Mon–Thurs 6:30–10:30am, noon–2pm, and 5:30–10pm; Fri–Sat 6:30–10:30am, noon–2pm, and 5:30–10:30pm; Sun 6:30–10:30am. Complimentary valet parking at dinner. CONTEMPORARY FRENCH.

In March 1998, Citronelle reopened after a $2-million renovation, with much fanfare provided by enthusiastic Washington foodies and Citronelle's ebullient chef/owner Michel Richard. Richard opened Citronelle in 1992, but left it in the hands of other good chefs while he returned to his flagship restaurant, the famed Citrus, in Los Angeles. Now the Frenchman has moved to Washington, happy to please the palates of Washingtonians, whose tastes he believes to be more sophisticated than Los Angelenos.

In terms of decor, the Citronelle transformation includes a wall that changes colors, a state-of-the-art wine cellar (a glass-enclosed room that encircles the dining room, displaying its 8,000 bottles and a collection of 18th- and 19th-century corkscrews), and a Provençal color scheme of mellow yellow and raspberry red.

Emerging from the bustling exhibition kitchen now are appetizers like the fricassee of escargots, sweetbreads, porcinis, and crunchy pistachios, and entrees like the crispy lentil-coated salmon. The dessert of choice: Michel Richard's rich, layered chocolate "bar" with sauce noisette. Citronelle's extensive wine list offers many premium by-the-glass selections, but with all those bottles staring out at you from the wine cellar, you may want to spring for a full bottle.

Seasons. In the Four Seasons Hotel, 2800 Pennsylvania Ave. NW. ☎ **202/ 944-2000.** Reservations recommended. Breakfast $10–$17.25, lunch $12.75– $21, dinner $21–$34. AE, DC, DISC, JCB, MC, V. Mon–Fri 7–11am, noon– 2:30pm, and 6–10:30pm; Sat–Sun 8am–noon and 6–10:30pm. Metro: Foggy Bottom. Free valet parking. AMERICAN.

Although Seasons is the signature restaurant of one of Washington's most upscale hotels, and a major celebrity haunt, it takes a casual approach to formal dining: relaxed atmosphere, no dress code, and friendly service. Seasons is candlelit at night and sunlit during the day and has windows overlooking the C&O Canal.

Scottish chef William Douglas McNeill's cuisine focuses on fresh market fare. Stellar entrees range from seared tuna with shiitake mushroom-mashed potatoes and peppercorn sauce, to mustard seed-encrusted roast rack of lamb served with Provençal veggies. A basket of scrumptious fresh-baked breads might include rosemary flat bread or sun-dried tomato bread drizzled with Parmesan. For dessert, consider a caramelized ginger crème brûlée. For the 11th consecutive year, *Wine Spectator* magazine has named Seasons' vast and carefully researched wine cellar one of the 100 best worldwide.

MODERATE

♦ **Bistrot Lepic.** 1736 Wisconsin Ave. NW. ☎ **202/333-0111.** Reservations recommended. Lunch $9–$12.25, dinner $14–$18. AE, DISC, MC, V. Tues– Thurs 11:30am–2:30pm and 5:30–10pm, Fri–Sat 11:30am–2:30pm and 5:30– 10:30pm, Sun 11:30am–2:30pm and 5:30–9:30pm. FRENCH.

So tiny it has no waiting area for new arrivals, Bistrot Lepic is the real thing, a charming French restaurant like one you might find on a Parisian side street. The atmosphere is bustling and cheery, and you hear a lot of French spoken—not just by the staff and the young proprietress, Cecile Fortin (her husband Bruno is chef), but by customers as well.

This is traditional French cooking, updated. The seasonal menu offers such seafood and meat entrees as grilled rockfish served with green lentils du Puy and aged balsamic sauce, and roasted rack of lamb with Yukon gold mashed potatoes and garlic juice. We opted for specials: tuna prepared quite rare, as it's supposed to be, and served on fennel with a citrusy vinaigrette, and grouper with a lightly spicy lobster sauce upon a bed of spinach.

The modest French wine list offers a fairly good range, but the house wine, Le Pic Saint Loup, is a nice complement to most menu choices and priced at less than $20 a bottle.

✪ **Martin's Tavern.** 1264 Wisconsin Ave. NW. ☎ **202/333-7370.** Reservations accepted. Breakfast $5.50–$11.95; brunch $5.50–$11.95; lunch $6.50–$10.95 (sandwiches and salads average $5.95); dinner $5.75–$19.95 (most items under $15). AE, CB, DC, DISC, MC, V. Sun–Thurs 8am–11pm, Fri–Sat 8am–1am. One hour free parking for lunch, 1¹/₂ hours for dinner, at Georgetown Inn. AMERICAN.

A good old-fashioned neighborhood pub—that's Martin's. Out-of-towners (especially French and Japanese) come here often, but Martin's has a loyal following of locals as well. I once heard a couple at the bar joking that they chose their new house on the basis of its proximity to Martin's. It has operated continuously since 1933, when it was opened by former New York Giants player William G. Martin, and his father, William S. These days, Billy Martin, great grandson of William S., is behind the bar and, as general manager, pretty much runs the show and supervises the staff, some of whom have been here for more than a decade. Sit at the bar, and you'll hear the lore about famous regulars over the years—from the Kennedys to Art Buchwald. If you crave intimacy, just ask for the "dugout." The menu mainstays are the crab cakes, steak sandwich, the shad and shad roe, and linguine with clam sauce. The place has lots of paneling, old photos, and draft beers on tap.

Miss Saigon. 3057 M St. NW. ☎ **202/333-5545.** Reservations recommended, especially weekend nights. Lunch $5.50–$7.95, dinner $6.95–$22.95. AE, DC, MC, V. Mon–Fri 11:30am–3pm and 3–11pm, Sat–Sun noon–11pm (dinner menu served all day). VIETNAMESE.

This is a charming restaurant, with tables scattered amid a forest of tropical foliage, with twinkly lights strewn upon the fronds of the potted palms and ferns.

The food here is delicious and authentic, although the service can be a trifle slow when the restaurant is busy. To begin, there is the crispy calamari, a favorite of Madeline Albright. House specialties include steamed flounder, caramel salmon, and "shaking beef" (Vietnamese steak): crusty cubes of tender beef marinated in wine, garlic, butter, and soy sauce, then sautéed with onions and potatoes, and served with rice and salad. There's a full bar. Desserts range from bananas flambé au rhum to ice cream with Godiva liqueur. Not to be missed is drip pot coffee, brewed tableside and served iced with sweetened condensed milk.

INEXPENSIVE

Music City Roadhouse. 1050 30th St. NW. ☎ **202/337-4444.** Reservations recommended. Family-style meal $12.95, $5.95 for children 6–12, children under 6 can share with adults; late night courses $3–$7.50; brunch $12.95. AE, CB, DC, DISC, MC, V. Tues–Sat 4:30pm–1am, Sun 11am–9pm (brunch 11am–2pm). SOUTHERN/AMERICAN.

The downstairs of Music City Roadhouse is a large and raucous two-room bar with pool tables. Upstairs is the restaurant where live, mostly blues bands play while you savor fried and barbecued chicken; barbecued spare ribs; fried catfish; pot roast; and country fried steak. The deal is, for $12.95 each, you may choose up to three entrees and three side dishes for your table. The sides, such as mashed regular and sweet potatoes, coleslaw, greens, and green beans with bacon, are replenishable.

The music is great, but so loud it overwhelms conversation, and the small tables are packed tightly next to each other (most seating is family style, at long tables). In good weather, try to sit out on the terrace, which overlooks the C&O Canal. The food is plentiful and tastes of the true South (that is, the greens are soggy), and the road-house validates your parking ticket from the underground garage, a rarity for Georgetown. *Note:* If you've got kids, make sure they go to the bathroom before you get here. The only rest room is downstairs in the bar, which, at 6:30 on a Saturday night is already noisy and jammed with beer-guzzling behemoths.

✪ **Old Glory Barbecue.** 3139 M St. NW. ☎ **202/337-3406.** Reservations recommended for 6 or more Sun–Thurs, reservations not accepted Fri–Sat. Main courses $6.50–$17; late-night entrees $5.25–$6.75; brunch buffet $11.95, $5.95 for kids 11 and under. AE, DC, DISC, MC, V. Sun 11:30am–1am (brunch 11am–3pm), Mon–Thurs 11:30am–1am, Fri–Sat 11:30am–3am. Metro: Foggy Bottom. AMERICAN/BARBECUE.

Raised wooden booths flank one side of the restaurant; an impos-ing, old-fashioned dark wood bar with saddle-seat stools extends down the other. Blues, rock, and country songs play in the background. Old Glory boasts the city's "largest selection of single-barrel and boutique bourbons," a claim that two buddies at the bar were confirming firsthand. In a few hours, when the two-story restaurant is packed with the young and the restless, these two may be swinging from the ceiling's tin-colander lampshade lighting fixtures.

In early evening, though, Old Glory is prime for anyone—singles, families, an older crowd. Come for the messy, tangy, delicious spare ribs; hickory smoked chicken; tender, smoked beef brisket; or marinated, wood-fried shrimp. Six sauces are on the table, the spiciest being the vinegar-based East Carolina and Lexington, the least spicy but most popular the sweet Memphis sauce. My southern-raised husband favored the Savannah version, which reminded him of that city's famous Johnny Harris barbecue sauce. The complimentary corn muffins and biscuits, side dishes of collard greens, succotash, potato salad, and desserts like apple crisp and coconut cherry cobbler all hit the spot.

7 Adams-Morgan

EXPENSIVE

Cities. 2424 18th St. NW (near Columbia Rd.). ☎ **202/328-7194.** Reservations recommended. Main courses $16.50–$24.95. AE, CB, DC, DISC, MC, V. Sun–Thurs 6–11pm, Fri–Sat 6–11:30pm. Bar open Sun–Thurs 5pm–2am, Fri–Sat 5pm–3am. INTERNATIONAL.

Housed in a century-old former five-and-dime store, Cities is a restaurant-cum-travelogue. A year-long, $1.2-million renovation has dressed up the place, with additions like suede drapes, touches of mahogany and Italian leather, and soft lighting provided by hundreds of hanging filament bulbs. Once a year, the restaurant is revamped to reflect the cuisine, character, and culture of a different city. Even the music reflects the city under consideration, and waiters are in native dress or some facsimile thereof. Until spring of 1999 or so, Cities will be embracing Paris, with photos of French street and cafe scenes on the walls and bouillabaisse and fillet of turbot with truffles on the menu. The wine and champagne list is small but expertly conceived, and premium wines are offered by the glass. The bar, at the front of the restaurant, is upscale and loungy, furnished with banquettes and the magnificent bar, and features light-fare specialties of the highlighted city, starting around $7.50.

Upstairs is Privé at Cities, "a private club dedicated to the new age of self-indulgence, available to the restaurant's elite clientele and

Adams-Morgan & Dupont Circle Dining

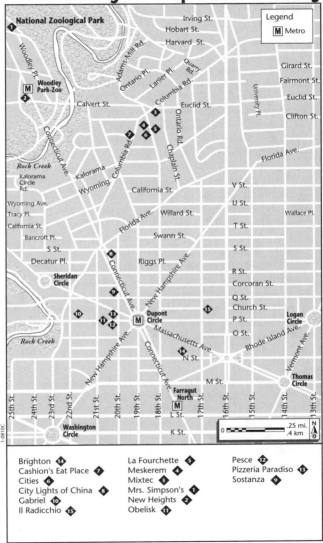

Legend

M Metro

National Zoological Park

Irving St.
Hobart St.
Harvard St.

Girard St.
Fairmont St.
Euclid St.
Clifton St.

Woodley Park-Zoo

Calvert St.

Florida Ave.

Rock Creek

Kalorama Circle Rd.

Kalorama

Wyoming

California St.

V St.

U St.

Wallace Pl.

Wyoming Ave.
Tracy Pl.
California St.
Bancroft Pl.

Willard St.

T St.

S St.

Decatur Pl.

Swann St.

S St.

Sheridan Circle

Riggs Pl.

R St.

Corcoran St.

Q St.
Church St.

Logan Circle

Rock Creek

Dupont Circle

P St.
O St.

Rhode Island Ave.

Thomas Circle

N St.

M St.

Farragut North

25th St. 24th St. 23rd St. 22nd St. 21st St. 20th St. 19th St. 18th St. 17th St. 16th St. 15th St. 14th St. 13th St.

L St.

Washington Circle

K St.

.25 mi.
.4 km

Woodley Pl.
Adams-Mill Rd.
Ontario Pl.
Lanier Pl.
Quarry Rd.
Columbia Rd.
Euclid St.
Ontario Rd.
Chaplain St.
University Pl.

Connecticut Ave.
Columbia Rd.
Florida Ave.
Connecticut Ave.
New Hampshire Ave.
New Hampshire Ave.
Massachusetts Ave.
Connecticut Ave.
Vermont Ave.

Brighton ⑭	La Fourchette ⑤	Pesce ⑫
Cashion's Eat Place ⑦	Meskerem ④	Pizzeria Paradiso ⑬
Cities ⑥	Mixtec ③	Sostanza ⑨
City Lights of China ⑧	Mrs. Simpson's ①	
Gabriel ⑩	New Heights ②	
Il Radicchio ⑮	Obelisk ⑪	

89

visiting celebrities." If you think you qualify, talk to your hotel concierge to arrange a visit.

MODERATE TO EXPENSIVE

✪ **Cashion's Eat Place.** 1819 Columbia Rd. NW (between 18th St. and Mintwood Place). ☎ **202/797-1819.** Reservations recommended. Brunch $6–$9, dinner $11–$17. MC, V. Tues 5:30–10pm, Wed–Sat 5:30–11pm, Sun 11:30am–2:30pm and 5:30–10pm. AMERICAN WITH EUROPEAN INFLUENCES.

A curving bar lies at the center of the agreeable Cashion's Eat Place, up a couple of steps from the main room. People sitting at tables inside the curve tend to prop their arms comfortably upon the half-wall and converse from time to time with the patrons seated in the dining area below.

Owner/chef Ann Cashion has gained renown for her stints at Nora, Austin Grill, and Jaleo. Her menu includes about eight entrees, split between seafood and meat—for example, grilled wild Chesapeake rockfish, or rabbit stew with dumplings and vegetables. The side dishes that accompany each entree, such as spiced red cabbage and chestnuts and sautéed foie gras, are worth as much attention. Desserts, like the chocolate cinnamon mousse and the lime tartalette, are worth saving room for.

The glass-fronted Cashion's opens invitingly on to the sidewalk in warm weather, but we were there on a frigid January day when each opening of the door blew a blast of cold over those of us seated at the front of the restaurant. A double door would take care of the problem. Go to Cashion's, but if it's a wintry day, ask for a table at the back.

La Fourchette. 2429 18th St. NW. ☎ **202/332-3077.** Reservations recommended on weekends. Main courses $8.95–$21.95. AE, DC, MC, V. Mon–Thurs 11:30am–10:30pm, Fri 11:30am–11pm, Sat 4–11pm, Sun 4–10pm. FRENCH.

Upstairs is no-smoking, but downstairs is where you want to be, among the French-speaking clientele and Adams-Morgan regulars. The waiters are suitably crusty and the ambience is as Parisian as you'll get this side of the Atlantic—so is the food. The menu lists escargots, onion soup, bouillabaisse, and mussels Provençal, along with specials like the grilled salmon on spinach mousse, and the shrimp niçoise, ever-so-slightly crusted and sautéed in a tomato sauce touched lightly with anchovy. A colorful mural covers the high walls, and wooden tables and benches push up against bare brick walls. La Fourchette is Washington's Paris cafe.

INEXPENSIVE

Meskerem. 2434 18th St. NW (between Columbia and Belmont road.).
☎ **202/462-4100.** Lunch $5–$10.50, dinner $8.50–$11.50. AE, DC, MC, V.
Mon–Fri noon–midnight, Sat–Sun noon–2am. ETHIOPIAN.

Washington has a number of Ethiopian restaurants, but this is probably the best. It's certainly the most attractive; the three-level, high-
ceilinged dining room (sunny by day, candlelit at night) has an oval
skylight girded by a painted sunburst and walls hung with African
art and musical instruments. On the mezzanine level, you sit at
messobs (basket tables) on low carved Ethiopian chairs or upholstered leather poufs. Ethiopian music (including live bands after
midnight on weekends) enhances the ambience.

Diners share large platters of food, which are scooped up with a
sourdough crepe-like pancake called *injera*. Items listed as *watt* are
hot and spicy; *alitchas* are milder and more delicately flavored. You
might also share an entree—perhaps *yegeb kay watt* (succulent lamb
in thick, hot berbere sauce)—along with a combination platter of
five vegetarian dishes served with tomato and potato salads. There
are also combination platters comprising an array of beef, chicken,
lamb, and vegetables. The restaurant has a full bar, and the wine list
includes Ethiopian wine and beer.

Mixtec. 1792 Columbia Rd. (just off 18th St.). ☎ **202/332-1011.** Main
courses $2.95–$9.95. MC, V. Sun–Thurs 11am–10:30pm, Fri–Sat 11am–11pm.
MEXICAN REGIONAL.

This cheerful Adams-Morgan eatery attracts a clientele of Hispan-
ics, neighborhood folks, and D.C. chefs, all of whom appreciate the
delicious authenticity of its regional Mexican cuisines. The kitchen
is open, the dining room colorfully decorated, and the music is lively
mariachi and other kinds of Mexican music.

Delicious made-from-scratch corn and flour tortillas enhance
whatever they're stuffed with. Small dishes called *antojitos* ("little
whims") are in the $2.50 to $4.95 range, including *queso fundido* (a
bubbling hot dish of broiled Chihuahua cheese topped with shredded spicy chorizo sausage and flavored with jalapeños and cilantro).
Also popular are the *enrollados Mexicanos*, which are large flour tortillas wrapped around a variety of fillings: grilled chicken, beef, vegetables, or salmon. The freshly prepared, from Mexican avocados,
guacamole is excellent. A house specialty, a full entree served with
rice and beans, is *mole Mexicano*—broiled chicken in a rich sauce of

---

ⅈⅈ   **Family-Friendly Restaurants**

Old Glory Barbecue (see p. 87)   A loud, laid-back place where the staff is friendly without being patronizing. Go early, because the restaurant becomes more of a bar as the evening progresses. There is a children's menu, but you may not need it; the barbecue, burgers, muffins, fries, and desserts are so good, everyone can order from the main menu.

Austin Grill (see p. 101)   Another easygoing, good-service joint, with great background music. Kids will probably want to order from their own menu here, and their drinks arrive in unspillable plastic cups with tops and straws, for taking with you if need be.

Il Radicchio (see p. 97)   A spaghetti palace to please the most finicky, at a price that should satisfy the family budget.

America (see p. 74)   The cavernous restaurant with its voluminous menu offers many distractions for a restless brood. No children's menu, but why would you need one, when macaroni and cheese, peanut butter and jelly, pizza, and chicken tenders are among the selections offered to everyone?

---

five peppers (the kitchen uses some 200 different spices!), sunflower and sesame seeds, onions, garlic, almonds, cinnamon, and chocolate. Choose from 30 kinds of tequila; tequila-mixed drinks; Mexican beers; and fresh fruit juices.

8 Dupont Circle

EXPENSIVE

✪ **Brighton.** In the Canterbury Hotel, 1733 N St. NW. ☎ **202/296-0665.** Reservations recommended. Lunch $8–$12.50, dinner $16.50–$22.50. AE, CB, DC, DISC, MC, V. Mon–Fri 11:30am–2pm and 6–10pm, Sat 6–10pm. Metro: Dupont Circle, Farragut North. AMERICAN.

Brighton lies below street level, in the Canterbury Hotel, and yet it is one of the brightest dining rooms you'll find. (If you want cozy, go upstairs to the Union Jack Pub and eat your Brighton dinner there.) Fabric colors are deep salmon and celery, the carpeting a grassy green, the walls lemon yellow. Little vases of fresh-cut yellow roses decorate each table. Diners tend to be locals more than hotel guests.

The food is sublime. First comes a basket of biscuits, sweet bread, and crusty peasant bread. The appetizers and entrees that follow live up to their dramatically artistic presentation. For an appetizer, try the iron-skillet-roasted mussels, with shaved garlic and diced tomato in a Riesling Dijon broth. Next up, sample the macadamia nut-encrusted Chilean sea bass in a ginger, lime, and coconut sauce. And for dessert, how about the banana, macadamia nut spring roll with ginger ice cream and chocolate sauce.

✪ **Gabriel.** In the Radisson Barceló Hotel, 2121 P St. NW. ☎ **202/956-6690.** Reservations recommended. Breakfast $8; breakfast buffet $10.18; lunch $8–$14; Mon–Fri lunch buffet $9.50; dinner $15–$22; tapas $3.75–$6.50; Sun brunch buffet $17.75, Wed–Fri happy-hour buffet $7.50. AE, DC, DISC, MC, V. Mon–Thurs 6:30am–10pm, Fri 6:30am–10:30pm, Sat 7am–10:30pm, Sun 7am–9pm (brunch 11am–3pm). Free valet parking. Metro: Dupont Circle. LATIN AMERICAN/MEDITERRANEAN.

Like Coco Loco (see "Downtown, East of 16th Street NW," above), Gabriel features Latin-accented fare, including tapas; while the former is funky/hip, however, this is a more traditional setting. A large, rectangular, mahogany bar is the centerpiece of a convivial lounge area; outdoors is a small patio cafe with umbrella tables. Noted Washington chef Greggory Hill spent months studying with major chefs in various parts of Spain and Mexico before creating Gabriel's dazzlingly innovative and ever-changing menu.

Sample a variety of tapas at the bar or begin a meal with them—plump chorizo-stuffed black figs or *gambas al ajillo* (shrimp in garlic oil). Entrees might include lamb with mole and sweet potato-plantain mash or pork tenderloin with black bean sauce on basmati rice. Crusty-chewy fresh-baked sourdough bread is great dipped in rosemary/garlic-infused olive oil. There's a well-chosen wine list, with several by-the-glass selections including dry and sweet sherries—the ideal complement to tapas. Incredible desserts here include a warm phyllo purse stuffed with papaya, pineapple, berries, and pistachio nuts, poised on cinnamon custard.

Obelisk. 2029 P St. NW. ☎ **202/872-1180.** Reservations recommended. Prix-fixe 5-course dinners only: $42–$45. DC, MC, V. Tues–Sat 6–10pm. Metro: Dupont Circle. ITALIAN.

In this pleasantly spare room decorated with 19th-century French botanical prints and Italian lithographs, owner/chef Peter Pastan presents his small prix-fixe menus of sophisticated Italian cuisine that uses the freshest possible ingredients. Pastan says his culinary philosophy is to "get the best stuff we can and try not to screw it up." Each night's menu offers diners two or three choices for each course. A recent dinner began with an antipasti of peppers with olivada and anchovies, followed by a Provençal sea bass soup seasoned with

Dining at Sightseeing Attractions

With so many great places to eat in Washington, I have a hard time recommending those at sightseeing attractions. Most of these are overpriced and too crowded, even if they are convenient. A few, however, are worth mentioning—for their admirable cuisine, noteworthy setting, or both.

CAPITOL HILL AREA Head to the Capitol's numerous restaurants for a chance to rub elbows with your senators and representatives, but keep in mind these spots are usually open only for lunch and can get very crowded; to lessen the chances of a long wait, try going about 30 minutes before the posted closing time. You'll find the **House of Representatives Restaurant** (also called the "Members' Dining Room") in Room H118, at the south end of the Capitol (☎ **202/225-6300**). This fancy, eatery, with chandeliers and gilt-framed pictures on the walls, is open to the public but doesn't take reservations (it's also open for breakfast). Senators frequent the **Senate Dining Room,** but you'll need a letter from your senator to eat here (jacket and tie required for men, no jeans for men or women). More accommodating is the **Refectory,** first floor, Room S112, Senate side of the Capitol (☎ **202/ 224-4870**), which serves sandwiches and other light luncheon fare.

Most Hill staffers eat at places like the **Longworth Building Cafeteria,** Independence Ave. and South Capitol St. SE (☎ **202/ 225-4410**), where they can just grab a bite and go, choosing from

saffron, and an artfully arranged dish of pan-cooked snapper with artichokes, thyme, and pancetta. Rather than cheese, I enjoyed a dessert of pear spice cake. Breads and desserts are all baked in-house and are divine. Pastan's carefully crafted wine list represents varied regions of Italy, as well as California vintages. The $40-ish prix-fixe menu seems a deal, but the cost of wine and coffees can easily double the price per person.

✪ **Sostanza.** 1606 20th St. NW. ☎ **202/667-0047.** Reservations recommended. Lunch $8–$12, dinner $15–$25. AE, CB, DC, MC, V. Daily noon–2pm and 6–10pm. Metro: Dupont Circle. SEAFOOD/ITALIAN.

This is the sort of place you'd hope to stumble upon as a stranger in town. It's pretty, with a sophisticated but relaxed atmosphere, the food is excellent, and the service professional. Although the restaurant has changed its name repeatedly since it opened in a fairly nice selection of food court booths, but by far the best deal for visitors is the **Dirksen Senate Office Building South Buffet Room,** 1st and C sts. NE (☎ **202/224-4249**). For just $9.50 per adult, $6.50 per child (including a nonalcoholic drink and dessert), you can choose from a buffet that includes a carving station and eight other hot entrees. It's often crowded, but they will take reservations for parties of more than 10.

In the same neighborhood, two institutions offering great deals and views (of famous sites or people) are the **Library of Congress's Cafeteria** (☎ **202/707-8300**), and its more formal **Montpelier Room** (☎ **202/707-8300**), where the buffet lunch is only $8.50; and the **Supreme Court's Cafeteria** (☎ **202/479-3246**), where you'll likely spy a justice or two enjoying the midday meal.

MUSEUM RESTAURANTS Among museum restaurants, the ones that shine are the Corcoran Gallery of Art's **Café des Artistes** (☎ **202/639-1786**); the National Air & Space Museum's two spots, **Flight Line** (☎ **202/371-8750**) and the **Wright Place** (☎ **202/371-8778**); the National Gallery of Art's **Terrace Café** (☎ **202/216-2492**) and **Garden Café** (☎ **202/216-5966**); the National Portrait Gallery's and the National Museum of American Art's restaurant, **Patent Pending** (☎ **202/357-2700**), situated in a corridor connecting the two museums; and the Phillips Collection's snug **Café** (☎ **202/387-2151**).

1980, (Vincenzo al Sole, Trattoria al Sole, and Vincenzo), it remains what it has always been, a reliable place to sample classic Italian cuisine. Conceived originally as an Italian steakhouse by owners Vince MacDonald and Roberto Donna, who reigns over a small dynasty of his own restaurants (see Galileo, Barolo, Il Radicchio, Pesce), Sostanza's menu has expanded to offer classic Italian pastas, fish, chicken, and veal dishes. For steak, think alla siciliano: grilled with capers, olives, and sweet pickled peppers. The soft-shell crabs in season, in late spring, are a treat, lightly breaded and fried. Daily specials number about 18, in addition to always-available meat and fish items. The antipasto selection is a holdover from the restaurant's early days, featuring roasted peppers with anchovies, stuffed zucchini, and the like.

At street level is Sostanza's slate terrace, where you can dine at umbrella tables; you go down a short flight of steps to reach Sostanza's exquisite dining room, which resembles a trattoria with its ochre and burnt sienna-toned walls, arched skylight, and tile floor. Across the long, narrow entry hall from the main dining room are the bar and more tables, where, if you're lucky, you can sit and shoot the breeze with owner Vince, who thinks of himself as Italian, though he is, in fact, American, with Italian roots.

MODERATE

✪ **Pesce.** 2016 P St. NW. ☎ **202/466-3474.** Reservations accepted for lunch, 6 or more at dinner. Main courses $16.50–$18. AE, DC, DISC, MC, V. Mon–Thurs 11:30am–2:30pm and 5:30–10pm, Fri 11:30am–2:30pm and 5:30–10:30pm, Sat noon–2:30pm and 5:30–10:30pm, Sun 5–9:30pm. Metro: Dupont Circle. SEAFOOD.

Nightly, from about 8:30 until 9:30, a line of people forms inside the cramped waiting area of this restaurant, sometimes trailing out the door, just to enjoy the marvelous grilled or sautéed fresh fish. If you get there earlier than 8:30, you may still have a wait, but not as long. This small, crowded restaurant has a convivial atmosphere, brought on, no doubt, by the collective anticipation of a pleasant meal. In this simple setting of exposed brick walls adorned with colorfully painted wooden fish, waiters scurry to bring you a basket of crusty bread, your wine selection, and the huge blackboard menu. Among the many appetizers are blue point oysters on the half shell and several tasty salads. Entrees always list several pastas along with the differently prepared fish. My grilled monkfish entree was firm but tender, and delicious upon its bed of potato purée and wild mushroom ragout. Jointly owned by chefs Roberto Donna and Jean-Louis Palladin, Pesce bears their mark of excellence, even though neither actually works in the kitchen. *Tip:* Try ordering your wine by the glass; depending on which wine you choose, your table may be able to enjoy four glasses of wine and still pay less than the cost of a whole bottle.

INEXPENSIVE

✪ **City Lights of China.** 1731 Connecticut Ave. NW (between R and S sts.). ☎ **202/265-6688.** Reservations recommended. Main courses $6.95–$11.95 at dinner (a few are pricier). AE, DC, DISC, MC, V. Mon–Thurs 11am–10:30pm, Fri 11:30am–11pm, Sat noon–11pm, Sun noon–10:30pm; Dinner from 3pm daily. Metro: Dupont Circle. CHINESE.

One of Washington's best Chinese restaurants outside of Chinatown, City Lights keeps getting bigger to accommodate its fans, who range from Mick Jagger to Natalie Cole to Jesse Jackson to Attorney General Janet Reno. White House workaholics frequently order deliveries of City Lights carryout. Favorite dishes prepared by Taiwanese chef (and part owner) Kuo-Tai Soug include crisp-fried Cornish hen prepared in a cinnamon-soy marinade and served with a tasty dipping sauce, Chinese eggplant with a garlic sauce, stir-fried spinach, crisp fried shredded beef, and the Peking duck. The setting is pretty but unpretentious—a three-tier dining room with much of the seating in comfortable pale-green leather booths and banquettes. Neat tables laid with white linen and set with peach napkins, cloth flower arrangements in lighted niches, and green neon track lighting complete the picture. There's a full bar.

✪ **Il Radicchio.** 1509 17th St. NW. ☎ **202/986-2627.** Main courses $5.50–$14.50. AE, DC, MC, V. Mon–Thurs 11:30am–10pm, Fri–Sat 11:30am–11pm, Sun 5–10pm. Metro: Dupont Circle, with a 10- to 15-minute walk. ITALIAN.

What a great idea: Order a replenishable bowl of spaghetti for the table at a set price of $6.50, and each of you chooses your own sauce from a long list, at prices that range from $1.50 to $4. Most are standards, like the carbonara of cream, pancetta, black pepper, and egg yolk, and the puttanesca of black olives, capers, garlic, anchovies, and tomato. It's a great deal.

The kitchen prepares daily specials, like Saturday's oven-baked veal stew with polenta, as well as sandwiches and an assortment of 14 wood-baked pizzas, with a choice of 25 toppings. I'd stick with the pizza, pasta, and salad.

Radicchio pops up on one of the thin-crusted pizzas, in salads like the radicchio and pancetta in balsamic vinaigrette, and in a pasta, with sausage, red wine, and tomato, all of which are recommended.

Ingredients are fresh and flavorful, the service quick and solicitous. This branch of the restaurant draws a neighborhood crowd to its long, warm, and cozy room decorated with wall murals of barnyard animals and radicchio leaves. The Georgetown Il Radicchio (1211 Wisconsin Ave. NW; ☎ **202/337-2627**) attracts college students and families. Il Radicchio on Capitol Hill (223 Pennsylvania Ave. SE; ☎ **202/547-5114**) caters to overworked, underpaid Hill staffers, who appreciate Il Radicchio's food and the price.

✪ **Pizzeria Paradiso.** 2029 P St. NW. ☎ **202/223-1245.** Pizzas $6.75–$15.95, sandwiches and salads $3.25–$6.25. DC, MC, V. Mon–Thurs 11am–11pm, Fri–Sat 11am–midnight, Sun noon–10pm. Metro: Dupont Circle. PIZZA AND PANINI.

Peter Pastan, master chef/owner of Obelisk, right next door, owns this classy, often crowded, 16-table pizzeria. Don't expect Domino's. Instead, an oak-burning oven at one end of the charming room produces exceptionally doughy but light pizza crusts. As you wait, you can munch on the mixed olives placed in a small bowl before you and gaze up at the ceiling painted to suggest blue sky peeking through ancient stone walls. Pizzas range from the plainest Paradiso, which offers chunks of tomatoes covered in melted mozzarella, to the robust Siciliano, a blend of 9 ingredients, including eggplant and red onion, or you can choose your own toppings from a list of 29. You can also order the daily special and be rewarded with an inspired creation, like potatoes roasted with goat cheese, red onions, and chives atop the chewy crust. Pizzas are available in two sizes, 8-inch and 12-inch, and most toppings cost 75¢ each on the 8-inch, $1.25 each on the 12-inch. As popular as pizza are the panini (sandwiches) of homemade focaccia stuffed with marinated roasted lamb and vegetables and other fillings, and the salads, such as tuna and white bean. Good desserts, but a limited wine list.

9 Foggy Bottom/West End

VERY EXPENSIVE

✪ **Aquarelle.** In the Watergate Hotel, 2650 Virginia Ave. NW. ☎ **202/ 298-4455.** Reservations recommended. Breakfast $10.75–$18; lunch $15.75– $19.75; dinner $17–$30; pretheater $38. AE, CB, DC, DISC, MC, V. Daily 7– 10:30am, 11:30am–2:30pm, and 5–10:30pm for dinner. Free valet parking. Metro: Foggy Bottom. AMERICAN.

The Watergate has a new chef in its new restaurant in the old spot that used to house Jean-Louis's Palladind. In Aquarelle's cheery room overlooking the Potomac, Chef Robert Wiedmaier presents his own version of "Euro-American" cuisine. The menu changes seasonally and focuses on game and fish. Wiedmaier is German-born and Belgian-trained, but he's thoroughly American in his exuberance, which shines in dishes like the flavorful grilled meats and fish, as well as in pastas topped with rich vegetable and garlic sauces. A timbale of salmon mousseline is a treat, as is anything Wiedmaier does with asparagus. Other appetizers might include lobster tail with fennel purée or flan of crabmeat in watercress butter with angel-hair potatoes. Recommended entrees are the rack of lamb and the veal chop with portobello mushroom and Stilton cheese, and for dessert: the crème brûlée. The Aquarelle is popular as a pretheater dinner spot for those going to the Kennedy Center, and wins the drama award for its in-kitchen dinners offered nightly.

EXPENSIVE

Goldoni. 1113 23rd St. NW. ☎ **202/293-1511.** Reservations recommended. Lunch $11–$19, dinner $17–$24. AE, CB, DC, DISC, MC, V. Mon–Thurs 11:30am–2pm and 5:30–10pm, Fri 11:30am–2pm and 5–11pm, Sat 5–11pm, Sun 5–10pm. Complimentary valet parking for dinner. Metro: Foggy Bottom. ITALIAN.

A lot of restaurants have occupied this space over the years, but with any luck, the year-old Goldoni is here to stay. It's dramatically large, high-ceilinged, and skylit; white walls display modern art evoking the Venetian carnival, and outbursts of operas play now and again during your meal.

The Fred Astaire-ish maitre' d, Julian Russell, escorts you past the bar to your table, where more drama awaits. A risotto with grape-fruit, basil, and baby shrimp is cradled in a grapefruit half. Chef/owner Fabrizio Aielli's signature dish, grilled whole fish (we had rockfish, but snapper, sea bass, and others may be available), arrives on a huge platter, served with polenta and shiitake mushrooms. A salad with radicchio, goat cheese, and ground walnuts is excellent. Sorbets are a specialty, as is the beautifully presented tiramisu. Bring a party of people; Goldoni is a good spot for a celebration.

✪ **Kinkead's.** 2000 Pennsylvania Ave. NW. ☎ **202/296-7700.** Reservations recommended. Lunch $10–$18, dinner $18–$26, Sun brunch $7.50–$13. AE, DC, DISC, MC, V. Daily 11:30am–11pm. Metro: Foggy Bottom. AMERICAN/SEAFOOD.

When a restaurant has been as roundly praised as Kinkead's, you start to think no place can be that good—but Kinkead's is. An appetizer like grilled squid with creamy polenta and tomato fondue leaves you with a permanent longing for squid. The signature dish, a pepita-crusted salmon with shrimp, crab, and chilies provides a nice hot crunch before melting in your mouth. Vegetables are simply prepared, usually steamed or sautéed with a touch of lemon or garlic oil.

The award-winning chef/owner Bob Kinkead is the star at this three-tier, 220-seat restaurant. He wears a headset and orchestrates his kitchen staff in full view of the upstairs dining room, where booths and tables neatly fill the nooks and alcoves of the town house. At street level is a scattering of tables overlooking the restaurant's lower level, the more casual bar and cafe, where a jazz group or pianist performs in the evening and at Sunday brunch. *Beware:* If the waiter tries to seat you in the "atrium," you should know that you'll be stuck at a table mall-side, just outside the doors of the restaurant.

Kinkead's menu features primarily seafood, but the menu (which changes daily for lunch and again for dinner) also includes at least one meat and one poultry entree. The wine list comprises more than 300 selections. You can't go wrong with the desserts either, like the chocolate dacquoise with cappuccino sauce.

Melrose. In the Park Hyatt Hotel, 1201 24th St. NW (at M St.). ☎ **202/ 955-3899.** Reservations recommended. Breakfast $9–$15.50; lunch $14– $22.50; dinner $23.75–$28; pretheater $26.95; Sun brunch $33 ($36 with champagne). AE, CB, DC, DISC, JCB, MC, V. Mon–Sat 6:30–11am, Sun 6:30– 10:30am; daily 11am–2:30pm and 5:30–10:30pm. Complimentary valet parking all day. Metro: Foggy Bottom. AMERICAN.

Situated in an upscale hotel, this pretty restaurant offers fine cuisine presented with friendly flourishes. In nice weather, dine outdoors on the beautifully landscaped, sunken terrace whose greenery and towering fountain protect you from traffic noises. The glass-walled dining room overlooks the terrace and is decorated with more greenery, grand bouquets of fresh flowers, and accents of marble and brass.

Brian McBride is the beguiling executive chef who sometimes emerges from the kitchen to find out how you like the angel-hair pasta with mascarpone and lobster, or his sautéed Dover sole with roasted peppers, forest mushrooms, and mâche. McBride, like Bob Kinkead (see above), is known for his seafood, which makes up most of the entrees and nearly all of the appetizers. Specialties of the house include shrimp ravioli with sweet corn, black pepper, tomato, and lemongrass beurre blanc, and Melrose crab cakes with grilled vegetables in a remoulade sauce. Desserts, like the raspberry crème brûlée or the chocolate bread pudding with chocolate sorbet, are excellent. The wine list offers 30 wines by the glass. Friday nights, the restaurant dispenses with corkage fees; feel free to bring your own bottle. Saturday nights, a quartet plays jazz, swing, and big-band tunes, 7–11pm; lots of people get up and dance.

Provence. 2401 Pennsylvania Ave. NW. ☎ **202/296-1166.** Reservations recommended. Lunch $13.50–$23, dinner $20.50–$34. AE, CB, DC, MC, V. Mon–Fri noon–2pm and 6–10pm, Sat 5:30–11pm, Sun 5:30–9:30pm. Complimentary valet parking evenings. Metro: Foggy Bottom. FRENCH.

With an exhibition kitchen arrayed with gleaming copper ware, Provence's interior is country French. Panels of rough-hewn stone are framed by rustic shutters, antique hutches display provincial pottery, and delicate chandeliers and shaded sconces provide a soft amber glow.

Yannick Cam's provincial cuisine "personalisée" refers to his unique interpretations of traditional Mediterranean recipes, which lose nothing in the way of regional integrity. An appetizer of pan-roasted young squid—stuffed with finely ground scallops and shrimp, sautéed shallots and garlic, wild mushrooms, parsley, toasted pine nuts, and lavender blossoms—was complemented by buttery pan juice. An entree of crisp-skinned organic roast chicken—perfumed with bay leaf, rosemary, sweet garlic, and a soupçon of anchovy—was accompanied by superb roasted potatoes and artichoke hearts in a sauce of red wine, citrus, tomato concassé, garlic, chopped olives, and rosemary-infused olive oil. For dessert, try the terrine of chocolate with walnut-hazelnut sauce. The knowledgeable staff can suggest appropriate wines from the 90%-French list.

10 Glover Park

MODERATE

Sushi-Ko. 2309 Wisconsin Ave. NW. ☎ **202/333-4187.** Reservations recommended. Lunch $6.50–$17, dinner $7.50–$18 at dinner. AE, MC, V. Mon 6–10:30pm, Tues–Fri noon–2:30pm and 6–10:30pm, Sat 5–10:30pm, Sun 5–10pm. JAPANESE.

This is the best place in Washington for sushi, and people know it; so even if you've reserved a table, you may have a wait (although an expansion completed in 1998 has helped the situation). The sushi choppers are fun to watch at the sushi bar, so try to sit there. At any rate, you can expect superb versions of sushi and sashimi standards, but the best items are those invented by former chef Kaz Okochi (now of Raku)—like a napoleon of diced sea trout layered between rice crackers, or a tuna tartare. If you're not one for sushi, you might enjoy this restaurant's excellent tempuras and teriyakis.

INEXPENSIVE

✪ **Austin Grill.** 2404 Wisconsin Ave. NW. ☎ **202/337-8080.** www.austingrill.com. Main courses $6–$15. AE, DC, DISC, MC, V. Mon 11:30am–10:30pm, Tues–Thurs 11:30am–11pm, Fri 11:30am–midnight, Sat 11am–midnight, Sun 11am–10:30pm. TEX-MEX.

Come with the kids, a date, or your friends for fun and good food. Austin Grill is loud; as the night progresses, conversation eventually drowns out the sound of the taped music (everything from Ry Cooder to Natalie Merchant).

Owner Rob Wilder opened his grill in 1988 to replicate the easy-going lifestyle, Tex-Mex cuisine, and music he'd loved when he lived in Austin. The grill is known for the fresh ingredients used to create outstanding crabmeat quesadillas; "Lake Travis" nachos (tostidas slathered with chopped red onion, refried beans, and cheese), a daily fish special (like rockfish fajitas), key lime pie, and excellent versions of standard fare (chicken enchiladas, guacamole, pico de gallo, and so on).

Austin Grill's upstairs overlooks the small bar area below. An upbeat decor includes walls washed in shades of teal and clay and adorned with whimsical coyotes, cowboys, Indians, and cacti. Arrive by 6pm weekends if you don't want to wait; weekdays are less crowded. This is the original Austin Grill; another District Austin Grill opened in May 1998 at 750 E St. NW. ☎ 202/393-3776; suburban locations are in Old Town Alexandria and West Springfield, Virginia, and in Bethesda, Maryland.

5

Exploring Washington, D.C.

As you plan your trip to Washington, you may start to wonder: Just how many memorials are there, anyway? The answer is a whopping 155, when you count those throughout the capital area.

As for numbers of museums, try more than 50. This figure includes the nine Smithsonian museums, joined by the National Gallery of Art, the United States Holocaust Museum, and the National Archives, all of which are clustered alongside the National Mall, a destination you, no doubt, have placed at the top of your itinerary.

The Mall rightfully belongs at the top of your list, but the many off-the-mall museums and attractions should not be far behind. These include the Smithsonian's National Portrait Gallery, National Museum of American Art (including the Renwick Gallery, the museum's American crafts annex near the White House), the Anacostia Museum, the National Zoo, and the National Postal Museum; privately funded museums, like the Corcoran Gallery of Art, the National Museum of Women in the Arts, and the Phillips Gallery; and other less famous sites, such as the Woodrow Wilson Historic House Museum, Dumbarton Oaks, and the Newseum (in Arlington).

If it's the Washington-as-the-nation's-capital side you'd most like to see, you should tailor your visit to accommodate tours of the White House, the Capitol, the Supreme Court, and the Library of Congress. If it's the Washington-as-a-historic city-of-neighborhoods side you'd prefer to get to know, explore on your own or take an organized tour (see "Organized Tours" section at the end of this chapter) that sends you in and out of historic homes, gardens, and neighborhoods throughout the city.

At long last, the city has a walk-in visitor center, complete with maps, visitor guides, interactive information kiosks, brochures, and live and talking information specialists, to help you get organized: It's The **Washington, D.C., Visitor Information Center** in the new Ronald Reagan Building and International Trade Center, at 1300 Pennsylvania Ave. NW (☎ **202/638-3222**), just 1 block from the White House Visitor Center.

1 The Three Major Houses of Government

Three of the most visited sights in Washington are the buildings housing the executive, legislative, and judicial branches of the U.S. government. All are stunning and offer considerable insight into the workings of America.

The White House. 1600 Pennsylvania Ave. NW (visitor entrance gate at E St. and E. Executive Ave.). ☎ **202/456-7041** or 202/208-1631. Free admission. Tues–Sat 10am–noon. Closed some days for official functions; check before leaving your hotel by calling the 24-hour number. Metro: McPherson Square (if you are going straight to the White House), Federal Triangle (if you are getting tour tickets from the White House Visitor Center).

If you think you're going to get the Monica Lewinsky tour, think again. Whether you visit the White House on a VIP guided tour or go through self-guided, you will see just what your escorts (Secret Service agents, by the way) want you to see, and that doesn't include the Oval Office. So forget scandal in the White House, if you can, and soak up the history of this house that has served as residence, office, reception site, and world embassy for every U.S. president since John Adams.

WHITE HOUSE TOURS AND TICKETS   It's not hard to get tickets to visit the White House, but there are a few things that you should know before heading out to the president's home. The White House is open mornings only, Tuesday through Saturday. Tickets are required year-round, although the National Park Service sometimes waives that requirement when things are really slow, usually between January and March.

There are two ways to get tickets: You can write to your congressperson or senator months in advance requesting tickets for the VIP tour (see "Visitor Information" in chapter 1 for more information), or, if you don't have VIP tour tickets, you can pick up your free tickets at the **White House Visitor Center,** 1450 Pennsylvania Ave., in the Department of Commerce Building, between 14th and 15th Streets. Tickets are timed for tours between 10am and noon and are issued on the day of the tour on a first-come, first-served basis starting at 7:30am. During the busy season (April through September), people start lining up before 7am, and although a multitude (approximately 4,500 are distributed) of tickets is available, it is essential that you arrive early (even before 7am, to ensure admission). One person may obtain up to four tickets. Each person who gets tickets, also receives an invisible hand stamp detectable only by some high-tech machine. To gain admittance on the tour, someone in your party must have the magic stamp. The ticket counter closes when the supply for that day is gone. Tickets are valid only for the day and time issued.

After obtaining your tickets, you'll probably have quite a bit of time to spare before your tour time; consider enjoying a leisurely breakfast at the **Old Ebbitt Grill,** (see chapter 4 for details).

Both the VIP tour and the not-so-VIP tour go through the same rooms; on the VIP tour, a Secret Service agent guides you; on the self-guided tour, Secret Service Agents are scattered throughout the rooms, and if you approach them, they'll even answer questions. Highlights of the tour include the following rooms:

The gold-and-white East Room   This room has been the scene of presidential receptions, weddings of presidents' daughters (Lynda Bird Johnson, for one), and other dazzling events. This is where the president entertains visiting heads of state and the place where seven of the eight presidents who died in office (all but Garfield) laid in state. Note the famous Gilbert Stuart portrait of George Washington that Dolley Madison saved from the British during the War of 1812.

The Green Room   Thomas Jefferson's dining room is today used as a sitting room. Green watered-silk fabric covers walls on which hang notable paintings by Gilbert Stuart and John Singer Sargent. Some of the early 19th-century furnishings are attributed to the famous cabinetmaker Duncan Phyfe.

The oval Blue Room   This room, decorated in the French Empire style chosen by James Monroe in 1817, is where presidents and first ladies have officially received guests since the Jefferson administration. Grover Cleveland, the only president to wed in the White House, was married here. Every year it's the setting for the White House Christmas tree.

The Red Room   Several portraits of past presidents—plus Albert Bierstadt's *View of the Rocky Mountains* and a Gilbert Stuart portrait of Dolley Madison—hang here. It's used as a reception room, usually for afternoon teas. The satin-covered walls and most of the Empire furnishings are red.

The State Dining Room   Modeled after late-18th-century neoclassical English houses, this room is a superb setting for state dinners and luncheons. Theodore Roosevelt, a big-game hunter, hung a large moose head over the fireplace and other trophies on the walls.

Note: All visitors, even those with VIP congressional tour passes, should call ☎ **202/456-7041** before setting out in the morning;

occasionally the White House is closed to tourists on short notice because of unforeseen events.

✪ **The Capitol.** At the east end of the Mall, entrance on E. Capitol St. and 1st St. NW. ☎ **202/225-6827.** Free admission. Mar–Sept daily 9am–8pm; guided tours Mon–Fri 9:30am–7pm and Sat 9:30am–3:30m, guides posted to assist but not guide you Sun 1–4:30pm. Sept–Feb daily 9am–4:30pm; guided tours Mon–Sat 9am–3:45pm. Closed Jan 1, Thanksgiving Day, and Dec 25. Parking at Union Station or on neighborhood streets. Metro: Union Station or Capitol South.

TOUR INFORMATION   For all tours, whether during peak season (March through August) or the slow season (September through February), find the east front side of the Capitol, whose sidewalks extend from the Capitol steps and plaza to 1st Street, across from the Library of Congress and Supreme Court. If you are visiting the Capitol in the off-season, you probably will be able to enter the Capitol without waiting in line: Walk up the long driveway and climb the central grand steps of the Capitol. After you pass through the security-check just inside the doors, you enter the Rotunda, where a Capitol Service Guide (a man or woman in a red jacket) will direct you where to stand if you're interested in a guided tour, or hand you the self-guiding brochure if you want to tour on your own.

During the peak season, you have three options if you'd like a guided tour of the Capitol. If you are part of a group of more than 15 people, you can call ☎ **202/224-4910** to reserve a guided tour time, thus avoiding a wait in line. Reservations are very limited, so call months in advance. When you make your reservation, you will be told to come to the east front side of the Capitol and look for any guide in the official red jacket, who will escort you off to the far right side, away from the other lines, and then take you inside for the tour. If you are touring as individuals or as a family, you can try to arrange ahead to obtain VIP tour tickets from the office of your representative or senator for the morning tours (departing at intervals between 8 and 8:45am). For these tours, you enter the Capitol through the Law Library door on the east front side of the Capitol, facing the Supreme Court, on the ground level, just to the right of the grand staircase. A Capitol Guide will meet you inside and take you on the tour.

Most people opt for just showing up at the Capitol, and if this is your plan, find the east front side of the Capitol and look for the signs posted at the end of either sidewalk flanking the Capitol. One sign designates the line for guided tours, the other denotes the

Capitol Hill

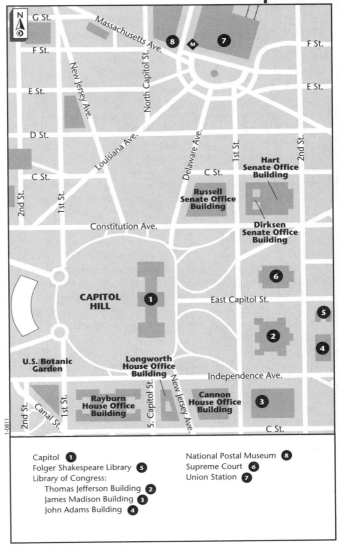

Capitol ❶
Folger Shakespeare Library ❺
Library of Congress:
    Thomas Jefferson Building ❷
    James Madison Building ❸
    John Adams Building ❹

National Postal Museum ❽
Supreme Court ❻
Union Station ❼

self-guided tours line. If you want the guided tour, step right up and stand in line; guided tours in peak season take place every 30 minutes and admit 50 people at a time. You may have a long wait, especially if you have arrived in the morning. Your best bet is to arrive midday, late afternoon, or early evening. If you'd rather walk through on your own, you will also have to wait in line in peak season, but this queue moves a little faster, admitting 15 people at a time in faster intervals. All tours are free, the guided tours last 20 to 30 minutes, and the self-guided tours last as long as you like. Whether you are self-guided or Capitol Guide Service–guided, you must have a ticket to enter the Capitol during the peak season; the tickets, which do not specify time and date, are handed to you just before you climb the steps and enter the Capitol, which means you're stuck in line and can't go and grab a bite to eat or tour another site in the interim.

The House and Senate galleries are always open to visitors, but passes are required when these galleries are in session. After 6pm, however, you may enter either gallery without a pass and watch the session to its conclusion. Once obtained, the passes are good through the remainder of the Congress. To obtain visitor passes in advance, contact your representative or senator (again, see chapter 1 for details). If you don't get advance tickets, and if you don't receive visitor passes in the mail (not every senator or representative sends them), they're obtainable at your senator's office on the Constitution Avenue side of the building or your representative's office on the Independence Avenue side. (Visitors who are not citizens can obtain a gallery pass by presenting a passport at the Senate or House appointments desk, located on the first floor of the Capitol). Call the Capitol switchboard at ☎ **202/224-3121** to contact the office of your senator or congressperson. You'll know when the House and/or the Senate is in session when you see flags flying over their respective wings of the Capitol, or you can check the weekday "Today in Congress" column in the *Washington Post* for details on times of the House and Senate sessions and committee hearings. This column also tells you which sessions are open to the public, allowing you to pick one that interests you. To visit the Hall of the House of Representatives Gallery, enter the Capitol through the south door at the end of the building facing Independence Avenue; to visit the Senate Chamber Gallery, enter the building through the Law Library door on the east front side of the Capitol facing the Supreme Court, on the ground level, just to the right of the central grand staircase.

The Capitol is as awesome up close at it is from afar. As the place where our elected representatives formulate, debate, and pass into law our country's policies and principles, the Capitol is perhaps the most important edifice in the United States. For 135 years it sheltered not only both houses of Congress but the Supreme Court, and for 97 years the Library of Congress as well. When you tour the Capitol, you'll learn about America's history as you admire the place in which it unfolded. Classic architecture, interior embellishments, and hundreds of paintings, sculptures, and other artworks are integral elements of the Capitol.

The **Rotunda**—a huge, 96-foot-wide, circular hall that is capped by a 180-foot-high dome—is the hub of the Capitol. The dome was completed, at Lincoln's direction, while the Civil War was being fought. Nine presidents and two heroic federal police officers have lain in state here. On the circular walls are eight immense oil paintings of events in American history, such as the presentation of the Declaration of Independence and the surrender of Cornwallis at Yorktown.

National Statuary Hall, originally the chamber of the House of Representatives, is filled with statues honoring individuals who played important roles in American history, such as Henry Clay, Ethan Allen, Daniel Webster, and even a woman or two, like Jeannette Rankin (the first woman to serve in Congress).

The south and north wings are occupied by the House and Senate chambers, respectively. The House of Representatives chamber is the largest legislative chamber in the world. The president delivers his annual State of the Union address here.

Supreme Court. East of the Capitol on 1st St. NE (between E. Capitol St. and Maryland Ave.). ☎ **202/479-3000.** Free admission. Mon–Fri 9am–4:30pm. Closed weekends and all federal holidays. Metro: Capitol South or Union Station.

The highest tribunal in the nation, the Supreme Court is charged with deciding whether actions of Congress, the president, the states, and lower courts are in accord with the Constitution, and with applying the Constitution's enduring principles to novel situations and a changing country. It has the power of "judicial review"—authority to invalidate legislation or executive action that conflicts with the Constitution. Out of the 6,500 cases submitted to it each year, the Supreme Court hears only about 100 cases, many of which deal with issues vital to the nation. The Court's rulings are final, reversible only by another Supreme Court decision, or in some cases, an Act of Congress or a constitutional amendment.

If you're in town when the Court is in session, try to see a case being argued (call ☎ **202/479-3211** for details). The Court meets Monday through Wednesday from 10am to noon and, on occasion, from 1 to 2pm, starting the first Monday in October through late April, alternating, in approximately 2-week intervals, between "sittings," to hear cases and deliver opinions, and "recesses," for consideration of business before the Court. Mid-May to late June, you can attend brief sessions (about 15 minutes) at 10am on Monday, when the justices release orders and opinions. You can find out what cases are on the docket by checking the *Washington Post's* "Supreme Court Calendar." Arrive at least an hour early—even earlier for highly publicized cases—to line up for seats, about 150 of which are allotted to the general public.

TOURING TIPS   If the Court is not in session during your visit, you can attend a free lecture in the courtroom about Court procedure and the building's architecture. Lectures are given every hour on the half hour from 9:30am to 3:30pm.

After the talk, explore the Great Hall and go down a flight of steps to see the 20-minute film on the workings of the Court. On the same floor is an exhibit displaying reproductions of the friezes adorning the tops of the courtroom walls, a gift shop, and a cafeteria that's open to the public and serves good food.

2 The Presidential Memorials

Tributes to American presidents appear in various guises all over the city, and the most recent additions honor Ronald Reagan: the immense new Ronald Reagan Building and International Trade Center at 1300 Pennsylvania Ave. NW and the Ronald Reagan National Airport (known until winter of 1998 as the Washington National Airport). Far fewer in the capital are presidential memorials intended as national shrines to honor the chief executive. In fact, there are four: the Washington Monument, Lincoln Memorial, Jefferson Memorial, and the Franklin Delano Roosevelt Memorial. Unfortunately, none of these lies directly on a Metro line, so you can expect a bit of a walk from the specified station.

Washington Monument. Directly south of the White House (at 15th St. and Constitution Ave. NW). ☎ **202/426-6841.** Free admission. Early Apr–Sept, daily 8am–midnight; Oct–Mar, daily 9am–5pm. Last elevators depart 15 minutes before closing (arrive earlier). Closed Dec 25, open till noon July 4. Metro: Smithsonian, then a 10-minute walk.

TICKET INFORMATION Tickets are required for admission to the Washington Monument in winter (roughly, September through March), from 9am to 5pm, and the rest of the year, from 8am to 8pm. If you come after 8pm in season, go to the Washington Monument and stand in line—always check first with a ranger or at the ticket booth to be sure, though. The ticket booth is located at the bottom of the hill from the monument, on 15th Street NW between Independence and Constitution Avenues. The tickets grant admission at half-hour intervals between the stated hours. You can obtain tickets on the day of the tour; if you want to save yourself the trouble and get them in advance (up to six tickets per person), call Ticketmaster (☎ **800/505-5040**), but you'll pay $1.50 per ticket plus a 50¢ service charge per transaction.

TOURING THE MONUMENT Don't be alarmed when you catch sight of the Washington Monument under wraps. Underneath its radical chic, transparent blue sheath (designed by celebrated architect Michael Graves), the 555-foot marble obelisk is undergoing exterior renovation. The interior was renovated in the spring of 1998, when the monument was closed for tours. Despite its appearance, the monument is open for regular tours; the elevator is refurbished; the climate-control system has been replaced; the 897 steps have been scrubbed; and the 193 carved commemorative stones are polished. The Washington Monument remains the city's most visible landmark, but now, and until at least the year 2000, you will see it through a bluish haze and scaffolding.

The idea of a tribute to George Washington first arose 16 years before his death, at the Continental Congress of 1783. But the new nation had more pressing problems, and funds were not readily available. It wasn't until the early 1830s, with the 100th anniversary of Washington's birth approaching, that any action was taken. Then there were several fiascoes. A mausoleum was provided for Washington's remains under the Capitol Rotunda, but a grandnephew, citing Washington's will, refused to allow the body to be moved from Mount Vernon. In 1830, Horatio Greenough was commissioned to create a memorial statue for the Rotunda. He came up with a bare-chested Washington, draped in classical Greek garb; a shocked public claimed he looked as if he were "entering or leaving a bath," and so the statue was relegated to the Smithsonian. Finally, in 1833, prominent citizens organized the Washington National Monument Society. Treasury Building architect Robert

Washington, D.C. Attractions

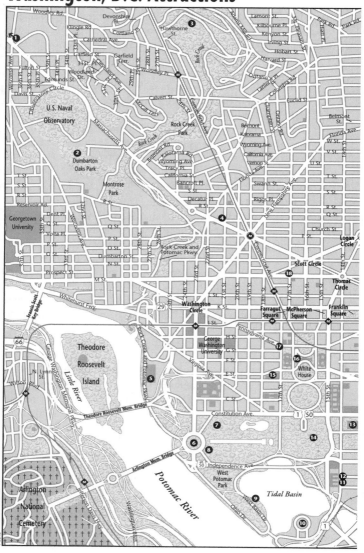

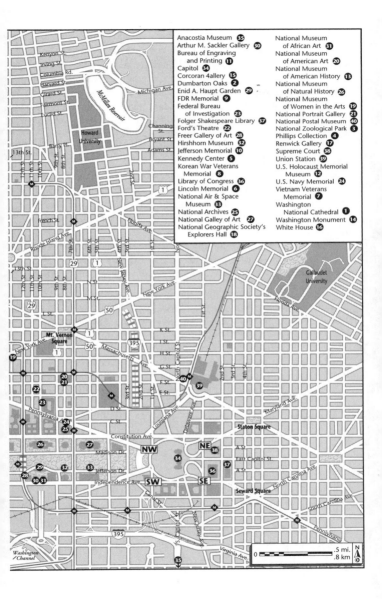

Anacostia Museum **35**
Arthur M. Sackler Gallery **30**
Bureau of Engraving
  and Printing **11**
Capitol **34**
Corcoran 4allery **15**
Dumbarton Oaks **2**
Enid A. Haupt Garden **29**
FDR Memorial **9**
Federal Bureau
  of Investigation **23**
Folger Shakespeare Library **37**
Ford's Theatre **22**
Freer Gallery of Art **28**
Hirshhorn Museum **32**
Jefferson Memorial **10**
Kennedy Center **5**
Korean War Veterans
  Memorial **8**
Library of Congress **36**
Lincoln Memorial **6**
National Air & Space
  Museum **33**
National Archives **25**
National Galley of Art **27**
National Geographic Society's
  Explorers Hall **18**

National Museum
  of African Art **31**
National Museum
  of American Art **20**
National Museum
  of American History **13**
National Museum
  of Natural History **26**
National Museum
  of Women in the Arts **19**
National Portrait Gallery **21**
National Postal Museum **40**
National Zoological Park **3**
Phillips Collection **4**
Renwick Gallery **17**
Supreme Court **38**
Union Station **39**
U.S. Holocaust Memorial
  Museum **12**
U.S. Navy Memorial **24**
Vietnam Veterans
  Memorial **7**
Washington
  National Cathedral **1**
Washington Monument **14**
White House **16**

Mills's design (originally with a circular colonnaded Greek temple base, which was later discarded for lack of funds) was accepted. The cornerstone was laid on July 4, 1848, and for the next 37 years, watching the monument grow, or not grow, was a local pastime. Declining contributions and the Civil War brought construction to a halt at an awkward 150 feet. The unsightly stump remained until 1876 when President Grant approved federal monies to complete the project. Dedicated in 1885, it was opened to the public in 1888.

The transparent blue covering will impede the spectacular view, but you should still be able to pick out the major sites. To the east are the Capitol and Smithsonian Buildings; to the north, the White House; to the west, the Lincoln and Vietnam Memorials, and Arlington National Cemetery beyond; and to the south, the gleaming-white shrine to Thomas Jefferson and the Potomac River. It's a marvelous orientation to the city.

Climbing the 897 steps is verboten, but the large elevator whisks visitors to the top in just 70 seconds. If, however, you're avid to see more of the interior, "Down the Steps" tours are given, subject to staff availability.

✪ **Lincoln Memorial.** Directly west of the Mall in Potomac Park (at 23rd St. NW, between Constitution and Independence aves.). ☎ **202/426-6842.** Free admission. Daily 8am–midnight, except Dec 25. Metro: Foggy Bottom, then about a 30-minute walk.

The Lincoln Memorial attracts some 1.5 million visitors annually. It's a beautiful and moving testament to a great American, its marble walls seeming to embody not only the spirit and integrity of Lincoln, but all that has ever been good about America.

A beautiful neoclassical templelike structure, similar in architectural design to the Parthenon in Greece, the memorial has 36 fluted Doric columns representing the states of the Union at the time of Lincoln's death, plus two at the entrance.

The memorial chamber, under 60-foot ceilings, has limestone walls inscribed with the Gettysburg Address and Lincoln's Second Inaugural Address. Two 60-foot murals by Jules Guerin on the north and south walls depict, allegorically, Lincoln's principles and achievements. Most powerful, however, is Daniel Chester French's 19-foot-high seated statue of Lincoln in deep contemplation in the central chamber.

TOURING TIPS   An information booth and bookstore are on the premises. Rangers present 20- to 30-minute programs as time permits throughout the day, year-round. Limited free parking is available along Constitution Avenue and south along Ohio Drive.

Jefferson Memorial. South of the Washington Monument on Ohio Dr. (at the south shore of the Tidal Basin). ☎ **202/426-6841.** Free admission. Daily 8am–midnight, except Dec 25. Metro: Smithsonian, with 20- to 30-minute walk, or by Tourmobile.

The site for the Jefferson Memorial, in relation to the Washington and Lincoln Memorials, was of extraordinary importance. The Capitol, the White House, and the Mall were already located in accordance with L'Enfant's plan, and there was no spot for such a project if the symmetry that guided L'Enfant was to be maintained. So the memorial was built on land reclaimed from the Potomac River, now known as the Tidal Basin. Franklin Delano Roosevelt, who laid the cornerstone in 1939, had all the trees between the Jefferson Memorial and the White House cut down, so he could see the memorial every morning and draw inspiration from it.

It's a beautiful memorial, a columned rotunda in the style of the Pantheon in Rome, whose classic architectural style Jefferson himself introduced to this country (he designed his home, Monticello, and the earliest University of Virginia buildings, in Charlottesville, Virginia). On the Tidal Basin side, the sculptural group above the entrance depicts Jefferson with Benjamin Franklin, John Adams, Roger Sherman, and Robert Livingston, all of whom worked on drafting the Declaration of Independence. The domed interior of the memorial contains the 19-foot bronze statue of Jefferson standing on a 6-foot pedestal of black Minnesota granite.

TOURING TIPS   Rangers present 20- to 30-minute programs throughout the day as time permits, year-round. Spring through fall, a refreshment kiosk at the Tourmobile stop offers snack fare. A new gift shop and bookstore opened in late 1998 on the bottom floor of the memorial. There's free 1-hour parking.

✪ **Franklin Delano Roosevelt Memorial.** In West Potomac Park, about midway between the Lincoln and Jefferson Memorials, on the west shore of the Tidal Basin. ☎ **202/426-6841.** Free admission. Ranger staff on duty 8am–midnight daily, except Dec 25. Free parking along W. Basin and Ohio Drives. Metro: Smithsonian, with a 30-minute walk. Transportation: Tourmobile (see "Getting Around," in chapter 2).

One year after it opened on May 2, 1997, the Franklin Delano Roosevelt had attracted twice as many visitors as any other memorial: 3 million. Its popularity has to do as much with the design as the man it honors. This is a 7¹/₂-acre, outdoor memorial that lies beneath a wide-open sky. It stretches out, rather than rising up, before you, leading you across the stone-paved floor. Granite walls define the four "galleries," each representing a different term in FDR's presidency, from 1933 to 1945. Architect Lawrence

Halprin's design includes waterfalls, sculptures (by Leonard Baskin, John Benson, Neil Estern, Robert Graham, Thomas Hardy, and George Segal), and Roosevelt's own words carved into the stone.

3   The Smithsonian Museums

The Smithsonian's collection of nearly 141 million objects encompasses the entire world and its history, as well as its peoples and animals (past and present) and our attempts to probe into the future. The sprawling institution comprises 14 museums (9 of them on the Mall) as well as the National Zoological Park in Washington, D.C., plus two additional museums in New York City.

It all began with a $500,000 bequest from James Smithson, an English scientist who had never visited this country. When he died in 1829, he willed his entire fortune to his nephew, stipulating that should the nephew die without heirs (which he did in 1835), the estate should go to the United States to found "at Washington . . . an establishment for the increase and diffusion of knowledge. . . ." Since then, other munificent private donations have swelled Smithson's original legacy many times over. Major gallery and museum construction through the years stands as testament to thoughtful donors.

In 1987, the Sackler Gallery (Asian and Near Eastern art) and the National Museum of African Art were added to the Smithsonian's Mall attractions. The National Postal Museum opened in 1993, and future plans call for moving the National Museum of the American Indian (currently in New York) here in 2001.

To find out information about any of the Smithsonian museums, you call the same number: ☎ **202/357-2700** or TTY 202/357-1729. The information specialists who answer are very professional and always helpful. As mentioned earlier, you can also access the Smithsonian Institution Web site at **www.si.edu,** which will get you to the individual home pages for each of the museums.

Smithsonian Information Center (the "Castle"). 1000 Jefferson Dr. SW. ☎ **202/357-2700** or TTY 202/357-1729. Daily 9am–5:30pm, info desk 9am–4pm. Closed Dec 25. Metro: Smithsonian.

Make your first stop the impressively high-tech and very comprehensive Smithsonian Information Center, located in the institution's original Norman-style red sandstone building, popularly known as the "Castle."

The main information area here is the Great Hall, where a 20-minute video overview of the institution runs throughout the day in two theaters. There are two large schematic models of the Mall (as well as a third in Braille), and two large electronic maps of Washington allow visitors to locate nearly 100 popular attractions and Metro and Tourmobile stops. Interactive videos, some at children's heights, offer extensive information about the Smithsonian and other capital attractions and transportation (the menus seem infinite).

The entire facility is accessible to persons with disabilities, and information is available in a number of foreign languages. Daily Smithsonian events appear on monitors; in addition, the information desk's volunteer staff (some of whom speak foreign languages) can answer questions and help you plan a Smithsonian sightseeing itinerary. Most of the museums are within easy walking distance of the facility.

Anacostia Museum. 1901 Fort Place SE (off Martin Luther King Jr. Ave.). ☎ **202/357-2700.** Free admission. Daily 10am–5pm. Closed Dec 25. Metro: Anacostia, then take a W1 or W2 bus directly to the museum.

This unique Smithsonian establishment was created in 1967 as a neighborhood museum. Expanding its horizons over the years, the museum is today a national resource devoted to the identification, documentation, protection, and interpretation of the African-American experience, focusing on Washington, D.C., and the Upper South. The permanent collection includes about 7,000 items, ranging from videotapes of African-American church services to art, sheet music, historic documents, textiles, glassware, and anthropological objects. In addition, the Anacostia produces a varying number of shows each year and offers a comprehensive schedule of free educational programs and activities in conjunction with exhibit themes. For instance, to complement an exhibition called "The African-American Presence in American Quilts," the museum featured a video about artist/quilt maker Faith Ringgold, quilting workshops for adults and children, talks by local quilting societies, and storytelling involving quilts.

Call for an events calendar (which always includes children's activities) or pick one up when you visit.

Arthur M. Sackler Gallery. 1050 Independence Ave. SW. ☎ **202/357-2700.** Free admission. Daily 10am–5:30pm; summer, Fri–Wed 10am–5:30pm, Thurs 10am–8pm. Closed Dec 25. Metro: Smithsonian.

Opened in 1987, the Sackler, a national museum of Asian art, presents traveling exhibitions from major cultural institutions in Asia, Europe, and the United States. In the recent past, these have focused

Parking Near the Mall

Don't drive, use the Metro. If you're hell-bent on driving on a week-day, though, set out early to nab one of the Independence or Constitution Avenues spots that become legal at 9:30am, when rush hour ends. Arrive about 9:15 and just sit in your car until 9:30am (to avoid getting a ticket), then hop out and stoke the meter. So many people do this, that if you arrive at 9:30 or later, you'll find most of the street parking spots gone.

on such wide-ranging areas as 15th-century Persian art and culture, contemporary Japanese woodblock prints and ceramics, photographs of Asia, and art highlighting personal devotion in India. Art from the permanent collection supplements the traveling shows: It includes Khmer ceramics, ancient Chinese jades, bronzes, paintings, and lacquerware; 20th-century Japanese ceramics and works on paper; ancient Near Eastern works in silver, gold, bronze, and clay; and stone and bronze sculptures from South and Southeast Asia. Since the museum's opening, 11th- to 19th-century Persian and Indian paintings, manuscripts, calligraphies, miniatures, and bookbindings from the collection of Henri Vever have enhanced Sackler's original gift.

The Sackler is part of a museum complex that also houses the National Museum of African Art, and it shares its staff and research facilities with the adjacent Freer Gallery, to which it is connected via an underground exhibition space.

The Sackler offers museum programs (including many wonderful experiences for children and families), free highlight tours given daily (highly recommended), films, events, and temporary exhibits.

Arts & Industries Building. 900 Jefferson Dr. SW (on the south side of the Mall). ☎ **202/357-2700.** Free admission. Daily 10am–5:30pm. Closed Dec 25. Metro: Smithsonian.

Completed in 1881 as the first U.S. National Museum, this redbrick and sandstone structure was the scene of President Garfield's Inaugural Ball. From 1976 through the mid-1990s, it housed exhibits from the 1876 United States International Exposition in Philadelphia—a celebration of America's centennial that featured the latest advances in technology. Some of these Victorian tools, products, art, and other objects are on permanent display, along with rotating exhibits, including "Speak to My Heart: Communities of Faith and

Contemporary African American Life," on view through February 28, 2001.

Singers, dancers, puppeteers, and mimes perform in the **Discovery Theater** (open all year except in August, with performances weekdays and on selected Saturdays—call ☎ **202/357-1500** for show times and ticket information; admission of about $5 is charged). Don't miss the charming Victorian-motif shop on the first floor. Weather permitting, a 19th-century carousel operates across the street.

✪ **Freer Gallery of Art.** On the south side of the Mall (at Jefferson Dr. and 12th St. SW). ☎ **202/357-2700.** Free admission. Daily 10am–5:30pm; summer, Fri–Wed 1am–8pm. Closed Dec 25. Metro: Smithsonian (Mall or Independence Ave. exit).

Charles Lang Freer, a collector of Asian art and American art from the 19th and early 20th centuries, gave the nation 9,000 of these works for the Freer Gallery's opening in 1923. Freer's original interest was, in fact, American art, but his good friend James McNeill Whistler encouraged him to collect Asian works as well. Eventually the latter became predominant. Freer's gift included funds to construct a museum and an endowment to add objects of the highest quality to the Asian collection only, which now numbers more than 28,000 objects. It includes Chinese and Japanese sculpture, lacquer, metalwork, and ceramics; early Christian illuminated manuscripts; Iranian manuscripts, metalwork, and miniatures; ancient Near Eastern metalware; and South Asian sculpture and paintings.

Among the American works are more than 1,200 pieces (the world's largest collection) by Whistler, including the famous **Peacock Room.** Other American painters represented in the collections are Thomas Wilmer Dewing, Dwight William Tryon, Abbott Henderson Thayer, John Singer Sargent, and Childe Hassam.

Housed in a recently renovated granite-and-marble building that evokes the Italian Renaissance, the pristine Freer has lovely skylit galleries. The main exhibit floor centers on a garden court open to

Information, Please

If you want to know what's happening at any of the Smithsonian museums, just get on the phone; **Dial-a-Museum** (☎ **202/357-2020** or 202/633-9126 for Spanish), a recorded information line, lists daily activities and special events. For other information, call ☎ **202/357-2700.**

the sky. An underground exhibit space connects the Freer to the neighboring Sackler Gallery, and both museums share the **Meyer Auditorium,** which is used for free chamber music concerts, dance performances, Asian feature films, and other programs. Inquire about these, as well as children's activities and free tours given daily, at the information desk.

Hirshhorn Museum & Sculpture Garden. On the south side of the Mall (at Independence Ave. and 7th St. SW). ☎ **202/357-2700.** Free admission. Daily 10am–5:30pm; summer, Fri–Wed 10am–5:30pm, Thurs 10am–8pm. Sculpture Garden 7:30am–dusk. Closed Dec 25. Metro: L'Enfant Plaza (Smithsonian Museums/Maryland Ave. exit).

This museum of modern and contemporary art is named after Latvian-born Joseph H. Hirshhorn, who, in 1966, donated his vast art collection—more than 4,000 drawings and paintings and some 2,000 pieces of sculpture—to the United States "as a small repayment for what this nation has done for me and others like me who arrived here as immigrants." At his death in 1981, Hirshhorn bequeathed an additional 5,500 artworks to the museum, and numerous other donors have since greatly expanded his legacy.

Constructed 14 feet aboveground on sculptured supports, the museum's contemporary cylindrical concrete-and-granite building shelters a verdant plaza courtyard where sculpture is displayed. The light and airy interior follows a simple circular route that makes it easy to see every exhibit without getting lost in a honeycomb of galleries. Natural light from floor-to-ceiling windows makes the inner galleries the perfect venue for viewing sculpture, second only, perhaps, to the beautiful tree-shaded sunken Sculpture Garden across the street (don't miss it). Paintings and drawings are installed in the outer galleries, along with intermittent sculpture groupings.

A rotating show of about 600 pieces is on view at all times. The collection features just about every well-known 20th-century artist and touches on most of the major trends in Western art since the late 19th century, with particular emphasis on our contemporary period. Among the best-known pieces are Rodin's *The Burghers of Calais* (in the Sculpture Garden); Hopper's *First Row Orchestra;* de Kooning's *Two Women in the Country;* and Warhol's *Marilyn Monroe's Lips.*

Pick up a free calendar when you enter to find out about free films, lectures, concerts, and temporary exhibits. An outdoor cafe is open during the summer. Free tours of the collection are given daily; call about these, and about tours of the Sculpture Garden.

✪ **National Air & Space Museum.** On the south side of the Mall (between 4th and 7th sts. SW), with entrances on Jefferson Dr. or Independence Ave. ☎ **202/357-2700,** or 202/357-1686 for IMAX ticket information. Free admission. Daily 10am–5:30pm. Free 1½-hour highlight tours daily at 10:15am and 1pm. Closed Dec 25. Metro: L'Enfant Plaza (Smithsonian Museums/Maryland Ave. exit).

The National Air & Space Museum is the most visited museum in the world. The museum chronicles the story of our mastery of flight, from Kitty Hawk to outer space, in 23 galleries filled with exciting exhibits. Plan to devote at least 3 or 4 hours to exploring these exhibits and, especially during the tourist season and on holidays, arrive before 10am to make a rush for the film-ticket line when the doors open. The not-to be-missed IMAX films shown in the Samuel P. Langley Theater here, on a screen five stories high and seven stories wide, are immensely popular, and tickets sell out quickly (although the first show seldom sells out). You can purchase tickets up to 2 weeks in advance; tickets are available only at the Langley Theater box office on the first floor. Five or more films play each day, most with aeronautical or space-exploration themes: *To Fly*, *Cosmic Voyage*, and *Magic of Flight* are the names of three. Tickets cost $5 for adults, $3.75 for ages 2 to 21 and seniors 55 and older; they're free for children under 2. You can also see IMAX films most evenings after closing (call for details and ticket prices, which are higher than daytime prices). At the same time, purchase tickets for a show at the Albert Einstein Planetarium.

In between shows, you can view the exhibits; audio tours are also available for rental. Interactive computers and slide and video shows enhance the exhibits throughout.

Highlights of the first floor include famous airplanes (such as the *Spirit of St. Louis*) and spacecraft (the *Apollo 11* Command Module); the world's only touchable moon rock; numerous exhibits on the history of aviation and air transportation; galleries in which you can design your own jet plane and study astronomy; and rockets, lunar-exploration vehicles, manned spacecraft, and guided missiles. **"How Things Fly,"** a gallery that opened in 1996 to celebrate the museum's 20th anniversary, includes wind and smoke tunnels, a boardable Cessna 150 airplane, and dozens of interactive exhibits that demonstrate principles of flight, aerodynamics, and propulsion. All the aircraft, by the way, are originals.

Kids love the **"walk-through" Skylab orbital workshop** on the second floor. Other galleries here highlight the solar system, U.S. manned space flights, sea-air operations, aviation during both world wars, and artists' perceptions of flight.

National Museum of African Art. 950 Independence Ave. SW. ☎ **202/ 357-2700.** Free admission. Daily 10am–5:30pm; summer, Wed–Fri 10am– 5:30pm, Thurs 10am–8pm. Closed Dec 25. Metro: Smithsonian.

Founded in 1964, and part of the Smithsonian since 1979, the National Museum of African Art moved to the Mall in 1987 to share a subterranean space with the Sackler Gallery (see above) and the Ripley Center. Its aboveground domed pavilions reflect the arch motif of the neighboring Freer.

The museum collects and exhibits ancient and contemporary art from the entire African continent, but its permanent collection of more than 7,000 objects (shown in rotating exhibits) highlights the traditional arts of the vast sub-Saharan region. Most of the collection dates from the 19th and 20th centuries. Also among the museum's holdings are the **Eliot Elisofon Photographic Archives,** comprising 300,000 photographic prints and transparencies and 120,000 feet of film on African arts and culture. Permanent exhibits include **"The Ancient West African City of Benin, A.D. 1300– 1897"; "The Ancient Nubian City of Kerma, 2500–1500 B.C."** (ceramics, jewelry, and ivory animals); **"The Art of the Personal Object"** (everyday items such as chairs, headrests, snuffboxes, bowls, and baskets); and **"Images of Power and Identity."**

Inquire at the desk about special exhibits; workshops (including excellent children's programs), storytelling, lectures, docent-led tours, films, and demonstrations. A comprehensive events schedule here (together with exhibitions) provides a unique opportunity to learn about the diverse cultures and visual traditions of Africa.

National Museum of American Art. 8th and G sts. NW. ☎ **202/ 357-2700.** Free admission. Daily 10am–5:30pm. Closed Dec 25. Metro: Gallery Place–Chinatown.

Don't wait to see the National Museum of American Art and the National Portrait Gallery: The two museums will close by the year 2000 for a 2-year overhaul. The National Museum of American Art owns more than 37,500 works representing 2 centuries of the nation's national art history. It is the largest collection of American art in the world. About 1,000 of these works are on display at any given time, along with special exhibits highlighting various aspects of American art. The museum is the country's oldest federal art collection—it was founded in 1829, predating the Smithsonian. The collection, along with the National Portrait Gallery (described below), is housed in the palatial quarters of the 19th-century Greek Revival Old Patent Office Building, partially designed by Washington Monument architect Robert Mills and Capitol dome architect

Thomas U. Walter. Fronted by a columned portico evocative of the Parthenon, the building was originally a multipurpose facility housing a jumble of items ranging from the original Declaration of Independence to a collection of shrunken heads.

On view are works of post–World War II artists such as de Kooning, Kline, Noguchi, and others; the works of mid- to late-19th-century artists such as Winslow Homer, Mary Cassatt, Albert Pinkham Ryder, and John Singer Sargent; and pieces by early American masters Charles Willson Peale, Benjamin West, and Samuel F. B. Morse.

When you enter, pick up a map and calendar of events and ask about current temporary exhibits at the information desk. Free walk-in tours are given at noon weekdays and at 2pm on weekends. The Patent Pending cafe lies in a hall connecting the museum to the National Portrait Gallery; in good weather, you can dine in the lovely courtyard that's enclosed within the walls of the museums.

✪ **National Museum of American History.** On the north side of the Mall (between 12th and 14th sts. NW), with entrances on Constitution Ave. and Madison Dr. ☎ **202/357-2700.** Free admission. Daily 10am–5:30pm. Closed Dec 25. Metro: Smithsonian or Federal Triangle.

The National Museum of American History deals with "everyday life in the American past" and the external forces that have helped to shape our national character. Its massive contents range from General George Washington's Revolutionary War tent to Archie Bunker's chair.

Exhibits on the **first floor** (enter on Constitution Avenue) explore the development of farm machinery, power machinery, transportation, timekeeping, phonographs, and typewriters.

If you enter from the Mall, you'll find yourself on the second floor, where **"After the Revolution"** focuses on the everyday activities of ordinary 18th-century Americans and **"Field to Factory"** tells the story of African-American migration, south to north, between 1915 and 1940 .

One of the most popular exhibits on the second floor is **"First Ladies: Political Role and Public Image,"** which displays the first ladies' gowns and tells you a bit about each of these women. Infinitely more interesting, I think, is the neighboring exhibit, **"From Parlor to Politics: Women and Reform in America, 1890–1925,"** which chronicles the changing roles of women as they've moved from domestic to political and professional pursuits.

Head for the third floor to view a vast collection of ship models, uniforms, weapons, and other military artifacts; and exhibits that focus on the experiences of GIs in World War II (and the postwar world), as well as the wartime internment of Japanese Americans.

Inquire at the information desk about highlight tours, films, lectures, and concerts, and hands-on activities for children and adults. The gift shop is vast—it's the largest of the Smithsonian shops.

✪ **National Museum of Natural History.** On the north side of the Mall, at 10th St. and Constitution Ave. NW, with entrances on Madison Dr. and Constitution Ave. ☎ **202/357-2700.** Free admission. Daily 10am–5:30pm. Closed Dec 25. Free highlight tours Mon–Thur 10:30am and 1:30pm, Fri 10:30am. Metro: Smithsonian or Federal Triangle.

Children refer to this Smithsonian showcase as the dinosaur museum (there's a great dinosaur hall), or sometimes the elephant museum (a huge African bush elephant is the first amazing thing you see if you enter the museum from the Mall). Whatever you call it, the National Museum of Natural History is the largest of its kind in the world, and one of the most visited of all of Washington's museums. It contains more than 120 million artifacts and specimens, everything from Ice Age mammoths to the legendary Hope Diamond.

A **Discovery Room,** filled with creative hands-on exhibits "for children of all ages," is on the first floor. Call ahead or inquire at the information desk about hours.

On the Mall Level, off the Rotunda, is the **fossil collection,** which traces evolution back billions of years with exhibits of a 3.5-billion-year-old stromatolite (blue-green algae clump) fossil—one of the earliest signs of life on Earth—and a 70-million-year-old dinosaur egg. **"Life in the Ancient Seas"** features a 100-foot-long mural depicting primitive whales, a life-size walk-around diorama of a 230-million-year-old coral reef, and more than 2,000 fossils that chronicle the evolution of marine life. The **Dinosaur Hall** displays giant skeletons of creatures that dominated the Earth for 140 million years before their extinction about 65 million years ago.

Upstairs is the popular **O. Orkin Insect Zoo,** where kids will enjoy looking at tarantulas, centipedes, and the like, and crawling through a model of an African termite mound. The **Ocean Planet** exhibit gives a video tour of what lies beneath the ocean surface, and teaches you about ocean conservation. The **Hope Diamond** is on display in the **Janet Annenberg Hooker Hall of Geology, Gems, and Minerals,** which includes all you want to know about earth science, from volcanology to the importance of mining in our daily lives.

National Portrait Gallery. 8th and F sts. NW. ☎ **202/357-2700.** Free admission. Daily 10am–5:30pm. Closed Dec 25. Metro: Gallery Place–Chinatown.

If the prospect of a gallery of "heroes and villains, thinkers and doers, conservatives and radicals" fascinates you, don't delay seeing the National Portrait Gallery because, along with the National Museum of American Art, this museum will close for a 2-year overhaul by the year 2000. The gallery enshrines those who have made "significant contributions to the history, development, and culture of the United States" in paintings, sculpture, photography, and other forms of portraiture. Although the museum didn't open until 1968, the concept of a national portrait gallery first arose in the mid-19th century when Congress commissioned G. P. A. Healy to paint a series of presidential portraits for the White House. American portraiture dates back even further, as evidenced by those predating the Revolution (of Pocahontas, among others), and of those by Rembrandt Peale. In May 1998, Peale's portraits of George and Martha Washington returned to the gallery after a 3-year stint at the Boston Museum of Fine Arts. It's great fun to wander these corridors, putting faces to famous names for the first time, and it's enlightening to discover portraits of accomplished Americans whose names you've never heard.

In addition to the Hall of Presidents (on the second floor), notable exhibits include Gilbert Stuart's famed *"Lansdowne"* portrait of George Washington; a portrait of Mary Cassatt by Edgar Degas; 19th-century silhouettes by French-born artist Auguste Edouart; Jo Davidson's sculpture portraits (including a Buddhalike Gertrude Stein); and photographs by Mathew Brady. On the mezzanine, the Civil War is documented in portraiture, including one of the last photographs ever taken of Abraham Lincoln. Take a look at the magnificent Great Hall on the third floor. Originally designed as a showcase for patent models, it later became a Civil War hospital, where Walt Whitman came frequently to "soothe and relieve wounded troops."

Pick up a calendar of events at the information desk to find out about the museum's comprehensive schedule of temporary exhibits, lunchtime lectures, concerts, films, and dramatic presentations. Walk-in tours are given at varying hours; inquire at the information desk.

✪ **National Postal Museum.** 2 Massachusetts Ave. NE (at 1st St.). ☎ **202/357-2700.** Free admission. Daily 10am–5:30pm. Closed Dec 25. Metro: Union Station.

This museum documents America's postal history from 1673 (about 170 years before the advent of stamps, envelopes, and mailboxes) to the present. In the central gallery, titled **"Moving the Mail,"** three planes that carried mail in the early decades of the 20th century are suspended from a 90-foot atrium ceiling. Here, too, are a railway mail car, an 1851 mail/passenger coach, a Ford Model A mail truck, and a replica of an airmail beacon tower. In **"Binding the Nation,"** historic correspondence illustrates how mail kept families together in the developing nation. Several exhibits deal with the famed Pony Express, a service that lasted less than 2 years but was romanticized to legendary proportions by Buffalo Bill and others. In the Civil War section, you'll learn about Henry "Box" Brown, a slave who had himself "mailed" from Richmond to a Pennsylvania abolitionist in 1856. **"The Art of Cards and Letters"** gallery displays rotating exhibits of personal (sometimes wrenching, always interesting) correspondence taken from different periods in history, as well as greeting cards and postcards, and an 800-square-foot gallery called **"Artistic License: The Duck Stamp Story,"** focuses on federal duck stamps (first issued in 1934 to license waterfowl hunters), with displays on the hobby of duck hunting and the ecology of American water birds. In addition, the museum houses a vast research library for philatelic researchers and scholars, a stamp store, and a museum shop. Inquire about free walk-in tours at the information desk.

National Zoological Park. Adjacent to Rock Creek Park, main entrance in the 3000 block of Connecticut Ave. NW. ☎ **202/673-4800** (recording) or 202/673-4717. Free admission. Daily May to mid-Sept (weather permitting): grounds 6am–8pm, animal buildings 10am–6pm. Daily mid-Sept to May: grounds 6am–6pm, animal buildings 10am–4:30pm. Closed Dec 25. Metro: Woodley Park–Zoo or Cleveland Park.

Established in 1889, the National Zoo is home to several thousand animals of some 500 species, many of them rare and/or endangered. A leader in the care, breeding, and exhibition of animals, it occupies 163 beautifully landscaped and wooded acres and is one of the country's most delightful zoos. Among the animals you'll see are cheetahs, zebras, camels, elephants, Hsing-Hsing (the rare giant panda from China), tapirs, antelopes, brown pelicans and other waterfowl, kangaroos, hippos, rhinos, giraffes, apes, orangutans, reptiles, invertebrates, lions, tigers, spectacled bears, beavers, hummingbirds and monkeys (in Amazonia, a rain forest habitat), seals, and sea lions.

Zoo facilities include stroller-rental stations, a number of gift shops, a bookstore, and several paid-parking lots. The lots fill up quickly, especially on weekends, so arrive early or take the Metro. Snack bars and ice-cream kiosks are scattered throughout the park.

Renwick Gallery of the National Museum of American Art. Pennsylvania Ave. and 17th St. NW. ☎ **202/357-2700.** Free admission. Daily 10am–5:30pm. Closed Dec 25. Metro: Farragut West or Farragut North.

A department of the National Museum of American Art (though nowhere near it), the Renwick, a showcase for American creativity in crafts, is housed in a historic mid-1800s landmark building of the French Second Empire style. The original home of the Corcoran Gallery, it was saved from demolition by First Lady Jacqueline Kennedy in 1963, when she recommended that it be renovated as part of the Lafayette Square restoration. Although the setting—especially the magnificent Victorian Grand Salon with its wainscoted plum walls and 38-foot skylight ceiling—evokes another era, the museum's contents are mostly contemporary. The rich and diverse display of objects here includes both changing crafts exhibits and contemporary works from the museum's permanent collection. Typical exhibits range from **"Uncommon Beauty: The Legacy of African-American Craft Art"** to **"Calico and Chintz: Antique Quilts from the Patricia Smith Collection."** The above-mentioned **Grand Salon** on the second floor, furnished in opulent 19th-century style, displays paintings by 18th- and 19th-century artists. (The great thing about this room, besides its fine art and grand design, is its cushiony, velvety banquettes, perfect resting places for the weary sightseer.)

The Renwick offers a comprehensive schedule of crafts demonstrations, lectures, and films. Inquire at the information desk, and check out the museum shop near the entrance for books on crafts, design, and decorative arts, as well as craft items, many of them for children.

4 Elsewhere on the Mall

National Archives. Constitution Ave. NW (between 7th and 9th sts.). ☎ **202/501-5000** for information on exhibits and films or 202/501-5400 for research information. www.nara.gov/nara/events/calendar/calendar.html. Free admission. Exhibition Hall Apr–Aug, daily 10am–9pm; Sept–Mar, daily 10am–5:30pm. Free tours weekdays 10:15am and 1:15pm by appointment only; call ☎ **202/501-5205.** Call for research hours. Closed Dec 25. Metro: Archives.

Keeper of America's documentary heritage, the National Archives display our most cherished treasures in appropriately awe-inspiring surroundings. Housed in the **Rotunda of the Exhibition Hall** are the nation's three charter documents—the Declaration of

Smithsonian Touring and Dining Tips

The Information Center opens 1 hour earlier than the museums. The Castle's 19th-century dining room, known as **The Commons,** is the site each Sunday for brunch, 11am to 3pm, featuring everything from omelets to baked ham, for $18.95 per person (less for children and senior citizens). Call ☎ **202/357-2957** before 10am or after 3pm to make a reservation.

Independence, the Constitution of the United States, and the Bill of Rights, as well as the 1297 version of the Magna Carta—each on permanent display to the public.

High above and flanking the documents are two larger-than-life murals painted by Barry Faulkner. One, entitled *The Declaration of Independence*, shows Thomas Jefferson presenting a draft of the Declaration to John Hancock, the presiding officer of the Continental Congress; the other, entitled *The Constitution*, shows James Madison submitting the Constitution to George Washington and the Constitutional Convention. In the display cases on either side of the Declaration of Independence are exhibits that rotate over a 3-year period, for instance, **"American Originals,"** which features 26 compelling American historical documents ranging from George Washington's Revolutionary War expense account to the Louisiana Purchase Treaty signed by Napoléon. There are also temporary exhibits in the **Circular Gallery.**

The Archives serve as much more than a museum of cherished documents. Famous as a center for genealogical research—Alex Haley began his work on *Roots* here—it is sometimes called "the nation's memory." This federal institution is charged with sifting through the accumulated papers of a nation's official life—billions of pieces a year—and determining what to save and what to destroy. The Archives' vast accumulation of census figures, military records, naturalization papers, immigrant passenger lists, federal documents, passport applications, ship manifests, maps, charts, photographs, and motion picture film (and that's not the half of it) spans 2 centuries. And it's all available for the perusal of anyone age 16 or over (call for details). If you're casually thinking about tracing your roots, stop by Room 400 where a staff member can advise you about the time and effort that will be involved, and, if you decide to pursue it, exactly how to proceed.

✪ National Gallery of Art. On the north side of the Mall, on Constitution Ave. NW, between 3rd and 7th sts. NW. ☎ **202/737-4215.** www.nga.gov. Free admission. Mon–Sat 10am–5pm, Sun 11am–6pm. Closed Jan 1 and Dec 25. Metro: Archives, Judiciary Square, or Smithsonian.

Most people don't realize it, but the National Gallery of Art is not part of the Smithsonian complex.

Housing one of the world's foremost collections of Western painting, sculpture, and graphic arts from the Middle Ages through the 20th century, the National Gallery has a dual personality. The original West Building, designed by John Russell Pope (architect of the Jefferson Memorial and the National Archives), is a neoclassic marble masterpiece with a domed rotunda over a colonnaded fountain and high-ceilinged corridors leading to delightful garden courts.

The West Building: On the main floor of the West Building, about 1,000 paintings are always on display. To the left (as you enter off the Mall) is the **Art Information Room,** housing the **Micro Gallery,** where those so inclined can design their own tours of the permanent collection and enhance their knowledge of art via user-friendly computers. Continuing to the left of the rotunda are galleries of 13th- through 18th-century Italian paintings and sculpture, including what is generally considered the finest Renaissance collection outside Italy; here you'll see the only painting by Leonardo da Vinci housed outside Europe, *Ginevra de' Benci.*

Note: The National Gallery Sculpture Garden, just across 7th Street from the West Wing, should have opened by the time you read this. The completed 6.1-acre park should include open lawns; a central pool with a spouting fountain (the pool is converted into an ice rink in winter); an exquisite, glassed-in pavilion housing a cafe; 20th century sculptures; and informally landscaped shrubs, trees, and plants.

The East Building: The 20th anniversary of the opening of this wing was celebrated in 1998. The wing was conceived as a showcase for the museum's collection of 20th-century art, including Picasso, Miró, Matisse, Pollock, and Rothko, and to house the art history research center. Always on display are the massive aluminum Calder mobile dangling under a seven-story skylight and an exhibit called **"Small French Paintings,"** which I love.

Pick up a floor plan and calendar of events at an information desk to find out about National Gallery exhibits; films; tours; lectures; and concerts. Highly recommended are the free highlight tours (call for exact times) and audio tours. The gift shop is a favorite. The gallery offers several good dining options, the best being the Terrace Café, which sometimes tailors its menu to complement a particular exhibit.

✪ **United States Holocaust Memorial Museum.** 100 Raoul Wallenberg Place (formerly 15th St. SW; near Independence Ave., just off the Mall). ☎ **202/488-0400.** www.ushmm.org. Free admission. Daily 10am–5:30pm. Closed Yom Kippur and Dec 25. Metro: Smithsonian.

When this museum opened in 1993, officials thought perhaps 500,000 people might visit annually. In fact, 2 million come here every year. On a daily basis, the number is 1,650, which is the maximum number of free timed tickets the museum gives out each day to visitors who come to tour the permanent exhibit. The museum opens its doors at 10am and the tickets are usually gone by 10:30am. It's best to get on line early in the morning (around 8am). Most visitors—80 percent— are not Jewish, 14 percent are foreigners, and 18 percent are repeats.

You will spend most of your time—anywhere from 1 to 5 hours—in the permanent exhibit, which takes up three floors, presenting the information chronologically. When you enter, you will be issued an identity card of an actual victim of the Holocaust. By 1945, 66% of those whose lives are documented on these cards were dead. The tour begins on the fourth floor, where exhibits portray the events of 1933 to 1939, the years of the Nazi uprising. On the third floor (documenting 1940 to 1944), exhibits illustrate the narrowing choices of people caught up in the Nazi machine. You board a Polish freight car of the type used to transport Jews from the Warsaw ghetto to Treblinka and hear recordings of survivors telling what life in the camps was like. This part of the museum documents the details of the Nazis' "Final Solution" for the Jews.

The second floor recounts a more heartening story: It depicts how non-Jews throughout Europe, by exercising individual action and responsibility, saved Jews at great personal risk.

Chartered by a unanimous Act of Congress in 1980 and located adjacent to the Mall, the museum strives to broaden public understanding of Holocaust history. In addition to its permanent and temporary exhibitions, the museum has a Resource Center for

Avoiding the Crowds at the National Gallery of Art

The best time to visit the National Gallery is Monday morning; the worst is Sunday afternoons.

educators, which provides materials and services to Holocaust educators and students; an interactive computer learning center; and a registry of Holocaust survivors, a library, and archives, which researchers may use to retrieve historic documents, photographs, oral histories, films, and videos.

The museum recommends not bringing children under 11; for older children, it's advisable to prepare them for what they'll see. There's a cafeteria and museum shop on the premises.

You can see some parts of the museum without tickets. These include two special exhibit areas on the first floor and concourse: **"Daniel's Story: Remember the Children"** and **"Hidden History of the Kovno Ghetto"** (this leaves in 1999); the **Wall of Remembrance** (Children's Tile Wall), which commemorates the 1.5 million children killed in the Holocaust, and the **Wexner Learning Center.**

5   Other Government Agencies

Bureau of Engraving & Printing. 14th and C sts. SW. ☎ **202/874-3188** or 202/874-2330. Free admission. Mon–Fri 9am–2pm (last tour begins at 1:40pm). Closed Dec 25–Jan 1 and federal holidays. Metro: Smithsonian (Independence Ave. exit).

This is where the cash is. A staff of 2,600 works around the clock churning it out at the rate of about 22.5 million notes a day. Everyone's eyes pop as they walk past rooms overflowing with fresh green bills. Although the money draws everyone in, it's not the whole story. The bureau prints many other products, including 25 billion postage stamps per year, presidential portraits, and White House invitations.

As many as 5,000 people line up each day to get a peek at all that moola, so arriving early, especially during the peak tourist season, is essential (unless you have secured VIP tickets from your senator or congressperson; details in chapter 1). April through September, you must obtain a same-day ticket specifying a tour time; the ticket booth on the 14th Street side of the building opens at 8am. The rest of the year no ticket is needed; you just have to line up on 14th Street.

The 40-minute guided tour begins with a short introductory film. Then you'll see, through large windows, the processes that go into the making of paper money: the inking, stacking of bills, cutting, and examination for defects. Most printing here is done from engraved steel plates in a process known as "intaglio," the hardest to

Holocaust Museum Touring Tips

Because so many people want to visit the museum, tickets specifying a visit time (in 15-minute intervals) are required. Reserve them via **Protix** (☎ 800/400-9373). There's a small service charge. You can also get them at the museum beginning at 10am daily (lines form earlier).

counterfeit, because the slightest alteration will cause a noticeable change in the portrait in use. Additional exhibits include bills no longer in use, counterfeit money, and a $100,000 bill designed for official transactions (since 1969, the largest denomination printed for the general public is $100).

Federal Bureau of Investigation. J. Edgar Hoover FBI Building, E St. NW (between 9th and 10th sts.). ☎ **202/324-3447.** Free admission. Mon–Fri 8:45am–4:15pm. Closed Jan 1, Dec 25, and other federal holidays. Metro: Metro Center or Federal Triangle.

At the height of the season, say mid-April, you might be standing in line with 300 people at 8 in the morning to tour the FBI Building—and not get in. If you're coming anytime between April and August, try to arrange for tickets ahead of time; even so, the tour office might tell you that they won't confirm your tickets until a week before your visit.

More than half a million visitors (many of them kids) come here annually to learn why crime doesn't pay. Tours begin with a short videotape presentation about the priorities of the bureau: organized crime; white-collar crime; terrorism; foreign counter-intelligence; illegal drugs; and violent crimes. En route, you'll learn about this organization's history (it was established in 1908) and its activities over the years. You'll see some of the weapons used by big-time gangsters such as Al Capone, John Dillinger, Bonnie and Clyde, and "Pretty Boy" Floyd; and an exhibit on counterintelligence operations. There are photographs of the 10 most-wanted fugitives (2 were recognized at this exhibit by people on the tour, and 10 have been located via the FBI-assisted TV show *America's Most Wanted*).

You'll also visit the **DNA lab;** the **Firearms Unit** (where it's determined whether a bullet was fired from a given weapon); the **Material Analysis Unit** (where the FBI can determine the approximate make and model of a car from a tiny piece of paint); the unit where hairs and fibers are examined; and a **Forfeiture and Seizure Exhibit**—a display of jewelry, furs, and other proceeds from illegal narcotics operations. The tour ends with a bang, lots of them in fact, when an agent gives a sharpshooting demonstration and discusses the FBI's firearm policy and gun safety.

✪ **Library of Congress.** 1st St. SE (between Independence Ave. and E. Capitol St.). ☎ **202/707-8000.** www/loc.gov/. Free admission. Madison Building Mon–Fri 8:30am–9:30pm, Sat 8:30am–6pm. Jefferson Building Mon–Sat 10am–5:30pm. Closed Sun and all federal holidays. Stop at the information desk inside the Jefferson Building's west entrance on First Street to obtain same-day, free tickets to tour the Library. Tours of the Great Hall Mon–Sat 11:30am, 1pm, 2:30pm, and 4pm. Metro: Capitol South.

The question most frequently asked by visitors to the Library of Congress is: "Where are the books?". And the answer is: On the 532 miles of shelves located throughout the library's 3 buildings. Established in 1800, "for the purchase of such books as may be necessary for the use of Congress," the library today serves the nation, with holdings for the visually impaired (for whom books are recorded on cassette and/or translated into braille), research scholars, and college students.

As impressive as the scope of the library's effects and activities is its original home, the ornate Italian Renaissance–style Thomas Jefferson Building, which reopened to the public May 1, 1997, after an $81.5 million, 12-year overhaul of the entire library. The Jefferson Building was erected between 1888 and 1897 to hold the burgeoning collection and establish America as a cultured nation with magnificent institutions equal to anything in Europe. Originally intended to hold the fruits of at least 150 years of collecting, the Jefferson was, in fact, filled up in 13. It is now supplemented by the James Madison Memorial Building and the John Adams Building.

If you have to wait for a tour, take in the 12-minute orientation film in the Jefferson's new visitors' theater or browse in its new gift shop. Pick up a calendar of events when you visit. Free concerts take place in the Jefferson Building's elegant Collidge Auditorium; find out more about them on the LOC concert Web site: **lcweb.loc.gov/ rr/perform/concert. The Madison Building** offers interesting exhibits and features classic, rare, and unusual films in its Mary Pickford Theater. It also houses a cafeteria and the more formal Montpelier Room restaurant, both of which are open for lunch weekdays.

FBI Touring Tips

To beat the crowds, arrive before 8:45am or write to a senator or congressperson for a scheduled reservation as far in advance as possible (details in chapter 2). Tours last 1 hour and are conducted every 20 to 30 minutes, depending upon staff availability. The building closes at 4:15pm, so you must arrive at least 1 hour before closing if you want to make the last tour (arrive even earlier in high season). Once inside, you'll undergo a security check.

6 War Memorials & Cemeteries

Arlington National Cemetery. Just across the Memorial Bridge from the base of the Lincoln Memorial. ☎ **703/607-8052.** Free admission. Apr–Sept, daily 8am–7pm; Oct–Mar, daily 8am–5pm. Metro: Arlington National Cemetery. If you come by car, parking is $1.25 an hour for the first 3 hours, $2 an hour thereafter. The cemetery is also accessible via Tourmobile.

Upon arrival, head over to the Visitor Center, where you can view exhibits, pick up a detailed map, use the rest rooms (there are no others until you get to Arlington House), and purchase a Tourmobile ticket ($4.75 per adult, $2.25 for children 4–11) allowing you to stop at all major sights in the cemetery and then reboard whenever you like. Service is continuous, and the narrated commentary is informative; this is the only guided tour of the cemetery offered. (See "Getting Around" in chapter 2 for details.) If you've got plenty of stamina, consider doing part or all of the tour on foot. Remember as you go that this is a memorial frequented not just by tourists but by those visiting the graves of beloved relatives and friends who are buried here.

The Tomb of the Unknowns, containing the unidentified remains of service members from both world wars, the Korean War, and the Vietnam War. The changing of the guard takes place every half-hour April to September and every hour on the hour October to March.

A 20-minute walk, all uphill, from the Visitor Center is **Arlington House** (☎ **703/557-0613**). For 30 years (1831–61) this was the legal residence of Robert E. Lee, where he and his family lived off and on until the Civil War. You tour the house on your own; park rangers are on-site to answer your questions. About 30% of the furnishings are original. Slave quarters and a small museum adjoin.

Admission is free. It's open daily 9:30am to 4:30pm but is closed January 1 and December 25.

Pierre Charles L'Enfant's grave was placed near Arlington House at a spot that is believed to offer the best view of Washington, the city he designed.

Below Arlington House, an 8-minute walk from the visitor center, is the **Gravesite of John Fitzgerald Kennedy.** Simplicity is the key to grandeur here, too. Jacqueline Kennedy Onassis rests next to her husband, and Senator Robert Kennedy is buried close by. The Kennedy graves attract streams of visitors. Arrive close to 8am to contemplate the site quietly; otherwise, it's mobbed. Looking north, there's a spectacular view of Washington.

About 1 1/2 miles from the Kennedy graves, the **Marine Corps Memorial,** the famous statue of the marines raising the flag on Iwo Jima, stands near the north (or Orde & Weitzel Gate) entrance to the cemetery as a tribute to marines who died in all wars. On Tuesday evenings in summer, there are military parades on the grounds at 7pm.

✪ In October 1997, the **Women in Military Service for America Memorial** (☎ 800/222-2294 or 703/533-1155) was added to Arlington Cemetery, to honor the more than 1.8 million women who have served in the armed forces from the American Revolution to the present. The impressive new memorial lies just beyond the gated entrance to the cemetery, a 3-minute walk from the Visitor Center. What you see as you approach the memorial is a large, circular reflecting pool, perfectly placed within the curve of the granite wall rising behind it. Arched passages within the 226-foot-long wall lead to an upper terrace and dramatic views of Arlington National Cemetery and the monuments of Washington; an arc of large glass panels (which form the roof of the memorial hall) contains etched quotations from servicewomen (and a couple from men). Behind the wall and completely underground is the **Education Center,** housing a **Hall of Honor,** a gallery of exhibits tracing the history of women in the military; a theater; and a computer register of servicewomen, which visitors may access for information about individual women, past and present, in the military. Hours are October through March 8am to 5pm and April through September 8am to 7pm. Stop at the reception desk for a brochure that details a self-guided tour through the memorial. The memorial is open every day but Christmas.

Arlington National Cemetery

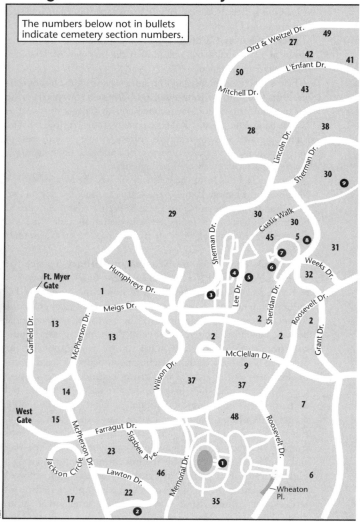

The numbers below not in bullets indicate cemetery section numbers.

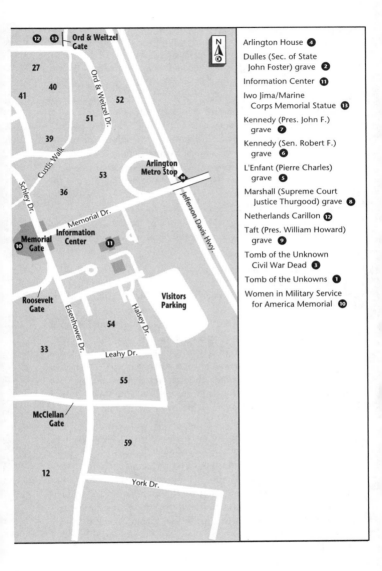

Arlington House **4**

Dulles (Sec. of State
John Foster) grave **2**

Information Center **11**

Iwo Jima/Marine
Corps Memorial Statue **13**

Kennedy (Pres. John F.)
grave **7**

Kennedy (Sen. Robert F.)
grave **6**

L'Enfant (Pierre Charles)
grave **5**

Marshall (Supreme Court
Justice Thurgood) grave **8**

Netherlands Carillon **12**

Taft (Pres. William Howard)
grave **9**

Tomb of the Unknown
Civil War Dead **3**

Tomb of the Unkowns **1**

Women in Military Service
for America Memorial **10**

The Korean War Veterans Memorial. Just across from the Lincoln Memorial (east of French Dr., between 21st and 23rd sts. NW). ☎ **202/426-6841.** Free admission. Rangers on duty 8am–midnight daily except Dec 25. Ranger-led interpretive programs are given throughout the day. Metro: Foggy Bottom.

This privately funded memorial founded in 1995 honors those who served in Korea, a 3-year conflict (1950–53) that produced almost as many casualties as Vietnam. It consists of a circular "Pool of Remembrance" in a grove of trees and a triangular "Field of Service." The latter is highlighted by lifelike statues of 19 infantrymen, who appear to be trudging across fields, their expressions and stances suggesting that their enemies lurk nearby. The scene is wholly compelling. In addition, a 164-foot-long black granite wall depicts the array of combat and combat support troops that served in Korea (nurses, chaplains, airmen, gunners, mechanics, cooks, and others); a raised granite curb lists the 22 nations that contributed to the UN's effort there; and a commemorative area honors KIAs, MIAs, and POWs.

United States Navy Memorial and Naval Heritage Center. 701 Pennsylvania Ave. NW. ☎ **800/723-3557** or 202/737-2300. Free admission. Mon–Sat 9:30am–5pm. Closed Thanksgiving, New Year's Day, and Dec 25. Metro: Archives–Navy Memorial.

Authorized by Congress in 1980 to honor the men and women of the U.S. Navy, this memorial comprises a 100-foot-diameter circular plaza bearing a granite world map flanked by fountains and waterfalls salted with waters from the seven seas. A statue *of The Lone Sailor* watching over the map represents all who have served in the navy, and two sculpture walls adorned with bronze bas-reliefs commemorate navy history and related maritime services.

The building adjoining the memorial houses a naval heritage center. The center's museum includes interactive video kiosks proffering a wealth of information about navy ships, aircraft, and history; the **Navy Memorial Log Room,** a computerized record of past and present navy personnel; the **Presidents Room,** honoring the six U.S. presidents who served in the navy and the two who became secretary of the navy; the **Ship's Store,** filled with nautical and maritime merchandise; and a wide-screen 70mm Surroundsound film called *At Sea* (by the makers of *To Fly*), which lets viewers experience the grandeur of the ocean and the adventure of going to sea on a navy ship. The 35-minute film plays every Monday through Saturday at 11am, 1pm, and 3pm; admission is $3.75 for adults, $3 for seniors and students 18 and under.

Guided tours are available from the front desk, subject to staff availability. The plaza is the scene of many free band concerts in spring and summer; call for details.

✪ **The Vietnam Veterans Memorial.** Just across from the Lincoln Memorial (east of Henry Bacon Dr. between 21st and 22nd sts. NW). ☎ **202/426-6841.** Free admission. Rangers on duty 8am–midnight daily except Dec 25. Ranger-led programs are given throughout the day. Metro: Foggy Bottom.

A most poignant sight in Washington is the Vietnam Veterans Memorial: two long, black granite walls inscribed with the names of the men and women who gave their lives, or remain missing, in the longest war in our nation's history. Even if no one close to you died in Vietnam, it's wrenching to watch visitors grimly studying the directories at either end to find out where their husbands, sons, and loved ones are listed. The slow walk along the 492-foot wall of names—it names close to 60,000 people, many of whom died very young—powerfully evokes the tragedy of all wars. It's also affecting to see how much the monument means to Vietnam veterans who visit it. Because of the raging conflict over U.S. involvement in the war, Vietnam veterans had received virtually no previous recognition of their service.

Yale senior Maya Ying Lin's design was chosen in a national competition open to all citizens over 18 years of age. It consists of two walls in a quiet, protected park setting, angled at 125° to point to the Washington Monument and the Lincoln Memorial. The wall's mirrorlike surface reflects surrounding trees, lawns, and monuments. The names are inscribed in chronological order, documenting an epoch in American history as a series of individual sacrifices from the date of the first casualty in 1959 to the date of the last death in 1975.

The park rangers at the Vietnam Veterans Memorial are very knowledgeable and are usually milling about—be sure to seek them out if you have any questions. Limited parking is available along Constitution Avenue.

7 More Fun Stuff to Do

✪ **Corcoran Gallery of Art.** 500 17th St. NW (between E St. and New York Ave.). ☎ **202/639-1700.** www.corcoran.com. Free admission. Wed and Fri–Mon 10am–5pm, Thurs 10am–9pm. Suggested contribution $3 adults, $1 students and senior citizens, $5 for families; children 12 and under are free. Free 45-minute tours daily at noon, Thurs 7:30, Sat–Sun 10:30am and 12:30pm. Closed Tues, Jan 1, and Dec 25. Some street parking. Metro: Farragut West or Farragut North.

The first art museum in Washington (and one of the first in the nation), the Corcoran Gallery was housed from 1869 to 1896 in the redbrick and brownstone building that is now the Renwick. The collection outgrew its quarters and was transferred in 1897 to its present beaux-arts building, designed by Ernest Flagg.

The collection, shown in rotating exhibits, focuses chiefly on American art. A prominent Washington banker, William Wilson Corcoran was among the first wealthy American collectors to realize the importance of encouraging and supporting this country's artists. Enhanced by further gifts and bequests, the collection comprehensively spans American art from 18th-century portraiture to 20th-century moderns like Nevelson, Warhol, and Rothko. Nineteenth-century works include Bierstadt's and Remington's imagery of the American West; Hudson River School artists like Cole, Church, and Durand; genre paintings; expatriates like Whistler, Sargent, and Mary Cassatt; and two giants of the late 19th century, Homer and Eakins.

The Corcoran is not exclusively an American art museum. On the first floor is the collection from the estate of Senator William Andrews Clark, an eclectic grouping of Dutch and Flemish masters, European painters, French impressionists, Barbizon landscapes, Delft porcelains, a Louis XVI *salon dore* transported in toto from Paris, and more. Don't miss the small, walnut-paneled room known as "Clark Landing," which showcases 19th-century French impressionist and American art; a room of exquisite Corot landscapes; another of medieval Renaissance tapestries; and numerous Daumier lithographs donated by Dr. Armand Hammer.

Ford's Theatre & Lincoln Museum. 517 10th St. NW (between E and F sts.). ☎ **202/426-6925.** Free admission. Daily 9am–5pm. Closed Dec 25. Metro: Metro Center.

On April 14, 1865, President Abraham Lincoln was in the audience of Ford's Theatre, one of the most popular playhouses in Washington. Everyone was laughing at a funny line from Tom Taylor's celebrated comedy, *Our American Cousin,* when John Wilkes Booth crept into the president's box, shot the president, and leapt to the stage, shouting "Sic semper tyrannis" (Thus ever to tyrants). With his left leg broken from the vault, Booth mounted his horse in the back alley and galloped off. Doctors carried Lincoln across the street to the house of William Petersen, where the president died the next morning.

Except when rehearsals or matinees are in progress (call before you go), visitors can see the theater and trace Booth's movements on that fateful night. Free 15-minute talks on the history of the theater and the story of the assassination are given throughout the day. Be sure to visit the Lincoln Museum in the basement, where exhibits—including the Derringer pistol used by Booth and a diary in which he outlines his rationalization for the deed—focus on events surrounding Lincoln's assassination and the trial of the conspirators. The theater stages productions most of the year.

National Geographic Society's Explorers Hall. 17th and M sts. NW. ☎ **202/857-7588.** Free admission. Mon–Sat and holidays 9am–5pm, Sun 10am–5pm. Closed Dec 25. Metro: Farragut North (Connecticut Ave. and L St. exit).

I don't know that I'd come here if I didn't have kids. Whatever, as my 11-year-old says. The truth is, anyone over 8 will find something fascinating or enjoyable at Explorers Hall.

The National Geographic Society was founded in 1888 for "the increase and diffusion of geographic knowledge." At Explorers Hall, dozens of fascinating displays, most of them using interactive videos, put that knowledge literally at your fingertips. In **Geographica,** on the north side of the hall, you can touch a tornado; find out what it's like inside the Earth; explore the vast Martian landscape; and study the origin of humankind. The major exhibit here is **Earth Station One,** an interactive amphitheater (centered on an immense free-floating globe) that simulates an orbital flight. You can also peer into a video microscope that zooms in clearly on slides showing such specimens as a hydra (a simple multicellular animal) or mosquito larva.

✪ **Phillips Collection.** 1600 21st St. NW (at Q St.). ☎ **202/387-2151.** Admission Sat–Sun $6.50 adults, $3.25 seniors and students, free for children 18 and under; contribution suggested Tues–Fri. Open Sept–May Tues–Wed and Fri–Sat 10am–5pm, Thurs 10am–8:30pm, Sun noon–5pm; June–Aug, noon–7pm. Free tours Wed and Sat 2pm. Closed Jan 1, July 4, Thanksgiving Day, and Dec 25. Metro: Dupont Circle (Q St. exit).

Conceived as "a museum of modern art and its sources," this intimate establishment, occupying an elegant 1890s Georgian Revival mansion and a more youthful wing, houses the exquisite collection of Duncan and Marjorie Phillips, avid collectors and proselytizers of modernism. Carpeted rooms, with leaded- and stained-glass windows, oak paneling, plush chairs and sofas, and frequently, fireplaces, establish a comfortable, homelike setting for the viewing of their art. Today the collection includes more than 2,500 works. Among the highlights: superb examples of Daumier, Dove, and Bonnard paintings; some splendid small Vuillards; five van Goghs; Renoir's

Luncheon of the Boating Party; seven Cézannes; and six works by Georgia O'Keeffe. Ingres, Delacroix, Manet, El Greco, Goya, Corot, Constable, Courbet, Giorgione, and Chardin are among the "sources" or forerunners of modernism represented. Modern notables include Rothko, Hopper, Kandinsky, Matisse, Klee, Degas, Rouault, Picasso, and many others.

On Thursdays, the museum stays open until 8:30pm for **Artful Evenings** with music, gallery talks, and a cash bar; admission is $5.

John F. Kennedy Center for the Performing Arts. New Hampshire Ave. NW (at Rock Creek Pkwy.). ☎ **800/444-1324,** or 202/416-8341 for information or tickets. Free admission. Daily 10am–midnight. Free guided tours Mon–Fri 10am–6pm, Sat–Sun between 10am and 2pm. Metro: Foggy Bottom (there's a free shuttle service from the station). Bus: no. 80 from Metro Center.

Opened in 1971, the Kennedy Center is both our national performing arts center and a memorial to John F. Kennedy. Carved into the center's river facade are several Kennedy quotations, including, "the New Frontier for which I campaign in public life can also be a New Frontier for American art." Set on 17 acres overlooking the Potomac, the striking $73-million facility, designed by noted architect Edward Durell Stone, encompasses an opera house, a concert hall, two stage theaters, a theater lab, and a film theater. The best way to see the Kennedy Center, including restricted areas, is to take a free 50-minute guided tour (see above for schedule). You can beat the crowds by writing in advance to a senator or congressperson for tickets for a VIP tour, which are given year-round Monday through Saturday 9:30am and 4:45pm, with a 9:45am tour added April through September (details in chapter 1).

If you'd like to attend performances during your visit, call the toll-free number above and request the current issue of *Kennedy Center News Magazine,* a free publication that describes all Kennedy Center happenings and prices.

✪ Washington National Cathedral. Massachusetts and Wisconsin aves. NW (entrance on Wisconsin Ave.). ☎ **202/537-6207.** Free admission, donations accepted for tours (see information below). Cathedral daily 10am–4:30pm; May 1–Labor Day, the nave level stays open weeknights until 9pm. Gardens open daily until dusk. Worship services vary throughout the year but you can count on a daily Evensong service at 4pm, a noon service Mon–Sat, and an 11am service every Sun; call for other service times. Metro: Tenleytown, then about a 20-minute walk. Bus: Any N bus up Massachusetts Ave. from Dupont Circle or any 30-series bus along Wisconsin Ave. Also: This is a stop on the Old Town Trolley Tour.

Pierre L'Enfant's 1791 plan for the capital city included "a great church for national purposes," but possibly because of early

America's fear of mingling church and state, more than a century elapsed before the foundation for Washington National Cathedral was laid. Its actual name is the Cathedral Church of St. Peter and St. Paul. The church is Episcopal, but it has no local congregation and seeks to serve the entire nation as a house of prayer for all people. It has been the setting for every kind of religious observance from Jewish to Serbian Orthodox.

A church of this magnitude—it's the sixth-largest cathedral in the world—took a long time to build. Its principal (but not original) architect, Philip Hubert Frohman, worked on the project from 1921 until his death in 1972. The foundation stone was laid in 1907 using the mallet with which George Washington set the Capitol cornerstone. Construction was interrupted by both world wars and by periods of financial difficulty. The cathedral was completed with the placement of the final stone atop a pinnacle on the west front towers on September 29, 1990, 83 years to the day it was begun.

English Gothic in style (with several distinctly 20th-century innovations, such as a stained-glass window commemorating the flight of *Apollo 11* and containing a piece of moon rock), the cathedral is built in the shape of a cross, complete with flying buttresses and gargoyles. It is, along with the Capitol and the Washington Monument, one of the dominant structures on the Washington skyline. Its 57-acre landscaped grounds have two lovely gardens (the lawn is ideal for picnicking); four schools, including the College of Preachers; an herb garden; a greenhouse; and two gift shops (one in the cathedral basement, the other in the "Herb Cottage").

The best way to explore the cathedral and see its abundance of art, architectural carvings, and statuary is to take a 30- to 45-minute guided tour. They leave continually, from the west end of the nave, Monday to Saturday 10–11:30am and 12:45–3:15pm, and Sunday 12:30–2:45pm. A suggested donation of $2 per adult, $1 per child is requested.

Allow additional time to tour the grounds or "close" and to visit the Observation Gallery where 70 windows provide panoramic views. Tuesday and Wednesday afternoon tours are followed by a high tea in the Observation Gallery.

The cathedral hosts numerous events: organ recitals; choir performances; an annual flower mart; calligraphy workshops; jazz, folk, and classical concerts; and the playing of the 53-bell carillon. Check the cathedral's Web site for upcoming events and other information at **www.cathedral.org/cathedral**.

GARDENS

Enid A. Haupt Garden. 10th St. and Independence Ave. SW. ☎ **202/357-2700.** Free admission. Late May–Aug daily 7am–8pm; Sept–mid-May; daily 7am–5:45pm. Closed Dec 25. Metro: Smithsonian.

Named for its donor, a noted supporter of horticultural projects, this stunning garden presents elaborate flower beds and borders, plant-filled turn-of-the-century urns, 1870s cast-iron furnishings, and lush baskets hung from reproduction 19th-century lampposts. Although on ground level, the garden is really a 4-acre rooftop garden above the subterranean Sackler and African Art Museums. A magnolia-lined parterre, framed by four floral swags, centers on a floral bed patterned after the rose window in the Commons of the Castle; it is composed of 30,000 green and yellow Alternanthera, supplemented by seasonal displays of spring pansies, begonias, or cabbage and kale. Additional features include wisteria-covered dome-shaped trellises, clusters of trees (Zumi crabapples, ginkgoes, and American hollies), a weeping European beech, and rose gardens. Elaborate cast-iron carriage gates made according to a 19th-century design by James Renwick, flanked by four red sandstone pillars, have been installed at the Independence Avenue entrance to the garden.

PARKS
POTOMAC PARK

West and East Potomac Parks, their 720 riverside acres divided by the Tidal Basin, are most famous for their spring display of cherry blossoms and all the hoopla that goes with it. The cherry trees lie along the portion of the Tidal Basin that runs alongside the FDR Memorial. If you're driving, you want to get on Independence Avenue and follow the signs posted near the Lincoln Memorial that show you where to turn to find parking and the FDR Memorial. If you're walking, you'll want to cross Independence Avenue where it intersects with W. Basin Drive (there's a stoplight and crosswalk), and follow the path to the Tidal Basin, where you'll find the trees. There is no convenient Metro stop near here.

West Potomac Park has 1,682 trees bordering the Tidal Basin. The blossoming of the cherry trees is the focal point of a week-long celebration. The trees bloom for a little less than 2 weeks beginning somewhere between March 20 and April 17; April 5 is the average date. Planning your trip around the blooming of the cherry blossoms is an iffy proposition, and I wouldn't advise it. One thing many people don't realize is that all it takes is one good rain and those cherry blossoms are gone. The cherry blossoms are not illuminated at night, and therefore, not truly visible, so if you think you're going to beat the crush of tourists touring the Tidal Basin during the day by going at night, you'll be out of luck. The National Park Service should consider backlighting the trees at night: Not only would it be a breathtaking sight, but it would help with the yearly stampede along the Tidal Basin. See the calendar of events in chapter 1 for further details on cherry blossom events.

East Potomac Park cherry trees number 1,681, and 11 varieties. The park also has picnic grounds, tennis courts, three golf courses, a large swimming pool, and biking and hiking paths by the water, all of which are described in "Outdoor Activities," below.

West Potomac Park encompasses Constitution Gardens; the Vietnam, Korean, Lincoln, Jefferson, and FDR Memorials; a small island where ducks live; and the Reflecting Pool.

ROCK CREEK PARK

Created in 1890, Rock Creek Park was purchased by Congress for its "pleasant valleys and ravines, primeval forests and open fields, its running waters, its rocks clothed with rich ferns and mosses, its repose and tranquillity, its light and shade, its ever-varying shrubbery, its beautiful and extensive views." A 1,750-acre valley within the District of Columbia, extending 12 miles from the Potomac River to the Maryland border (another 2,700 acres), it's one of the biggest and finest city parks in the nation. Parts of it are still wild; it's not unusual to see a deer scurrying through the woods in more remote sections.

For full information on the wide range of park programs and activities, call the Rock Creek Nature at ☎ **202/426-6829**, Wednesday to Sunday 9am to 5pm; or Park at ☎ **202/282-1063**, weekdays 7:45am to 4:15pm. To get to the Nature Center by public transportation, take the Metro to Friendship Heights and transfer to bus no. E2 or E3 to Military Road and Oregon Avenue/Glover Road.

There's convenient free parking throughout the park.

8 Organized Tours

If you have the time and the inclination, start your sightseeing with an organized tour.

BY FOOT

TourDC, Walking Tours of Georgetown (☎ **301/588-8999;** Web site www.tourdc.com) conducts 90-minute ($12) and 2-hour

($15) walking tours of Georgetown, telling about the neighborhood's history up to the present and taking you past the homes of notable residents.

Weekend Walks in Georgetown (☎ 301/294-9514) offers 2-hour walks through the streets of Georgetown, guided by author/ historian Anthony S. Pitch. Rates are $9 per person, seniors and students $6.

D.C. Heritage Tours (☎ 202/639-0908), co-sponsored by the D.C. Heritage Tourism Coalition and the Discovery Store, leave twice daily from the front of the Discovery Channel Store in the MCI Center, in downtown Washington. A costumed guide tells tales about 19th-century Washington as she takes you in and out of historic sites and through Chinatown, showing you a side of Washington you won't find out about otherwise. Tours last 90 minutes and cost $7.50 per adult, $5 per child under 6 and per senior 55 and older. Before the tour starts, you might want to see the 15-minute film *Destination DC,* shown on the top floor of the Discovery store; the charge is $2.50 per adult, $1.50 per child under 6 and senior.

BY BUS

The Gray Line (☎ 202/289-1995) offers a variety of tours, among them: "Grand Homes and Gardens" (co-sponsored by the D.C. Chamber of Commerce and the D.C. Heritage Tourism Coalition, each tour lasts 4 hours and costs $30 per person), featuring a choice of 3 neighborhoods—Georgetown, Lafayette Park, or Dupont Circle; "Washington After Dark" (3 hours; $25 per adult, $12 per child), focusing on night-lit national monuments and federal buildings; and the "Washington, D.C., All-Day Combination Tour" ($42 per adult, $21 per child), which includes major Washington sights plus Arlington National Cemetery, Mount Vernon, and Alexandria.

Consider, too, Tourmobile and Old Town Trolley tours (see "Getting Around" in chapter 2 for details).

BY BOAT

Since Washington is a river city, why not see it by boat? Potomac cruises allow sweeping vistas of the monuments and memorials, Georgetown, the Kennedy Center, and other Washington sights.

Some of the following boats leave from the Washington waterfront and some from Old Town Alexandria:

Spirit of Washington Cruises, Pier 4 at 6th and Water Streets SW (☎ 202/554-8000; Metro: Waterfront), offers a variety of trips daily from early March through October, including evening dinner, lunch and brunch, and moonlight dance cruises, as well as a half-day excursion to Mount Vernon and back. Lunch and dinner cruises include a 40-minute, high-energy musical revue. Prices range from $23.50 for a sightseeing (no meals) excursion to Mount Vernon, which takes 5^{1}/$_{2}$ hours in all, including a 2-hour tour break, to $65.30 for a Friday or Saturday dinner cruise, drinks not included. Call to make reservations in advance.

The **Capitol River Cruise's** *Nightingale II* (☎ **800/405-5511** or 301/460-7447) is a historic 65-foot steel riverboat that can accommodate up to 90 people. The *Nightingale II*'s narrated jaunts depart Georgetown's Washington Harbour every hour on the hour, from noon until 8pm weekdays and 9pm weekends, April through October. The 50-minute narrated tour travels past the monuments and memorials as you head to National Airport and back. A snack bar on board sells light refreshments, beer, wine, and sodas; you're welcome to bring your own picnic aboard. The price is $10 per adult, $5 per child ages 3 to 12. To get here, take the Metro to Foggy Bottom and then walk into Georgetown, following Pennsylvania Avenue, which becomes M Street. Turn left on 31st Street NW, which dead-ends at the Washington Harbour complex.

9 Outdoor Pursuits

BICYCLING   Both **Fletcher's Boat House** and **Thompson's Boat Center** (see "Boating," below) rent bikes, as does **Big Wheel Bikes,** 1034 33rd St. NW, right near the C&O Canal just below M Street (☎ **202/337-0254**). The rate is $5 per hour, with a 3-hour minimum, or $25 for the day. Shop opens at 10am daily, closing times vary. There's another Big Wheel shop on Capitol Hill at 315 7th St. SE (☎ **202/543-1600**); call for hours. Photo ID and a major credit card are required to rent bicycles.

On Fridays, the *Washington Post* "Weekend" section lists cycling trips. Rock Creek Park has an 11-mile paved bike route from the Lincoln Memorial through the park into Maryland. On weekends and holidays, a large part of it is closed to vehicular traffic. The C&O Canal and the Potomac Parks, described earlier in "Parks & Gardens," also have extended bike paths.

BOATING   Thompson's Boat Center, 2900 Virginia Ave. at Rock Creek Parkway NW (☎ **202/333-4861** or 202/333-9543; Metro: Foggy Bottom with a 10-minute walk), rents canoes, kayaks, rowing shells (recreational and racing), and bikes. They also offer sculling and sweep-rowing lessons. Photo ID and a credit card are required for rentals. They're open for boat rentals usually from early May to the end of September, daily 8am to 6pm. Bike rentals range from $4 for the most basic to $22 for the fanciest.

Late March to mid-September, you can rent paddleboats on the north end of the Tidal Basin off Independence Avenue (☎ **202/ 479-2426**). You have the choice of renting a four-seater for $14 an hour or a two-seater for $7 an hour. Hours are 10am to about an hour before sunset daily.

GOLF   Within the District **East Potomac Park** and **Rock Creek Park** have the only public courses. Fees run from $9 weekdays for 9 holes to $19 weekends for 18 holes. The 18-hole Rock Creek Golf Course and clubhouse, at 16th and Rittenhouse Streets NW (☎ **202/882-7332**), are open to the public daily year-round from dawn to dusk. You will find a snack bar on the premises, and you can rent clubs and carts.

East Potomac Park has one 18-hole, par-72 layout, and two 9-hole courses. For details, call ☎ **202/554-7660.**

JOGGING   A parcourse jogging path, a gift from Perrier, opened in Rock Creek Park in 1978. Its $1^{1}/_{2}$-mile oval route, beginning near the intersection of Calvert Street NW and Rock Creek Parkway (directly behind the Omni Shoreham Hotel), includes 18 calisthenics stations with instructions on prescribed exercises. There's another Perrier parcourse, with only four stations, at 16th and Kennedy Streets NW. Other popular jogging areas are the C&O Canal and the Mall.

10 Spectator Sports

TICKETS   For tickets to most events, call ☎ **800/551-SEAT** or 202/432-SEAT.

BASEBALL   Lovely 48,000-seat Camden Yards, 333 W. Camden St. (between Howard and Conway Streets), Baltimore (☎ **410/ 685-9800**), is home to the American League's Baltimore Orioles. Unlike recent ultramodern sports stadiums and ugly domes, Camden Yards is an old-fashioned ballpark, unafraid to incorporate features of its urban environment, such as the old B&O Railroad yards. A renovated brick warehouse serves as a striking visual backdrop beyond the right-field fence.

Tickets (which range from $9 to $35) were once impossible to get; now it's possible but still tough, so call ☎ **800/551-SEAT** or 410/481-SEAT well in advance of your visit if you want to catch a game. There are usually scalpers outside the stadium before a game; use your judgment if you try this option. There's a D.C. ticket office as well, at 914 17th St. NW (☎ **202/296-2473**). From Union Station in Washington, take a MARC train to Baltimore, where you are let off right at the ballpark. If you're driving, take I-95 north to Exit 53.

BASKETBALL The Washington Wizards (née Bullets) and the Georgetown Hoyas play home games at the newly opened MCI Center (☎ **202/628-3200**), at 7th and F Streets NW, adjacent to the Gallery Place Metro station in downtown Washington. Tickets cost $19 to $65 for the Wizards and $5 to $16 for the Hoyas.

FOOTBALL The Washington Redskins played their last home game at RFK Stadium in 1997 and now play at the new Jack Kent Cooke Stadium, 1600 Raljohn Rd., Raljohn, MD 20785 (☎ **301/276-6050;** Metro: Addison Road, with bus shuttle to stadium). Tickets for Redskins games have been sold out since Lyndon Johnson was in the White House, so forget about getting your hands on one, unless you're willing to shove out $250 for a club-level seat.

The Baltimore Ravens (formerly the Cleveland Browns, until Art Modell moved the team and broke the city's heart) started off the 1998–1999 season in their new home, the Ravens Stadium, right next to Camden Yards. Tickets cost $17 to $75; for more information, call ☎ **410/261-7283.**

HOCKEY Home ice for the NHL's Washington Capitals is now the MCI Center (☎ **202/628-3200**), at 7th and F Streets NW, adjacent to the Gallery Place Metro station. Tickets cost $19 to $50.

6

Shopping the District

*T*here's no such thing as a Washington shopping district—shops and boutiques are scattered throughout the city, from Union Station or Capitol Hill, to the streets of Georgetown.

1 Shopping A to Z

ANTIQUES

While you won't find many bargains in Washington area antique stores, you will see beautiful and rare decorative furniture, silver, jewelry, art, and fabrics, from Amish quilts to Chinese silks. Antique shops dot the greater Washington landscape, but the richest concentrations are in **Old Town Alexandria; Capitol Hill; Georgetown; Adams-Morgan;** and **Kensington, Maryland**.

Antiques-on-the-Hill. 701 North Carolina Ave. SE. ☎ **202/543-1819.** Metro: Eastern Market.

A Capitol Hill institution since the 1960s, this place sells silver; furniture; glassware; jewelry; porcelain; and lamps.

✪ **The Brass Knob Architectural Antiques.** 2311 18th St. NW. ☎ **202/332-3370.** Metro: Dupont Circle.

When early homes and office buildings are demolished in the name of progress, these savvy salvage merchants spirit away saleable treasures, from chandeliers to wrought-iron fencing. Cross the street to its other location: The Brass Knob's Back Doors, 2329 Champlain St. NW (☎ **202/265-0587**).

Cherishables. 1608 20th St. NW. ☎ **202/785-4087.** www.washingtonpost. com/yp/cherishables. Metro: Dupont Circle.

An adorable shop specializing in 18th- and 19th-century American furniture, folk art, quilts, and decorative accessories. The furniture is displayed in roomlike settings. The store stocks a world-renowned line of Christmas ornaments designed each year around a new theme: the garden, architecture, and breeds of dogs are some from years past.

ART GALLERIES

Art galleries abound in Washington, but they are especially prolific in the **Dupont Circle** and **Georgetown neighborhoods** and along 7th Street, downtown. For a complete listing of local galleries, get your hands on a copy of *Galleries,* a monthly guide to major galleries and their shows; the guide is available free at many hotel concierge desks and at each of the galleries listed in the publication. Here's a selection of top places.

DUPONT CIRCLE

For all galleries listed below, the closest Metro stop is Dupont Circle.

Addison/Ripley Gallery, Ltd.. 9 Hillyer Court NW. ☎ **202/328-2332.** Metro: Dupont Circle.

This gallery displays contemporary paintings, sculpture, and drawings by Americans, some but not all by locals. Edith Kuhnle, Richard Hunt, and Wols Kahn are a few of the artists represented here. There is a second location at 1670 Wisconsin Ave. NW (☎ **202/ 333-3335**).

GEORGETOWN

If you're not driving, take a cab, a "30" series bus, or the Metro. If you Metro it, hop off at the Foggy Bottom station, walk up to Washington Circle, turn left and follow Pennsylvania Avenue, which becomes M Street, into Georgetown.

Govinda Gallery. 1227 34th St. NW. ☎ **202/333-1180.**

You read about this one in the newspaper because it often shows pictures of celebrity musicians taken by well-known photographers.

SEVENTH STREET ARTS CORRIDOR

A renaissance is taking place on 7th Street, which lies at the heart of downtown Washington, in the general vicinity of the MCI Center. These galleries were here before (in the case of the Michelson Gallery, try 40 years before) there was even talk of an MCI Center, and where once these galleries languished among office buildings, their neighbors now are trendy restaurants and bars.

406 Group. 406 7th St. NW, between D and E sts. Metro: Archives–Navy Memorial.

Several first-rate art galleries, some interlopers from Dupont Circle, occupy this historic building, with its 13-foot-high ceilings and spacious rooms. They include **David Adamson Gallery** (☎ **202/**

628-0257), which is probably the largest gallery space in D.C., with two levels showing the works of contemporary artists, including locals Kevin MacDonald and rising star Renee Stout, and prints and drawings by David Hockney; and the very expensive **Baumgartner Galleries** (☎ **202/347-2211**), displaying national and international artists. Although this gallery gets a lot of good press, other galleries have works every bit as impressive, or more so. Try **Touchstone Gallery** (☎ **202/347-2787**), which is a self-run co-op of 15 artists who take turns exhibiting their work.

BEAUTY

With a few exceptions, the best salons are in **Georgetown** and cater to both men and women. If you don't want to take a chance, these are the places to go. Expect to spend a little money.

Interiano Salon. 1025 31st St. NW. ☎ **202/333-3455.** Metro: Foggy Bottom with a 15-minute walk.

Gloria (Interiano) has been cutting my husband's hair for 20 years now and mine about half that time. Other patrons are often Washington insiders whose names, if not faces, you will recognize. Gloria, herself, is pretty down to earth, and so are her rates: $35 for men, $60 for women.

✪ **Okyo.** 2903 M St. NW. ☎ **202/342-2675.** Metro: Foggy Bottom, with a 10-minute walk, or take one of the 30-series buses (30, 32, 34, 36, 38B) from downtown into Georgetown.

Owner Bernard Portelli colored Catherine Deneuve's hair in France, and he's so booked that he isn't taking any new clients. They only do hair here, at surprisingly reasonable rates: cuts start at $50 for women, $30 for men.

BOOKS

Washingtonians are readers, so bookstores pop up throughout the city. An increasingly competitive market means that stores besides Crown Books offer discounts. Here are favorite bookstores in general, used, and special-interest categories.

Barnes & Noble. 3040 M St. NW. ☎ **202/965-9880.**

This is a wonderful three-story shop that discounts all hardcovers 10%, *New York Times* hardcover best-sellers 30%, and *New York Times* paperback best-sellers 20%. It has sizable software, travel-book, and children's sections. A cafe on the second level hosts concerts. Open daily 9am to 11pm.

B. Dalton. Union Station. ☎ **202/289-1750.** Metro: Union Station.

Your average all-round bookstore, heavy on the best-sellers. They sell magazines, too.

Borders Books & Music. 1800 L St. NW. ☎ **202/466-4999.** Metro: Farragut North.

With its overwhelming array of books, records, videos, and magazines, this outpost of the rapidly expanding chain has taken over the town. Most hardcovers are 10% off; *New York Times* and *Washington Post* hardcover best-sellers are 30% off. People hang out here, hovering over the magazines or sipping espresso in the cafe as they read their books. The store often hosts performances by local musicians.

Kramerbooks & Afterwords Café. 1517 Connecticut Ave. NW. ☎ **202/387-1400.** Metro: Dupont Circle.

The first bookstore/cafe in the Dupont Circle area, this place has launched countless romances. It's jammed and often noisy, stages live music Wednesday through Saturday evenings, and is open all night on weekends. Paperback fiction takes up most of its inventory, but the store carries a little of everything. It does not offer discounts.

Olsson's Books and Records. 1239 Wisconsin Ave. NW, between M and N sts. ☎ **202/338-9544.**

This 21-year-old, independent, quality bookstore chain has about 60,000 to 70,000 books on its shelves. Members of the helpful staff know what they're talking about and will order books the store doesn't have in stock. Competition has forced them to offer discounts: 25% off *Washington Post* best-sellers, 20% off certain hardcover books, and 10% off certain paperbacks that are promoted as "good reads" by store staff. Similar discounts exist for tapes and CDs. Regular prices are pretty good. Open Monday to Thursday 10am to 11pm, Friday and Saturday 10am to midnight, Sunday 11am to 11pm.

Travel Books & Language Center. 4437 Wisconsin Ave. NW. ☎ **800/220-2665** or 202/237-1322. Metro: Tenleytown.

Its move in November 1997 to new digs tripled the space of this 14-year-old travel bookstore, which has the best-in-the-area assortment of guidebooks and maps covering the entire world, as well as language dictionaries and learning tapes, travel diaries, memoirs, and novels famous for their evocation of particular places.

Trover Shop. 227 Pennsylvania Ave. SE. ☎ **202/543-8006.** Metro: Capitol South.

The only general bookstore on Capitol Hill, Trover's strengths are its political selections and its magazines. The store discounts 20% on *Washington Post* hardcover fiction and nonfiction best-sellers, computer books, and cookbooks.

CAMERAS & PHOTOGRAPHIC EQUIPMENT

Ritz Camera Centers. 1740 Pennsylvania Ave. NW. ☎ **202/466-3470.** Metro: Farragut West.

This place sells camera equipment and develops film with 1-hour processing for the average photographer. Call for other locations— there are many throughout the area.

CRAFTS

American Hand Plus. 2906 M St. NW. ☎ **202/965-3273.**

This crafts shop features exquisite contemporary handcrafted American ceramics and jewelry, plus international objets d'art. Open Monday to Saturday 11am to 6pm, Sunday 1 to 5pm.

Appalachian Spring. 1415 Wisconsin Ave. NW, at P St. ☎ **202/337-5780.**

This store brings country crafts to citified Georgetown. You'll find pottery, jewelry, newly made pieced and appliqué quilts, stuffed dolls and animals, candles, rag rugs, hand-blown glassware, an incredible collection of kaleidoscopes, glorious weavings, and wooden kitchenware. Everything in the store is made by hand in the United States. There's another branch in Union Station (☎ **202/682-0505**). Open Monday to Saturday 10am to 8pm, Sunday noon to 6pm.

Indian Craft Shop. Department of the Interior, 1849 C St. NW, Room 1023. ☎ **202/208-4056.** Weekday hours only. Metro: Farragut West or Foggy Bottom.

The Indian Craft Shop has represented authentic Native American artisans since 1938, selling their handwoven rugs and handcrafted baskets, jewelry, figurines, paintings, pottery, and other items. You need a photo ID to enter the building.

The Phoenix. 1514 Wisconsin Ave. NW. ☎ **202/338-4404.** Metro: Foggy Bottom, with a 30-minute walk, or take one of the 30-series buses (30, 32, 34, 36, 38B) from downtown into Georgetown.

Around since 1955, the Phoenix still sells those embroidered Mexican peasant blouses popular in hippie days; Mexican folk and fine

art; handcrafted, sterling silver jewelry from Mexico and all over the
world; clothing in natural fibers from Mexican and American
designers like Eileen Fisher and Flax; collector-quality masks; and
decorative doodads in tin, brass, copper, and wood.

DEPARTMENT STORES

Hecht's. Metro Center, 1201 G St. NW. ☎ **202/628-6661.** Metro: Metro
Center.

Everything from mattresses to electronics, children's underwear to
luggage, can be bought in this mid-priced emporium.

Lord & Taylor. 5255 Western Ave. NW. ☎ **202/362-9600.** Metro: Friendship Heights.

This is another lesser version of a New York chain, although lately
the store has vastly improved its selections. The staff, too, seems
more professional and helpful than in the past. Its women's clothing and accessories departments are probably its strong suit; go elsewhere for gadgets and gifts.

Macy's. Fashion Center at Pentagon City, 1000 S. Hayes St., Arlington, VA.
☎ **703/418-4488.** Metro: Pentagon City.

A household name for many East Coasters, this Macy's (although
nowhere near the size of its Manhattan counterpart) hopes to ful-
fill the same role for Washington customers. Expect mid- to upscale
merchandise and prices.

✪ **Nordstrom.** Fashion Center at Pentagon City, 1400 S. Hayes St., Arlington,
VA. ☎ **703/415-1121.** Metro: Pentagon City.

This Seattle-based retailer's reputation for exceptional service is well
deserved—a call to the main information number confirms this. In
keeping with the store's beginnings as a shoe store, this location has
three entire departments devoted to women's shoes (designer, dressy,
and just plain fun); if you can't find your size or color, they'll
order it.

FARMERS' & FLEA MARKETS

Alexandria Farmers' Market. 301 King St., at Market Sq. in front of the city
hall, in Alexandria. ☎ **703/370-8723.** Sat 5:30–10am. Metro: King St., then
take the DASH bus (AT2 or AT5) eastbound to Market Square.

The oldest continually operating farmers' market in the country
(since 1752), this market offers the usual assortment of locally grown
fruits and vegetables, along with delectable baked goods, cut flowers, and plants.

✪ **Eastern Market.** 225 7th St. SE, between North Carolina Ave. and C St. ☎ **202/546-2698.** Metro: Eastern Market.

This is the one everyone knows about, even if they've never been here. Located on Capitol Hill, Eastern Market is an inside/outside bazaar of stalls, where greengrocers, butchers, bakers, farmers, artists, crafts people, florists and other merchants vend their wares daily (except Monday), but especially on weekends. Saturday morning is the best time to go. On Sundays, the food stalls become a flea market.

✪ **Georgetown Flea Market.** In a parking lot bordering Wisconsin Ave., between S and T sts. NW. ☎ **202/223-0289.** Open Mar–Dec, Sun 9am–5pm. Metro: Foggy Bottom, with a 30- to 40-minute walk, or take one of the 30-series buses (30, 32, 34, 36, 38B) from downtown into Georgetown.

Grab a coffee at Starbucks across the lane and get ready to barter. The Georgetown Flea Market is an institution frequented by all types of Washingtonians looking for a good deal—they often get it—on antiques, painted furniture, vintage clothing, and decorative garden urns. Nearly 100 vendors sell their wares here.

MALLS

The Shops at Georgetown Park. 3222 M St. NW. ☎ **202/342-8180.** Metro: Foggy Bottom, then a 20-minute walk.

This is a deluxe mall, where you'll see beautiful people shopping for beautiful things, and paying stunning prices at stores with European names: Nicolo (men's clothes), Arpelli's (leather goods). The diplomatic set and well-heeled foreign travelers favor these stores, so you're bound to hear a number of languages, especially French and Italian. Wander here, then set off for the streets of Georgetown for more shopping.

Mazza Gallerie. 5100 Wisconsin Ave. NW. ☎ **202/966-6114.** Metro: Friendship Heights.

Undergoing a renovation scheduled for completion in 1999, the mall is looking down at its heels right now, despite the presence of Neiman-Marcus, and the fact that McDonald's is the mall's main restaurant doesn't help. With sprucing up, the Mazza should return as an attractive shopping center, with its skylit atrium and stores like Ann Taylor and Benetton's. The mall has theaters on the lower level, and there is access to Chevy Chase Pavilion, the subway, and to the Hecht's department store via the Metro tunnel.

The Pavilion at the Old Post Office. 1100 Pennsylvania Ave. NW. ☎ **202/ 289-4224.** Metro: Federal Triangle.

This is a tourist trap with souvenir shops and a food court. Noon-time concerts are a draw, as is the view of the city from the building's clock tower, 315 feet up.

Potomac Mills. 30 miles south on I-95. Accessible by car, or by shuttle bus leaving from designated places throughout the area, including Dupont Circle and Metro Center. Call ☎ **800/VA-MILLS** or **1-703/490-5948** for information about Potomac Mills; call ☎ **1-703/551-1050** for information about the shuttle bus service.

When you are stuck in the traffic that always clogs this section of I-95, you may wonder if a trip to Potomac Mills is worth it. Believe it or not, this place attracts more visitors than any other in the Washington area, and twice as many as the next top draw, the Smithsonian's National Air & Space Museum. It's the largest indoor outlet mall around, with more than 225 shops, including New York's Barney's, DKNY, Nordstrom's, IKEA, Samsonite, and Jones New York.

Union Station. 50 Massachusetts Ave. NE. ☎ **202/371-9441.** Metro: Union Station.

After the National Air & Space Museum, this is the next most popular stop in Washington. The architecture is magnificent. The mall's more than 120 shops include the Nature Company, Brookstone, and Appalachian Spring; among the places to eat are America, B. Smith, and an international food court. There's also a nine-screen movie theater complex.

MEN'S CLOTHES & SHOES

Brooks Brothers. 1840 L St. NW. ☎ **202/659-4650.** Metro: Farragut West or Farragut North.

This is where to go for the K Street/Capitol Hill pinstriped power look. Brooks Bros. sells the fine line of Peal's English shoes. This store made the news as the place where Monica Lewinsky bought a tie for President Clinton. The store has other locations at Potomac Mills (see "Malls," above) and at 5500 Wisconsin Ave., in Chevy Chase, MD.

Burberry's. 1155 Connecticut Ave. NW. ☎ **202/463-3000.** Metro: Farragut North.

Here you'll find those plaid-lined trench coats, of course, along with well-tailored but conservative English clothing for men and women.

Gianfranco Ferre. 5301 Wisconsin Ave. NW. ☎ **202/244-6633.** Metro: Friendship Heights.

Shop here for the sleek and sexy European look. This store also features interesting suits and some casual wear.

POLITICAL MEMORABILIA

Capitol Coin and Stamp Co. Inc. 1701 L St. NW. ☎ **202/296-0400.** Metro: Farragut North.

A museum of political memorabilia—pins, posters, banners—and all of it is for sale. This is also a fine resource for the endangered species of coin and stamp collectors.

✪ **Political Americana.** Union Station. ☎ **202/547-1685.** Metro: Union Station.

This is another great place to pick up souvenirs from a visit to D.C. The store sells political novelty items; books; bumper stickers; old campaign buttons; and historical memorabilia. A second location is at 685 15th St. NW (☎ **202/547-1817**).

RECORDS, TAPES & CDS

Borders Books & Music. 1800 L St. NW. ☎ **202/466-4999.** Metro: Farragut North.

Besides being a fabulous bookstore, Borders offers the best prices in town for CDs and tapes and a wide range of music.

HMV. 1229 Wisconsin Ave. NW. ☎ **202/333-9292.** Metro: Foggy Bottom, with a 20-minute walk.

This London-based record and tape store is fun to visit, with its cunning clientele, party atmosphere, and headphones at the ready for easy listening. But you can get a better deal almost anywhere else.

Melody Record Shop. 1623 Connecticut Ave. NW. ☎ **202/232-4002.** Metro: Dupont Circle, Q St. exit.

CDs, cassettes, and tapes are discounted 10% to 20% here, new releases 20% to 30%. Melody offers a wide variety of rock, classical, jazz, pop, show, folk music, and international selections. This is also a good place to shop for discounted portable electronic equipment, blank tapes, and cassettes. The knowledgeable staff is a plus.

Olsson's Books & Records. See entry above under "Books."

Tower Records. 2000 Pennsylvania Ave. NW. ☎ **202/331-2400.** Metro: Foggy Bottom.

When you need a record at midnight on Christmas Eve, you go to Tower. The large, funky store, across the street from George Washington University, has a wide choice of records, cassettes, and compact discs in every category—but the prices are high.

WOMEN'S CLOTHES & SHOES

Ann Taylor. Union Station. ☎ **202/371-8010.** Metro: Union Station.

Specializes in American-style, chic clothing, Joan and David and other footwear, and accessories. Other locations include 1720 K St. NW (☎ **202/466-3544**), 600 13th St. NW (☎ **202/737-0325**), and Georgetown Park, 3222 M St. NW (☎ **202/338-5290**).

Betsy Fisher. 1224 Connecticut Ave. NW. ☎ **202/785-1975.** Metro: Dupont Circle.

A walk past the store is all it takes to know that this shop is a tad different. Its window front and racks show off whimsically feminine fashions, including hats, of new American Designers.

Commander Salamander. 1420 Wisconsin Ave. NW. ☎ **202/337-2265.** Metro: Foggy Bottom, with a 20-minute walk.

Too cool. Commander Salamander has a little bit of everything, including designer items, some of which are quite affordable: Dolce and Gabanna dresses; Jean Paul Gaultier and Oldham creations; $1 ties; and handmade jackets with Axl jewelry sewn on, for more than $1000. Loud music, young crowd, funky and sweet.

7

Washington, D.C., After Dark

*I*n Washington, you'll find a cornucopia of entertainment options, from attending a Shakespeare play to laughing it up at the Improv Comedy Club. The venues for every type of theater, dance, and musical entertainment are here, with new ones opening everyday. If your idea of relaxation involves a visit to a bar or a nightclub, you won't be disappointed, either

In addition to the listings below, check the Friday "Weekend" section of the *Washington Post*, which will inform you about children's theater, sports events, flower shows, and all else. The *City Paper*, available free at restaurants, bookstores, and other places around town, is another good source.

TICKETS

TICKETplace, Washington's only discount, day-of-show, ticket outlet, has one location: in the Old Post Office Pavilion, 1100 Pennsylvania Ave. NW (Metro: Federal Triangle). Call ☎ **202/ TICKETS** for information. TICKETplace is a service of the Cultural Alliance of Greater Washington. On the day of performance only (except Sunday and Monday, see below), you can buy half-price tickets (with cash, select debit cards, or traveler's checks) to performances at most major Washington area theaters and concert halls. TICKETplace is open Tuesday to Saturday from 11am to 6pm; half-price tickets for Sunday and Monday shows are sold on Saturday. Although you purchase the ticket for half price, you will have to pay a service charge, 10% of the full face value of the ticket.

Full-price tickets for most performances in town can be bought through **Ticketmaster** (☎ **202/432-SEAT**) at Hecht's Department Store, 12th and G Streets NW, and at George Washington University's Lisner Auditorium, 1730 21st St. NW (at H Street; Metro: Foggy Bottom). You can purchase tickets to Washington theatrical, musical, and other events before you leave home by calling ☎ **800/551-SEAT.** Another similar ticket outlet is **Protix** (☎ **800/955-5566** or 703/218-6500).

1   Theater

Theatrical productions in Washington, D.C., are first-rate and varied. Almost anything on Broadway has either been previewed here or will eventually come here. Washington, D.C., also has several nationally acclaimed repertory companies and a theater specializing in Shakespearean productions.

Ford's Theatre. 511 10th St. NW (between E and F sts.). ☎ **202/347-4833**, TDD 202/347-5599 for listings, 800/955-5566 or 703/218-6500 to charge tickets. Tickets $27–$40; discounts available for families, also for senior citizens at matinee performances and any time on the "day of" for evening shows; both seniors and students with ID can get "rush" tickets an hour before performances if tickets are available. Metro: Metro Center or Gallery Place.

This is the theater where, on the evening of April 14, 1865, actor John Wilkes Booth shot President Abraham Lincoln. The assassination marked the end of what had been John T. Ford's very popular theater; it remained closed for more than a century. In 1968, Ford's reopened, completely restored to its 1865 appearance, based on photographs, sketches, newspaper articles and samples of wallpaper and curtain material from museum collections.

Ford's season is more or less year-round (it's closed for a while in the summer). Several of its productions have gone on to Broadway and off-Broadway.

National Theatre. 1321 Pennsylvania Ave. NW. ☎ **202/628-6161** or 800/447-7400 to charge tickets by phone. Tickets $30–$75; discounts available for students, seniors, military personnel, and people with disabilities. Metro: Metro Center.

The luxurious, Federal-style National Theatre is the oldest continuously operating theater in Washington (since 1835) and the third-oldest in the nation. It's exciting just to see this stage where Sarah Bernhardt, John Barrymore, Helen Hayes, and so many other notables have performed. The National is the closest thing Washington has to a Broadway-style playhouse. Managed by New York's Shubert Organization, it presents star-studded hits, often pre- or post-Broadway, most of the year.

The National also offers free Saturday-morning children's theater (puppets, clowns, magicians, dancers, and singers), summer films, and Monday-night showcases of local groups and performers. Call ☎ 202/783-3372 for details.

Shakespeare Theatre. 450 7th St. NW (between D and E sts.). ☎ **202/393-2700.** Tickets $14–$56, $10 for standing-room tickets sold 1 hour before sold-out performances; discounts available for students, groups, and senior citizens. Metro: Archives–Navy Memorial or Gallery Place.

This internationally renowned classical ensemble company, which for 2 decades performed at the Folger Shakespeare Library, moved to larger quarters at the above address in 1992. The company also offers one admission-free, 2-week run of a Shakespeare production at the Carter Barron Amphitheatre in Rock Creek Park (see listing for Carter Barron below, under "Outdoor Pavilions & Stadiums").

Source Theatre Company. 1835 14th St. NW (between S and T sts.). ☎ **202/462-1073** for information or 301/738-7073 to charge tickets. Tickets $20–$25, OFF HOURS shows $15, Washington Theatre Festival shows $8–$15.

Washington's major producer of new plays, the Source also mounts works of established playwrights. The theater is also used for an OFF HOURS series of productions geared to a contemporary urban audience. Annual events here include the **Washington Theatre Festival** each July, a 4-week showcase of about 50 new plays.

2 Other Performing Arts

The following listings are a potpourri of places offering a mixed bag of theater, opera, classical music, headliners, jazz, rock, dance, and comedy. Here you'll find some of the top entertainment choices in the district.

MULTICULTURAL FACILITIES

DAR Constitution Hall. 18th and D sts. NW. ☎ **202/628-4780**, 800/551-SEAT or 202/432-SEAT to charge tickets. Tickets $15–$50. Metro: Farragut West.

Housed within a beautiful, turn-of-the-century, beaux-arts–style building is this fine, 3,746-seat auditorium. Its excellent acoustics make it a prime venue for hearing the eclectic music that plays here from the Boston Symphony to John Hiatt.

The Folger Shakespeare Library. 201 E. Capitol St. SE. ☎ **202/544-7077.** Students and seniors receive discounts with proof of ID. Call for information about ticket prices, which can range from $5 to $40, depending upon the event. Metro: Capitol South.

The Folger Shakespeare Library is open year-round for exhibits in and tours of its Tudor-style great rooms. Its theatrical programs and special events generally coincide with the academic year, from October through May. Among the offerings are the **Folger Consort,** a music ensemble that performs medieval, Renaissance, and baroque music; troubadour songs; madrigals; and court ensembles. Between October and May, the group gives 30 concerts over the course of 7 weekends.

The Folger presents theatrical and musical performances, lectures, readings, and other events in its Elizabethan Theatre, which is styled after the innyard theatre from Shakespeare's time.

John F. Kennedy Center for the Performing Arts. At the southern end of New Hampshire Ave. NW and Rock Creek Pkwy. ☎ **800/444-1324** or 202/ 467-4600. kennedy-center.org. 50% discounts are offered (for most attractions) to students, seniors 65 and over, people with permanent disabilities, and enlisted military personnel with a valid ID. Garage parking $8. Metro: Foggy Bottom (it's a fairly short walk, but a free shuttle between the station and the Kennedy Center departs every 15 minutes from 7pm to midnight). Bus: 80 from Metro Center.

Our national performing arts center, the hub of Washington's cultural and entertainment scene, is actually made up of six different theaters. You can find out what is scheduled during your stay (and charge tickets) before leaving home by calling the above toll-free number. Half-price tickets are available for full-time students, senior citizens, enlisted military personnel, people with disabilities, and persons with fixed, low income (call ☎ **202/416-8340** for details).

The Kennedy Center's free concert series, known as **"Millennium Stage,"** features daily performances by area musicians, staged each evening at 6pm in the center's Grand Foyer. The Friday "Weekend" section of the *Washington Post* lists the free performances scheduled for the coming week. Also call about "pay what you can" performances, scheduled throughout the year on certain days, for certain shows.

Opera House This plush red-and-gilt, 2,300-seat theater is designed for ballet, modern dance, and musical comedy, as well as opera.

Eisenhower Theater A wide range of dramatic productions, solo performances, and dance presentations can be seen here.

Concert Hall This is the home of the National Symphony Orchestra, which presents concerts from September to June. Tickets are available by subscription and for individual performances. Guest artists have included Itzhak Perlman, Vladimir Ashkenazy, Zubin Mehta, Pinchas Zukerman, André Previn, Jean-Pierre Rampal, and Isaac Stern. Headliner entertainers such as Ray Charles, Patti LuPone, Bill Cosby, and Harry Belafonte also have appeared here.

Terrace Theater   Small chamber works, choral recitals, musicals, comedy revues, cabarets, and theatrical and modern-dance performances are among the varied provinces of the 500-seat Terrace Theater, a bicentennial gift from Japan.

Theater Lab and More   By day, the Theater Lab is Washington's premier stage for children's theater. Evenings it becomes a cabaret, now in a long run of *Shear Madness*, a comedy whodunit (tickets are $25 to $29).

Parking   Limited underground parking at the Kennedy Center is $8 for the entire evening after 5pm; if that lot is full, go to the Columbia Plaza Garage, at 2400 Virginia Ave. NW, which runs a free shuttle back to the facility.

Warner Theatre. 1299 Pennsylvania Ave. NW (entrance on 13th St., between E and F sts.). ☎ **800/551-SEAT,** 202/783-4000, or 202/432-SEAT to charge tickets. www.warnertheatre.com. Play tickets $20–$60. Metro: Metro Center. Parking is available in the Warner Building PMI lot on 12th St. NW, for $6.

Opened in 1924 as the Earle Theatre (a movie/vaudeville palace) and restored to its original appearance in 1992 at a cost of $10 million, this stunning neoclassical-style theater features a 2,000-seat auditorium that offers year-round entertainment, alternating dance performances and Broadway/off-Broadway shows with headliner entertainment (Sheryl Crow; k. d. lang; Natalie Merchant; Chris Isaak; Wynton Marsalis).

ARENAS

MCI Center. 601 F St. NW, where it meets 7th St. ☎ **202/628-3200.** To charge tickets by phone, call 800/551-SEAT or 202/432-SEAT. Very limited parking on-site, surface lots and garages in neighborhood, but your best bet is the Metro. The Gallery Place stop lies just beneath the building.

Set on 5 acres in a prime downtown location, the MCI Center is open 365 days a year, not just as a sports facility, but as a location for rock and country music concerts and business conferences. Within the three-story complex are a 25,000 square-foot Discovery Channel, Destination D.C. retail store, a National Sports Gallery (an interactive sports museum), and three restaurants.

US Airways Arena. 1 Harry S Truman Dr., Exit 15A or 17A off the Capital Beltway in Landover, MD. ☎ **800/551-SEAT** or 301/350-3400.

This 19,000-seat arena hosts a variety of concerts and headliner entertainment, ranging from Pavarotti to AC/DC; it's also home to the Washington Warthogs indoor soccer games, Washington International Horse Show, and monster truck events.

OUTDOOR PAVILIONS & STADIUMS

Carter Barron Amphitheater. 4850 Colorado Ave. NW, at 16th St. ☎ **202/ 260-6836.** Take Metro to Silver Spring, transfer to bus no. S2 or S4, with "Federal Triangle" destination sign, and let the driver know you wish to hop off at the 16th St. bus stop nearest the Carter Barron; the amphitheater is a 5-minute walk from that stop.

Way out on 16th Street (near the Maryland border) is this 4,250-seat amphitheater in Rock Creek Park. Summer performances include a range of gospel, blues, and classical entertainment, though each year is different. You can always count on Shakespeare: **The Shakespeare Theatre Free for All** takes place at the Carter Barron usually for 2 weeks in June, Tuesday through Sunday evenings. The free tickets are available the day of performance only, on a first-come, first-served basis (call ☎ **202/628-5770** for details).

Robert F. Kennedy Memorial Stadium/D.C. Armory. 2400 E. Capitol St. SE. ☎ **202/547-9077;** 800/551-SEAT or 202/432-SEAT to charge tickets. Metro: Stadium-Armory.

Until 1998, RFK was the home stadium for the Washington Redskins football team, who now play at the new Jack Kent Cooke facility in Raljohn, Maryland. The stadium continues as a spring, summer, fall event facility, packing crowds of 55,000-plus into its seats to hear concerts by the Rolling Stones, the Eagles, and other big name groups, and to watch D.C. United Major League soccer and college football.

The D.C. Armory, right next door, is a year-round venue for the Ringling Brothers Barnum and Bailey Circus, antique shows, and other events that require space for as many as 10,000 people.

3 The Club & Music Scene

The best nightlife districts are **Adams-Morgan;** the area around **U and 14th Streets NW,** a newly developing district yet still a relatively dangerous part of town; the **7th Street NW corridor** near Chinatown and the MCI Center; and **Georgetown**. As a rule, while city-clubbing—even in Georgetown—stick to the major thoroughfares and steer clear of deserted side streets. The best source of information about what's doing at bars and clubs is *City Paper*, which is available free at bookstores, movie theaters, drugstores, and other locations.

COMEDY

In addition to Chelsea's, be sure to catch **Gross National Product,** a political satire troupe that appears at Chief Ike's Mambo Room every Saturday night. (See Chief Ike's listing in this section.) Big-name comedians also perform around town at such places as Constitution Hall.

Chelsea's. 1055 Thomas Jefferson St. NW (in the Foundry Building on the C&O Canal). ☎ **202/298-8222.** $50 for dinner and show, $33.50 for show only. Fri and Sat nights. Metro: Foggy Bottom, with a 10-minute walk. Complimentary parking in building garage.

This nightclub in the Foundry Building on the C&O Canal is home base for the Capitol Steps comedy satire troupe, whose claim to fame is poking fun at Washington institutions through song. Their shows are at 5:30pm Saturday, 6pm Friday. See Chelsea's listing under "International Sounds," in this chapter, for information about Latino and Arabic music and dancing nights here.

POP/ROCK

The Ballroom. 1015 Half St. SE (at K St.). ☎ **202/554-1500.** www.cellardoor.com. Cover: Fri–Sat $9–12; Sun–Thurs $8–$30, depending on the performer. Open most weekend nights, and often weeknights, depending upon performance schedule. Metro: Navy Yard.

Occupying a vast converted boiler-company warehouse consisting of a cavernous space, a bigger cavernous space, and a half dozen bars, this place is generally a Gen-X mecca (although some performers attract an older crowd). It's also D.C.'s largest club, accommodating upward of 1,500 people a night.

The Bayou. 3135 K St. NW (under the Whitehurst Fwy., near Wisconsin Ave.). ☎ **202/333-2897.** www.cellardoor.com. Cover: $5–$25. Open most weekend nights, and often weeknights, depending upon performance schedule. Metro: Foggy Bottom, with 25-minute walk.

This lively nightclub, located on the Georgetown waterfront, features a mixed bag of live musical entertainment, mostly progressive, reggae, and alternative sounds. Discounts $2 off the $5 cover if you're dressed in disco attire.

Black Cat. 1831 14th St. NW (between S and T sts.). ☎ **202/667-7960.** Cover: $5–$10 for concerts; no cover in the Red Room. Open nightly, with concerts held 4 or 5 nights a week. Metro: U St.–Cardozo.

This comfortable, low-key, everyone-in-black-clothes bar has a large, funky, red-walled living-roomy lounge with booths and tables, a red-leather sofa, pinball machines, a pool table, and a jukebox stocked with a really eclectic collection. College crowds gather here on weekends, but you can count on seeing a 20- to 30-something bunch here most nights, including members of various bands who like to stop in for a drink. There's live music in the adjoining room, essentially a large dance floor (it accommodates about 400 people) with stages at both ends. Entertainment is primarily alternative rock.

Chief Ike's Mambo Room. 1725 Columbia Rd. NW. ☎ **202/332-2211.** www.tlac.net/users/chiefike. Cover: $3 Sat–Sun. Open from 4pm–2am or 3am nightly. Metro: Woodley Park–Zoo, with a 20-minute walk.

In early 1998, Chief Ike's served as a location shot for a scene in Will Smith's movie *Enemy of the State*. Its more usual role is as a place where professional musicians jam on Tuesday nights; local DJ legend Stella Neptune spins dance tunes once or twice a week; and the Gross National Product, a political satire troupe, performs Saturday nights.

Club Heaven and Hell. 2327 18th St. NW. ☎ **202/667-HELL** (club phone), or 703/522-4227 (for bookings and information). Cover in Heaven: $3 Tues, $3 Wed, $5 Thurs, $5 Fri and Sat; no cover in Hell. Hell open daily, Heaven is closed Sun–Mon. Metro: Dupont Circle (Q St. exit) or Woodley Park–Zoo, with a 20- to 30-minute walk.

This schizophrenic club is in Adams-Morgan. Heaven (upstairs, of course) is a psychedelic version of paradise with black walls and strobe lights, Buddhas, Egyptian art, and paintings based on Michelangelo's *David* and *God Creating Adam*. The balcony allows an escape from the dense mob of dancers and very loud music. Weather permitting Thursday through Saturday, you can go up on the rooftop patio, one of the larger ones, in Adams-Morgan at least.

Metro Café. 1522 14th St. NW. ☎ **202/518-7900,** for advance tickets, call ☎ 202/884-0060. Cover: $5 until 12:30am. Shows usually start daily at 9pm. Free parking across the street. Metro: Dupont Circle, about 5 blocks away.

The space at the Metro fits about 100 people in a room that holds a big stage, an L-shaped bar, red velvet curtains, and high ceilings. Acts range from hip-hop to good local rock bands, to national acts like Holly Cole. The club, a newcomer, seems to be attracting all ages, everyone in black. Like several other nightclubs (State of the Union for one; see p. 168), the Metro is also into drama and presenting short plays on various nights.

9:30 Club. 815 V St. NW. ☎ **202/393-0930.** Tickets $5–$40,depending on the performer. Open days of performance only. Metro: U St.–Cardozo.

Housed in yet another converted warehouse, this major live-music venue hosts frequent record-company parties and features a wide range of top performers. In 1998, the concert trade publication *Pollstar* named the 9:30 the nightclub of the year. It's only open when there's a show on (call ahead), and, obviously, the crowd varies with the performer. There are four bars, two on the main dance-floor level, one in the upstairs VIP room (anyone is welcome here unless the room is being used for a private party), and another in the distressed-looking cellar. The 9:30 Club is a standup place, literally; there are no seats. Tickets to most shows are available through Protix (☎ **800/955-5566** or 703/218-6500).

State of the Union. 1357 U St. NW. ☎ **202/588-8810.** Cover: generally $5–$7. Open through 2am Sun–Thurs, 3am Fri–Sat. Metro: U St.–Cardozo.

DJ and live music highlight reggae, hip-hop, and acid jazz sounds in this nightclub that plays on a Soviet Union theme: hammer and sickle sconces, a bust of Lenin over the bar, and a big painting of Rasputin on a back wall. The hip crowd is diverse, "different every half hour," says a bartender.

JAZZ/BLUES

Blues Alley. 1073 Wisconsin Ave. NW (in an alley below M St.). ☎ **202/337-4141.** Cover: $13–$40, plus $7 food or drink minimum, plus $1.75 surcharge. Open nightly. Metro: Foggy Bottom, with a 20-minute walk.

Blues Alley, in Georgetown, has been Washington's top jazz club since 1965, featuring such artists as Nancy Wilson and Wynton Marsalis. There are usually two shows nightly, at 8 and 10pm; some performers also do midnight shows on weekends. Reservations are essential (call after noon), and because seating is on a first-come, first-served basis, it's best to arrive no later than 7pm and have dinner.

City Blues. 2651 Connecticut Ave. NW. ☎ **202/232-2300.** Cover: $5 Thurs–Sat. Open Nightly. Metro: Woodley Park–Zoo.

This is a neighborhood club that offers live entertainment 7 nights a week, mostly blues and some jazz, performed mainly by locals but with big names sitting in from time to time. Look for groups like the Mary Ann Redmond Band, and names like Timothy Ford, who plays piano with the Marianna Previti Band.

Columbia Station. 2325 18th St. NW. ☎ **202/462-6040.** No cover, but a $6 minimum. Breakfast served Fri–Sat 1am–5am. Open weeknights until 1:30am. Metro: Dupont Circle (Q St. exit) or Woodley Park–Zoo, with a 20- to 30-minute walk.

Another fairly intimate club in Adams-Morgan, this one showcases live blues and jazz nightly.

Madam's Organ. 2461 18th St. NW. ☎ **202/667-5370.** Cover: never more than $5–$8. Open Sun–Thurs 5am–2am, Fri–Sat 5pm–3am. Metro: Dupont Circle (Q St. exit) or Woodley Park–Zoo, with a 20- to 30-minute walk.

This beloved Adams-Morgan hangout fulfills owner Bill Duggan's definition of a good bar: where there's great sound and people sweating. The great sounds are provided courtesy of jazz guitarist Peter Beck on Mondays, bluesman Ben Andrews on Tuesdays, bluegrass open mike on Wednesday, and live R&B, including the likes of Bobby Parker, on Friday and Saturday provides the great sounds. You provide the sweat. DJ and local "character" Stella Neptune spins funk and dance tunes on Thursday nights.

New Vegas Lounge. 1415 P St. NW. ☎ **202/483-3971.** Cover: $7–$10. Open Sat–Sun, Tues–Sat. Sun–Thurs 8pm–2am, Fri–Sat 8pm–3am. Metro: Dupont Circle.

When the Vegas Lounge is good, it's very good. When it's bad, it's laughable. If you're lucky, you might find a blues band out of Chicago playing Otis Redding's "Try a Little Tenderness," making the room swoon, and eventually putting everyone on their feet dancing.

One Step Down. 2517 Pennsylvania Ave. NW. ☎ **202/955-7141.** Cover: $5 Mon–Thurs, typically $12.50 or 13.50 Sat–Sun; 2-drink minimum every night. Open Mon–Thurs 5:30pm–1am, Sat–Sun until 2am. Live music 6 nights a week. Metro: Foggy Bottom.

This quintessential, hole-in-the-wall jazz club showcases the talents of names you often recognize, and some you don't: sax player Paul Bollenbeck, the Steve Wilson Quartet, Ronnie Wells, and Ron Elliston. The people who come to the One Step tend to be jazz enthusiasts who stay quiet during the sets.

INTERNATIONAL SOUNDS

Chelsea's. 1055 Thomas Jefferson St. NW (in the Foundry Building on the C&O Canal). ☎ **202/298-8222.** Cover: $10. Open Wed–Mon. Complimentary parking in the building garage. Metro: Foggy Bottom, with a 10-minute walk.

Wednesday and Sunday, 10pm to 2am, are Arabic nights, here, featuring an Arabic band and a belly dancer. Thursday through Saturday nights are devoted to Latino music, with a DJ playing disco Latino tunes Thursdays 10:30pm to 2am, and bands playing live music 10:30pm to 4am on Friday and Saturday nights.

Coco Loco. 810 7th St. NW (between H and I sts.). ☎ **202/289-2626.** Cover: $5–$10. Open every night but Sunday. Metro: Gallery Place.

This is one of D.C.'s liveliest clubs, heralded by marquee lights. On Friday and Saturday nights, you can come for a late tapas or mixed-grill dinner (see chapter 4 for details) and stay for international music and dancing, with occasional live bands. On Saturday nights, the entertainment includes a sexy 11pm floor show featuring Brazilian exhibition dancers who begin performing in feathered and sequined Rio Rita costumes and strip down to a bare minimum.

Habana Village. 1834 Columbia Rd. NW. ☎ **202/462-6310.** Cover $5 only on Friday and Saturday nights after 10pm, and only for men. Open Wed–Sat 6:30pm–2am. Metro: Dupont Circle, with a 15-minute walk, or Woodley Park–Zoo, with a 20-minute walk.

The 2-story nightclub holds a bar/restaurant on the first floor, a dance floor and bar on the second level. Salsa and merengue lessons are given every Wednesday and Thursday evening, from 7 to 9:30pm, tango lessons every Friday and Saturday evening, same time; each lesson is $10. When dance lessons are not taking place, a DJ plays danceable Latin jazz tunes.

Kala Kala. 2439 18th St. NW. ☎ **202/232-5433.** After midnight –Sat, a $5 cover charge, for men only, includes 1 drink. Open Mon–Thurs until 2am, Fri–Sat until 3am.

The owner of this Adams-Morgan African club originally hails from Madagascar. A DJ plays African reggae, zouk (French Caribbean), soca (from Trinidad), salsa, and the occasional Top 40 tune.

Latin Jazz Alley. 1721 Columbia Rd. NW, on the 2nd floor of the El Migueleno Cafe. ☎ **202/328-6190.** $5 for salsa instruction; $5 for beginner, $8 for intermediate mambo lesson; or 2-drink minimum. Open Wed–Thurs 6pm–midnight, Fri–Sat 6pm–3am. Metro: Dupont Circle (Q St. exit) or Woodley Park–Zoo, with a 20- to 30-minute walk.

Another place to get in on Washington's Latin scene, this one in Adams-Morgan. At the Alley, you can learn to dance: salsa for beginners on Wednesday, Friday, and Saturday nights at 7:30pm; and mambo, rumba, and cha-cha on Thursday nights at 7:30pm. Friday, and Saturday nights, from about 10pm to 2am, a DJ plays Latin jazz; there's no cover but there is a 2-drink minimum.

GAY CLUBS

Dupont Circle is the gay hub of Washington, D.C., with at least 10 gay bars within easy walking distance of one another. At either of the two Dupont Circle locales listed below, you'll find natives happy to tell you about (or take you to) the others.

The Circle Bar & Tavern. 1629 Connecticut Ave. NW (between Q and R sts.). ☎ **202/462-5575.** No cover. Sun–Thurs until 2am, Fri– Sat until 3am. Metro: Dupont Circle.

This impressively slick-looking three-story club is the largest gay bar in the Dupont Circle area. It attracts a racially mixed gay and lesbian crowd (about 80% male), mostly in the 25 to 35 age range.

J.R.'s. 1519 17th St. NW (between P and Q sts.). ☎ **202/328-0090.** No cover. Sun–Thurs until 2am, Fri–Sat until 3am. Metro: Dupont Circle.

More intimate than the above, this casual all-male Dupont Circle club draws a crowd that is friendly, upscale, and very attractive.

Tracks. 1111 1st St. SE. ☎ **202/488-3320.** Cover: $5–$10. Metro: Navy Yard.

This vast, high-energy club (a converted auto dealership, with 21,000 square feet inside and a 10,000-square-foot patio) is a favorite place to dance in D.C.

4 The Bar Scene

Asylum. 2471 18th St. NW. ☎ **202/319-9353.** No cover. Sun–Wed 8pm–2am, Thurs 5pm–2am, Fri 5pm–3am, Sat 7pm–3am. Metro: Dupont Circle, with a 15-minute walk, or Woodley Park–Zoo, with a 20-minute walk, that takes you across the Calvert St. Bridge.

This below-street joint has room for about 100 people; plays rock CDs; and has a pool table, a bar, tables for sitting and drinking, and an atmosphere made fun by the youngish patrons.

The Bar. 1416 U St. NW. ☎ **202/588-7311.** No cover. Wed–Thurs 7:30–2am, Fri–Sat 7:30–3am. Metro: U St.–Cardozo.

Open Wednesday and Thursday 8pm to 2am and Saturday and Sunday 8pm to 3am, the Bar is a mellow place to get comfortable and listen to good music. It's cozy, with candles, sofas, and brick walls topped with a mural of dancers, diners, card players; platters of food, and bottles of wine. Musicians, usually jazz, set up in the front window. The bartender is amiable and the food not bad.

The Big Hunt. 1345 Connecticut Ave. NW (between N St. and Dupont Circle). ☎ **202/785-2333.** No cover. Sun–Thurs until 2am, Fri–Sat until 3am. Metro: Dupont Circle.

This casual and comfy Dupont Circle hangout for the 20- to 30-something crowd—billing itself as a "happy hunting ground for humans"—has a kind of *Raiders of the Lost Ark*/explorer/jungle theme.

Brickskeller. 1523 22nd St. NW. ☎ **202/293-1885.** No cover. Wed–Thurs 7:30–2am, Fri 11:30am–3am, Sat 6:30pm–3am, Sun 6:30pm–2am. Metro: Dupont Circle or Foggy Bottom.

If you like beer and you like a choice, head for Brickskeller, which has been around for nearly 40 years and offers about 1,000 beers from the world over.

Café Milano. 3251 Prospect St. NW. ☎ **202/333-6183.** No cover. noon–1am daily. Metro: Foggy Bottom, with a 25-minute walk.

Located just off Wisconsin Avenue in lower Georgetown, Café Milano has gained a reputation for attracting beautiful people. You might see a few glamorous faces, and then again, you might see a bunch of people on the prowl for glamorous faces. It's often crowded, especially Thursday through Saturday nights. The food is good; in fact, Café Milano could rightfully be included in the restaurant section. Salads and pastas are excellent.

The Dubliner. In the Phoenix Park Hotel, at 520 N. Capitol St. NW, with its own entrance on Massachusetts Ave. NW. ☎ **202/737-3773.** No cover. Sun–Thurs 11am–1am, Fri–Sat 11am–2:30am. Metro: Union Station.

This is your old Irish pub, the port you can blow into in any storm, personal or weather-related. It's got the dark wood paneling and tables, the etched-and-stained glass windows, Irish-accented staff from time to time, and, most importantly, the Auld Dubliner Amber Ale.

Fadó. 808 7th St. NW. ☎ **202/789-0066.** No cover. Open daily until 2am. Metro: Gallery Place/Chinatown.

Another Irish pub, this one opened in the spring of 1998, in Chinatown of all places. It's gotten a lot of attention from the start, partly because it was designed and built by the Irish Pub Company of Dublin, who shipped everything—the stone for the floors, the etched glass, and the milled wood—from Ireland.

Fox and Hounds. 1533 17th St. NW (between Q and Church sts.). ☎ **202/232-6307.** No cover. Mon–Thurs 11:30am–1:30am, Fri 11:30am–2:30am, Sat 9am–2:30am, Sun 9am–1:30am. Metro: Dupont Circle.

Although it's in the heart of the Dupont Circle gay district, Fox and Hounds is a basically straight and very friendly neighborhood bar that offers pretty good singles action. In the beery-smelling interior, the walls are hung with fox-hunting prints and posters from the Disney movie *The Fox and the Hound.*

Lucky Bar. 1221 Connecticut Ave. NW. ☎ **202/331-3733.** No cover. Mon–Thurs 3pm–2am, Fri–Sat noon–3am. Metro: Dupont Circle or Farragut North.

You used to be able to dance here, when the place was known as Planet Fred. As the name has changed, so has the focus: to sitting back and relaxing. DJ or jukebox music plays, but never so loud that you can't carry on a conversation.

Mr. Smith's of Georgetown. 3104 M St. NW. ☎ **202/333-3104.** No cover. Sun–Thurs 11:30am–1:30am, Fri–Sat 11:30am–2:30am. Metro: Foggy Bottom, with a 15-minute walk.

Mr. Smith's bills itself as the Friendliest Saloon in Town, but the truth is that it's so popular among regulars, you're in danger of being ignored if the staff doesn't recognize you. The bar, which opened about 30 years ago, has a front room with original brick walls, wooden seats, and a long bar, at which you can count on finding pairs of newfound friends telling obscene jokes, loudly. At the end of this room is a large piano around which customers congregate each night to accompany the pianist. (Have a daiquiri—Mr. Smith's is known for them.)

Ozio, Martini and Cigar Lounge. 1835 K St. NW. ☎ **202/822-6000.** Cover: $20 Fri–Sat after 10:30pm. Open Mon–Wed until 2am, Fri–Sat until 3am. Closed Sun. Happy hour weekdays 4–7pm. Metro: Farragut West, Farragut North.

Winston Churchill's rule of life reigns here: "Smoking cigars and drinking of alcohol before, after, and if need be, during all meals, and intervals between them." Ozio has a whimsical/upscale art-deco interior, with distressed walls and columns, Persian rugs strewn on concrete floors, and comfortable seating in plush armchairs, sofas, and banquettes. The lighting is nightclubby, and the music mellow (light jazz; blues; Sinatra; Tony Bennett). People dance wherever they can find a space. Ozio is the kind of place where limos are parked out front, and the suit-and-tie crowd is comprised of senators, hotshot professionals, and local sports figures.

The Rock. 717 6th St. NW. ☎ **202/842-7625.** No cover. Mon–Thurs 3pm–2am, Fri–Sat noon–3am, Sun noon–2am. Metro: Gallery Place.

The Rock is the district's newest sports bar, situating itself in probably the best location a sports establishment could have: across the street from the MCI Center. The 3-floor bar fills a former warehouse, its decor a montage of pre-existing exposed pipes and concrete floors, and TV screens, pool tables, and sports memorabilia. The most popular spot is the third floor, where the pool tables and a cigar lounge are located. In good weather, folks head to the rooftop bar.

The Tombs. 1226 36th St. NW. ☎ **202/337-6668.** Cover sometimes on Tuesday nights, never more than $5. Open Mon–Fri 11:30am–1:30am, Sat 11am–1:30am, Sun 10:30am–1:30am. Metro: Foggy Bottom, with a 40-to-45-minute walk.

Housed in a converted 19th-century Federal-style home, the Tombs, which opened in 1962, is a favorite hangout for students and faculty of nearby Georgetown University. (Bill Clinton came here during his college years.) GU types tend to congregate at the central bar and surrounding tables, while local residents tend to head for "the Sweeps," the room that lies down a few steps and has red-leather banquettes.

The Tune Inn. 33¹/₂ Pennsylvania Ave. SE. ☎ **202/543-2725.** No cover. Sun–Thurs 8am–2am, Fri–Sat 8am–3am. Metro: Capitol South.

Capitol Hill has a number of bars that qualify as "institutions," but the Tune Inn is probably the most popular. Capitol Hill staffers and their bosses, apparently at ease in dive surroundings, have been coming here since it opened in 1955, or maybe it's the cheap beer and greasy burgers that draw them. Anyway, stop in.

Tunnicliff's Tavern. 222 7th St. SE. ☎ **202/546-3663.** www. tunnicliffs.com. No cover. noon–2am daily. Metro: Eastern Market.

Directly across from Eastern Market is another Capitol Hill institution, named for the original, circa-1796 Tunnicliff's Tavern. (This Tunnicliff's opened in 1988.) An outdoor cafe fronts the tavern, which includes a great bar and a partly set-apart dining room. You're likely to see Hill people here; the last time I was there, Louisiana Senator John Breaux and his wife stopped by. Proprietress Lynne Breaux, though not related to the senator, hails from New Orleans and cultivates a Mardi Gras atmosphere that includes live music (no cover) on Saturday nights.

XandO. 1350 Connecticut Ave. NW. ☎ **202/296-9341.** No cover. Mon–Thurs 6:30am–1am, Fri 6:30am–2am, Sat 7am–2am, Sun 7am–1am. Metro: Dupont Circle, 19th St. exit.

Popular from the start, XandO (pronounced "zando") is a welcoming place in the morning for a coffee drink, and even more inviting for a cocktail as the day progresses. Men, you'll see a lot of cute girls hanging here, drawn perhaps, by the s'mores, which you make yourselves, and other delicious desserts. (XandO also serves sandwiches and soups.) The music is loud, the decor a cross between bar and living room.

5 More Entertainment

FREE SHOWS

In D.C., some of the best things at night are free—or very cheap. See information earlier in this chapter about the free performances staged by the **Kennedy Center,** the **Shakespeare Theatre,** and the **Carter Barron Amphitheater.**

The city comes especially alive in summer when numerous outdoor concerts take place all around town. Choose a night, any night, and you will find a military band playing at one of three locations in Washington, D.C.: the **U.S. Capitol,** the **Sylvan Theater** on the grounds of the Washington Monument, or the **Navy Memorial Plaza.** These bands perform jazz, show tunes, blues, music for strings—you name it. The concerts begin at 8pm and continue every night June through Labor Day. For details about military events, call the individual branches: the U.S. Army Band, "Pershing's Own" (☎ **703/696-3399**); the U.S. Navy Band (☎ **202/433-2525** for a 24-hour recording or 202/433-6090); the U.S. Marine Band, "The President's Own" (☎ **202/433-4011** for a 24-hour recording or 202/433-5809); and the U.S. Air Force Band, "America's International Musical Ambassadors" (☎ **202/767-5658** for a 24-hour recording or 202/767-4310).

Index

See also Accommodations & Restaurants indexes below.

Page numbers in italics refer to maps.

ACCOMMODATIONS

FROMMER'S® COMPLETE TRAVEL GUIDES

Alaska
Amsterdam
Arizona
Atlanta
Australia
Austria
Bahamas
Barcelona, Madrid & Seville
Belgium, Holland &
   Luxembourg
Bermuda
Boston
Budapest & the Best of
   Hungary
California
Canada
Cancún, Cozumel &
   the Yucatán
Cape Cod, Nantucket &
   Martha's Vineyard
Caribbean
Caribbean Cruises & Ports
   of Call
Caribbean Ports of Call
Carolinas & Georgia
Chicago
China
Colorado
Costa Rica
Denver, Boulder &
   Colorado Springs
England
Europe
Florida

France
Germany
Greece
Greek Islands
Hawaii
Hong Kong
Honolulu, Waikiki & Oahu
Ireland
Israel
Italy
Jamaica & Barbados
Japan
Las Vegas
London
Los Angeles
Maryland & Delaware
Maui
Mexico
Miami & the Keys
Montana & Wyoming
Montréal & Québec City
Munich & the Bavarian Alps
Nashville & Memphis
Nepal
New England
New Mexico
New Orleans
New York City
Nova Scotia, New Brunswick
   & Prince Edward Island
Oregon
Paris
Philadelphia & the
   Amish Country

Portugal
Prague & the Best of the
   Czech Republic
Provence & the Riviera
Puerto Rico
Rome
San Antonio & Austin
San Diego
San Francisco
Santa Fe, Taos &
   Albuquerque
Scandinavia
Scotland
Seattle & Portland
Singapore & Malaysia
South Pacific
Spain
Switzerland
Thailand
Tokyo
Toronto
Tuscany & Umbria
USA
Utah
Vancouver & Victoria
Vermont, New Hampshire
   & Maine
Vienna & the Danube Valley
Virgin Islands
Virginia
Walt Disney World &
   Orlando
Washington, D.C.
Washington State

FROMMER'S® DOLLAR-A-DAY GUIDES

Australia from $50 a Day
California from $60 a Day
Caribbean from $60 a Day
England from $60 a Day
Europe from $50 a Day
Florida from $60 a Day

Greece from $50 a Day
Hawaii from $60 a Day
Ireland from $50 a Day
Israel from $45 a Day
Italy from $50 a Day
London from $75 a Day

New York from $75 a Day
New Zealand from $50 a Day
Paris from $70 a Day
San Francisco from $60 a Day
Washington, D.C.,
   from $60 a Day

FROMMER'S® PORTABLE GUIDES

Acapulco, Ixtapa &
   Zihuatanejo
Alaska Cruises & Ports of Call
Bahamas
California Wine Country
Charleston & Savannah
Chicago

Dublin
Las Vegas
London
Maine Coast
New Orleans
New York City
Paris

Puerto Vallarta, Manzanillo
   & Guadalajara
San Francisco
Sydney
Tampa & St. Petersburg
Venice
Washington, D.C.

FROMMER'S® NATIONAL PARK GUIDES

Family Vacations in the
National Parks
Grand Canyon

National Parks of the
American West
Yellowstone & Grand Teton

Yosemite & Sequoia/
Kings Canyon
Zion & Bryce Canyon

FROMMER'S® GREAT OUTDOOR GUIDES

New England
Northern California

Southern California & Baja
Pacific Northwest

FROMMER'S® MEMORABLE WALKS

Chicago
London

New York
Paris

San Francisco
Washington D.C.

FROMMER'S® IRREVERENT GUIDES

Amsterdam
Boston
Chicago

London
Manhattan

New Orleans
Paris

San Francisco
Walt Disney World
Washington, D.C.

FROMMER'S® DRIVING TOURS

America
Britain
California

Florida
France
Germany

Ireland
Italy
New England

Scotland
Spain
Western Europe

THE COMPLETE IDIOT'S TRAVEL GUIDES

Boston
Cruise Vacations
Planning Your Trip to Europe
Hawaii

Las Vegas
London
Mexico's Beach Resorts
New Orleans

New York City
San Francisco
Walt Disney World
Washington D.C.

THE UNOFFICIAL GUIDES®

Branson, Missouri
California with Kids
Chicago
Cruises
Disney Companion

Florida with Kids
The Great Smoky &
Blue Ridge
Mountains

Las Vegas
Miami & the Keys
Mini-Mickey
New Orleans

New York City
San Francisco
Skiing in the West
Walt Disney World
Washington, D.C.

SPECIAL-INTEREST TITLES

Born to Shop: Caribbean Ports of Call
Born to Shop: France
Born to Shop: Hong Kong
Born to Shop: Italy
Born to Shop: New York
Born to Shop: Paris
Frommer's Britain's Best Bike Rides
The Civil War Trust's Official Guide
 to the Civil War Discovery Trail
Frommer's Caribbean Hideaways
Frommer's Europe's Greatest Driving Tours
Frommer's Food Lover's Companion to France
Frommer's Food Lover's Companion to Italy
Frommer's Gay & Lesbian Europe

Israel Past & Present
Monks' Guide to California
Monks' Guide to New York City
New York City with Kids
New York Times Weekends
Outside Magazine's Guide
 to Family Vacations
Places Rated Almanac
Retirement Places Rated
Washington, D.C., with Kids
Wonderful Weekends from Boston
Wonderful Weekends from New York City
Wonderful Weekends from San Francisco
Wonderful Weekends from Los Angeles